TRANSFORMATIVE TEACHING AND LEARNING IN FURTHER EDUCATION

Key Issues in Social Justice: Voices from the Frontline

Series Editors: **Kalwant Bhopal**, University of Birmingham, **Martin Myers**, University of Nottingham, **Karl Kitching**, University of Birmingham and **Kenzo Sung**, Rowan University

---

How do issues of social justice, inclusion and equity shape modern-day society? This series delivers a forum for perspectives from historically marginalised and minoritised communities to challenge contemporary dominant discourses about social justice, inclusion and equity in the social sciences and aligned disciplines.

Also in the series:

Hidden Voices:
Lived Experiences in the Irish Welfare Space
By **Joe Whelan**

Forthcoming in the series:

Low-income Female Teacher Values and Agency in India:
Implications for Reflective Practice
By **Ruth Samuel**

Find out more at

bristoluniversitypress.co.uk/
key-issues-in-social-justice

TRANSFORMATIVE TEACHING AND LEARNING IN FURTHER EDUCATION

Pedagogies of Hope and Social Justice

Rob Smith and Vicky Duckworth

With a foreword by
Alan Tuckett

First published in Great Britain in 2022 by

Policy Press, an imprint of
Bristol University Press
University of Bristol
1–9 Old Park Hill
Bristol
BS2 8BB
UK
t: +44 (0)117 374 6645
e: bup-info@bristol.ac.uk

Details of international sales and distribution partners are available at
policy.bristoluniversitypress.co.uk

© Bristol University Press 2022

British Library Cataloguing in Publication Data
A catalogue record for this book is available from the British Library

ISBN 978-1-4473-6232-6 hardcover
ISBN 978-1-4473-6233-3 paperback
ISBN 978-1-4473-6235-7 ePdf
ISBN 978-1-4473-6234-0 ePub

Cover design: Liam Roberts Design
Front cover image: iStock/Gang Zhou
Bristol University Press and Policy Press use environmentally responsible
print partners.
Printed and bound in Great Britain by CMP, Poole

Rob:
This book is dedicated to Blanche and to the memory
of M.J. and C.H. Smith

Vicky:
This book is dedicated to the memory of my kid brother Matthew David
Duckworth (Our Matt). Always in my heart your soul journeys on x

Contents

Series editors' preface

Debates about social justice, inclusion and equity in the early twenty-first century have become increasingly more contentious and problematical. This should not come as a surprise and reflects Western social, economic and political climates driven by neoliberal narratives: the rapid expansion of European Union membership followed by signs of its impending potential dissolution; the election of Donald Trump as 45th President of the United States of America in 2016; the growing populism of nationalist political parties in almost every Western democracy. At the same time the global South has seen economic expansion on a scale undreamt of a generation ago that threatens to undermine the hegemony of the West.

This original book series delivers a forum for marginalised and minoritised perspectives in the social sciences. It challenges contemporary dominant discourses about social justice, inclusion and equity from the perspective of marginalised and minoritised communities. Drawing upon the work of researchers, theorists and practitioners from Europe, the USA and the Global South, the series adopts a broad interdisciplinary approach including disciplines such as education, sociology, social policy and childhood studies. The titles in the series are published on broad topics, underpinned by research and theory.

The series draws upon definitions of social justice that identify the marginalisation and exclusion of groups and communities of people based on their difference from the majority population. The series seeks to understand how such processes should be disrupted and subverted. Social justice in this respect is both the subject matter of the book series but also its practical contribution to academic scholarship. By providing an outlet for scholarship that itself emerges from under-represented voices, the books published in the series contribute to addressing rather than simply commenting on social justice issues. The series centres social justice, inclusion and equity as a key focus; gives voice to those from marginalised communities and groups; places a spotlight on the work of under-represented (minority ethnic, religious, disabled, female, LGBTQ) academics; and challenges hegemonic narratives that underpin Western discourses about how best to reach a socially just world.

A key strength of the series includes a broad range of topics from different disciplines in the social sciences including education, sociology, social policy, gender studies, migration and international relations, politics and childhood studies. The series draws on themes which include race/ethnicity, gender, class, sexuality, age, poverty, disability and other topics which address and challenge inequalities. It includes a range of different theoretical perspectives including addressing intersectional identities.

Transformative Teaching and Learning explores the important hidden stories of transformative teaching and learning, specifically focusing on further and adult education and how this impacts on the lives of students, their families and the local and wider communities. A key strength of the book is the profound and compelling case studies which show the depth of experiences of students from diverse backgrounds and those of teachers who support the students. Each of the chapters eloquently draw on different aspects and themes based on the case studies. Smith and Duckworth expertly bring together the key issues in how transformative education can contribute to a social justice agenda. This book provides an original contribution to debates on further and adult education. Clear, sharp and challenging, the book centres the importance of why a socially just society is one which must ensure that all groups are included in their right to a decent, quality education.

Kalwant Bhopal
Martin Myers
Karl Kitching
Kenzo Sung
19 January 2022

List of figures

About the authors

Rob Smith is Professor of Education at Birmingham City University. His work explores the impact of funding regimes and marketisation in education. Recent research focuses on transformative teaching and learning. Other research interests include social justice, educational space, leadership in education, race and higher education and English as a subject for critical citizenship.

Vicky Duckworth is Professor of Further Education at Edge Hill University. Vicky's research is in Adult Education and Literacy, and she is deeply committed to challenging inequality through critical and emancipatory approaches to education, widening participation, inclusion, community action and engaging in research with a strong social justice agenda. Vicky is a trustee for the Helena Kennedy Foundation (https://www.hkf.org.uk/); she was a member of the 2019 Lifelong Learning Commission (https://labour.org.uk/wp-content/uploads/2019/11/Lifelong-Learning-Report-2019.pdf) and is a founder member of the Right2Learn (https://right2learn.co.uk/our-team/).

Acknowledgements

A very special thanks to the learners and their families and communities, teachers, employers and everyone who has contributed to this research project.

We would also like to offer a special thanks to Matt Waddup and the Universities and Colleges Union for commissioning the research and being encouraging and responsive in its development and throughout the research process.

Many thanks to Laura Nicholson, Senior Research Fellow at Edge Hill University, for her excellent input into the development and analysis of the surveys.

Thanks to the reviewers of the manuscript for helpful guidance.

Foreword

Alan Tuckett

This book grows out of the inspiring Transforming Lives project, in which tutors and students bear witness, through video sessions, to the powerful impact on their lives of learning and teaching in further education. It constitutes a passionate, polemical yet reasoned case for major change in the over-regulated and data-driven fiscal and assurance processes that shape current British policy. Drawing on the thinking of Paulo Freire, Jack Mezirow, Gert Biesta and others, Rob Smith and Vicky Duckworth ground their approach to transformative teaching and learning in a commitment to education in pursuit of social justice. It is an approach that seeks to reassert the centrality of students' experiences, of the need to start from where they are, to build critical enquiry through dialogue, and uses evidence from learners and teachers to argue against the narrow utilitarianism of government skills policies, to assert the right of everyone not only to have access to education, but also to help shape it. They argue that 'every student's encounter with knowledge has the potential to critique it, to change it, to build on it, to reach beyond it' (121), but that this is currently achieved despite the system, rather than because of it, as teachers are burdened by ever growing forms of accountability – a view of UK further education incidentally critiqued by the Organisation for Economic Co-operation and Development – and college leaders are increasingly caught between meeting the needs of local communities and economies and the demands of an ever-more centralised system.

At the heart of the book is the evidence of learners whose lives have been enriched and transformed through their experience at further education colleges. No-one reading their testimonies can be left without a strong conviction that exam results alone fail to capture the complexity and richness of the learning journeys of people juggling their studies with caring and parental responsibilities, problems with housing, mental health, and for some not having enough to eat. Yet, despite the severe constraints on colleges and their teachers and students, the testimonies in the book exude agency, energy, confidence and a passion for what comes next. As Herbert who struggled through school with undiagnosed dyslexia put it, 'When you are at school it feels like it's for the government. Whereas when you are at college you feel this is for me, it's my livelihood. It's going to be my future.' He describes his brilliant college teacher as the reason for his transformation, and the way she helped him see his dyslexia as a talent and source of creativity. That story is repeated time after time, and clearly shows how important what Herbert calls 'time for people' is beyond the formal curriculum.

Transforming Teaching and Learning also makes a powerful case for locality – for further education colleges at the heart of communities, and responding to their needs. How far that responsiveness to place is achievable within the present, funding, accountability and performance measures that shape so much of colleges' work takes the authors back to their central argument – that further education deserves a system responsive not only to the vocational studies needed for labour market entry, but also to the needs of people returning to learning and seeking afresh, in the words of Raymond Williams, to understand, to adapt and help shape their, and our, lives.

Introduction

Who is this book for?

This book is for all teachers of young people and adults, researchers, policy makers and those interested in the power of education to challenge intergenerational inequity locally, nationally and globally. At the heart of this book are two very different perspectives on how further and adult education is currently shaped (in England and the UK more generally) and the potential of what it could be. One view, an external view held by government ministers, civil servants and policy makers, positions further education in particular as the 'handmaiden of British industry' (Ainley and Bailey, 1997), the skills development arm of the national economy – almost as though colleges were little factories whose sole purpose is to churn out a nameless, faceless, identity-less flexible workforce of skilled labour.

This view arises from a particular historical moment. Sometime in the last quarter of the twentieth century, in response to globalisation, politicians in England began focusing on productivity and growth as central economic concerns. Arguably, it's a view that originates in the so-called Great Debate speech in 1976 (see *Guardian*, 2001) in which the then Prime Minister Jim Callaghan appeared to criticise teachers and schools for not being focused enough on the needs of employers. It's also clearly visible in many of Tony Blair's speeches (see Blair, 1996) and forms the backbone of the Leitch Review of 2006 (Leitch, 2006).

This didn't just happen in England but across the world. We all recognise this story because it so dominates our media, we have come to believe it is the only possible way of viewing what's happening in the world. To that extent, it also shapes the way we see our future and the communities around us on this planet. Further education and education in general have been caught up in this economic 'purposing' and are still entangled in it and fuelled by it.

The other view, which is opposing in many ways, arises from local contexts and from the embodied experience of teachers and students. It is smaller (from a neoliberal perspective), but also, ultimately much bigger than the first story. It sees further and adult education as being about real people with real lives and families and communities. These people have often been badly served by our system of schooling and may feel they have been written off by a system which is driven by meritocracy and fails to address issues of structural inequality that can shape communities' choices or lack of choices on their learning trajectories (Duckworth and Smith, 2018c).

This is the view of further and adult education that most of the people who work in it have. Many of them, most of them even, relate only distantly to the grand economic story about providing essential skills for the nation. Of course, they care about the towns and cities where they live and work and they dedicate their working lives to helping their students become active working members of those communities; that's what motivates them; that's what gets them out of bed in the morning. Filtered through an economic lens, the bigger picture is something they understand and something they worry about – but it is a story that in the telling, makes them feel powerless; while it may be supposed to provide a purpose, what it actually does is make them feel like an insignificant cog in some gigantic mechanism. A mysterious mechanism, moreover, whose workings few people seem to understand and that seems to run out of control damaging economies and lives on a regular basis. It's a bigger picture not because it's more significant (though it claims to be), but because it looms over their work, disrupts it and even undermines it. In their hearts, they know that their best contribution is at the local level and that's where they focus their efforts. Sadly and disturbingly, those efforts receive little or no recognition from the great machine that claims to give meaning to their work.

Every day though, that bigger picture, that story about the national economy, the need for a more 'productive' workforce with essential skills and a positive mind-set pushes its way into their consciousness. It demands attention: through the pressure to recruit more students and put 'bums on seats', through the pressure to chase up students to maintain high attendance levels (even during a pandemic) and of course the pressure to push students through their assessment. While all of these aspects of education are important, they contribute to an unending burden of paperwork: the incessant bureaucracy teachers are forced to undertake in pursuit of funding. These are the ways that the bigger picture makes itself visible, makes itself felt and paradoxically, these are also the things that interfere with teachers getting on with what they really want to do: their job teaching students, feeling the reward of seeing people learn, grow, thrive and seeing their lives change.

These two different views of further and adult education exist at the same time. In the research underpinning this book, in every example we cite and in every story we recount, both versions are there. What's tragic is that the first story, the story that has been imagined by the people who oversee budgets and who drive changes in qualifications and who have starved further and adult education (in England) of the funding it needs for more than a decade often threatens to blot out the real human stories, the stories that give meaning and value to the work of teachers. This bigger story typically sees teachers (and some colleges) in deficit terms: as 'requiring improvement' as though they are obstacles or impediments that are slowing down or damaging what would otherwise be an efficient and effective delivery process.

This book is an attempt to challenge those perspectives. It is a book that calls out to all teachers in colleges and other further and adult education providers, to the teachers who work in prisons, who work for charities, who work in English for speakers of other languages (ESOL) classrooms and with excluded school students, to the teachers who work with 16–19-year-olds who feel that they're 'thick' and unable to learn. This book reaches out to teachers who work in education settings across the UK and the world to acknowledge the work they do as a resource of hope that affirms their value and to reassure them that their energies and commitment are worthwhile – however much they feel undermined by the external meanings being imposed on their labour.

The words on the pages are markers of our attempt and deep commitment to redress the balance, to reverse the current polarity and assert the supreme value of further and adult education as something more miraculous than a skills factory or a handmaiden to industry, and instead as an engine for individual, community-based and social change. It proposes a model of education after schooling that reaches beyond national boundaries as a new imagining of education as a space for nurturing hope and change.

Further and adult education

In the UK context, the book seeks to provide insights relevant to both adult and further education contexts. Further and adult education overlap but are often viewed as distinct. The differences are mainly to do with governance and control, and over the last 30 years since incorporation (in March 1993), government policy rhetoric and the system of funding have consolidated a view of further education as being mainly or exclusively for 16–19-year-olds overwhelmingly pursuing vocational qualifications and training programmes (Smith, 2015). The clarity of that distinction was blurred during a period under New Labour in which the idea of lifelong learning and the Skills for Life initiative positioned adult provision as an integral feature of further education; but it has been reasserted since 2010 and the remaining adult education providers have found themselves under sustained funding pressures.

Adult education has a tradition, culture and heritage that is distinct from what is now popularly understood to be further education (see Hyland and Merrill, 2003). Local authorities used to oversee a massive amount of provision. When one of us (Rob) first began teaching in 1988 in a secondary school in Lozells, Birmingham, there was an option to take an evening adult literacy class; the school was one of thousands of local adult education centres' that ran a range of 'liberal, general, multi-purpose' courses (Tuckett, 1991, 25) across the country. By the end of the 1980s the reduction of funding from central government to local authorities had lessened expenditure on this kind of provision. Facilitated by the seeming disinterest of an increasingly instrumentalist orthodoxy, in some areas all such classes were cut.

Over the last decade, adult education has experienced even greater reductions in funding than further education colleges (see Belfield et al, 2018). Indeed, some curriculum areas that have featured historically in the adult education curriculum, for example trade union studies, have been defunded altogether. The reason for this could well lie in the view of education as a social good for collective and social benefit that sits at the heart of the adult education tradition and that many adult educators hold dear. This clashes with the government's preferred human capital view and indeed is in many ways inimical to it.

Adult education institutions (now called Specialist Designated Institutions – and including Fircroft College, Northern College, Ruskin College, and the Workers' Educational Association and a small handful of London colleges like City Lit) are founded on a model of pedagogy that positions students as rounded, whole human beings. In addition, over almost a century (until 2016 when through merger it became the Learning and Work Institute), the National Institute of Adult Continuing Education (NIACE) became a powerful advocate for adult and continuing education. Through focusing on research and development to provide a strong evidence base for adult education, NIACE gave adult education a heart and a voice that helped in the preservation of historical and cultural continuity. The last decade of education policy since 2010 has put this heritage in jeopardy.

Jarvis (2004, 195) talks about teaching in adult education as centering on a moral relationship:

> Once these moral elements enter teaching and the focus is on the humanity of the learners much of the instrumentality of teaching disappears. It is about enabling human beings to achieve their own potential, without imposing on them predetermined outcomes, although we recognize the importance of what is learned in the process. Fundamentally, teaching is a human process, in which the teachers themselves may well be the best instruments that they have in helping learners to both learn their subject and achieve their potential.

Thinking such as this is at the heart of this book. In that sense then, our argument about what makes teaching and learning transformative could be said to have its roots in adult education. Looked at another way though, this book is simply underlining that in the heavily instrumentalised and skills-dominated 'sector' of further education, the moral purpose and deeply human and individualised pedagogical approaches espoused by the adult education tradition in England are still very much in evidence. To use (ironically) a term that has become popular in policy discourse since the introduction of austerity measures, these pedagogical approaches have remained remarkably resilient.

The research that this book is founded on crosses the boundaries between further and adult education. Acknowledging the importance of adult education in its pedagogical tradition and social history, we juxtapose these two areas. Adults are learning in colleges on a range of courses: access to higher education (HE), foundation degrees, off-the-job training for apprenticeships, community and family learning, English for Speakers of Other Languages and the examples of transformative educational experiences we cite are drawn from further education colleges but also from adult education settings. The orientation of locally determined adult provision and its ability to directly address issues of social justice in particular are certainly a distinguishing feature. But in the students' stories that follow, we will illustrate how transformative experiences occur in both settings. In addition, these stories almost always have a dimension that connects them to issues of social justice.

Much of the policy focus in this book concentrates on the English context. Devolution means that different systems and policies operate in each part of the UK. Our policy critique centres on further education policy as it relates to England, but the research aspect does extend beyond English borders, and we hope this doesn't create confusion. An obvious reason why we haven't been able to adhere strictly to only stories from England is that the project's digital presence has spread more widely, and the internet is no respecter of national boundaries. While this book originates in English further and adult education settings, we hope the issues it grapples with will resonate across many different national and international contexts. That's largely because education is currently shaped by a particular view on its purpose, a reductive ideology that has often marginalised groups of learners and their communities and damaged the experiences of millions of children, young people and adults.

The structure of this book

The book is organised in chapters that all look at different aspects of the Transforming Lives project. Chapter 1 introduces the central focus of the book: the notion of transformative teaching and learning and its particular resonance in contemporary further and adult education contexts. We provide examples from our research to illustrate the breadth but also the layered aspects of our analysis. This opening chapter will also provide a policy frame for the book as a whole giving an insight into the structural factors and forces affecting further education and adult education in England over the last two decades and more. Important aspects we touch on in this chapter also include the instrumentalist way young people are represented in policy documents and, a central concern of much of the book, the damaging effects of the funding, accountability and performance apparatus (FAP) that shape (and we would argue undermine) educational experiences in further and adult education.

The focus of Chapter 2 will be to provide detailed insights into how we carried out the research and the way we gathered additional material. The contextualisation of the research will be a key focus. The diversity of the participants necessitated an exploration of their views framed by a commentary on the wider educational landscape. Participants engaged with the project because they had a positive story to tell so we develop a rationale for using a qualitative approach and explore the use of narrative while foregrounding the principle of seeing and undertaking research as a social practice. Finally, we develop a justification for extending the research through the use of two quantitative surveys and present some of the findings from them.

Chapter 3 will focus on our use of digital technologies when researching with a methodological approach centred on social justice and in the sharing of our participants' stories. We provide an overview of the way the project used video (recording and editing), the website and a Twitter account to gather data but also to share it and to broaden the impact of the research. The website in particular we see as facilitating the co-production of a 'third space' in which further and adult education can be collectively reimagined by the staff and students who constitute it.

At the heart of the book, Chapter 4 will present the voices of students and teachers from the research as they have recounted their experiences to us but also, where relevant, the voices of parents and employers that sometimes assume great importance within these narratives. For us, these stories communicate how further and adult education is a force not just for individual development but for addressing social inequality. These are powerful and affecting stories of the triumph of individuals over difficult circumstances. They illustrate how transformative teaching and learning has a positive ripple effect into families and communities. The examples we present highlight the importance of the teacher's role, how transformative educational experiences connect with parenthood and can take place even in areas of provision (like apprenticeships) in which students are structurally and discursively positioned in objectified ways.

In Chapter 5 we address the contested meaning of social justice and go on to develop our thinking about transformative teaching and learning and how it connects with a range of connected issues. We explore how the academic/vocational divide in education feeds social division and inequality and further and adult education's role in reifying as well as challenging that. Drawing on participants' stories, we explore how further and adult education offers a unique and cohesive space in which people from different ethnic backgrounds can forge hybrid identities in relation to people of other different backgrounds. We also reframe the concept of social mobility through participants' stories and show how further and adult education can offer hope and benefit mental health and well-being for people caught up in difficult socio-economic circumstances.

Chapter 6 explores the implications of the research findings for the ways in which leadership and governance play out and are typically conceptualised in further (and to a lesser extent adult) education settings. As part of this, we critique the recent area reviews and discuss what they tell us about the breakdown of the architecture of further and adult education. Rather than viewing leadership as the psychological characteristic or property of individuals in senior positions, this chapter conceptualises it as a characteristic of the actions of staff at all levels within colleges. To illustrate this, we draw on teachers' accounts from the project, showing how a transformative educational experience depends on teachers building relationships with students in a co-produced differential space that is actively distanced from and buffered against the destructive effects of funding, accountability and performance-driven cultures. Leadership as the enabled agency of all staff in a further and adult education provider is necessary if the conditions conducive to transformative teaching and learning are to be met.

Chapter 7 will revisit current theorisations of transformative teaching and learning and position our work within that field. Drawing on the heritage of the British adult education tradition, we flesh out a distinctive, contextualised theorisation of transformative education. We survey a range of theoretical perspectives as we pull together the themes from the teachers and learners' chapters and probe the interconnected nature of teaching and learning in transformative education. This involves engaging with the principles of critical pedagogy, the debate around powerful knowledges, looking at symbolic violence and embodiment in educational experiences. The strong aspects of transformative teaching and learning are addressed by exploring the role of affect, spatiality and the triad of belief, hope and care in transformative teaching and learning. Finally, we return to purposes: do we want a further and adult education orientated to maintaining the (flawed) social inequalities of the past, or do we instead need to reimagine it as a space for creating the collective personal development and socially just changes that we need in order to face the enormous challenges of the future?

Chapter 8, the concluding chapter, suggests what needs to be done to build and strengthen transformative teaching and learning in further and adult education. It offers important re-imaginings of some of the major structural change that is necessary for the potential of post-schooling transformative education to be fully realised.

It proposes the changes to funding, leadership and the influence of local as opposed to central government that are necessary to create the conditions in which transformative teaching and learning can flourish and contribute fully to bringing about a more socially just society.

What this book argues

This book argues that further and adult education as currently thought of – by policy makers in particular – is too narrowly conceived. The reasons for such a narrow view may be historical in that further education colleges have for a long time been chiefly associated with technical and vocational education, and since 1945 have also been seen as having a role in industrial development. The consequences of viewing it in this narrow way, combined with cultures of performativity and accountability practices that originate in neoliberalism and marketisation (to be expanded further) are causing ongoing damage and limiting the powerful impact on individuals and communities that the stories at the heart of this book evidence.

For us, further and adult education in all its breadth is educational provision that has a role much greater than simply as a supplier of 'skills' for employers. In our view, that instrumentalist view is hugely restrictive and neglects a much broader role that local further education colleges in particular built and developed up to incorporation in 1993 and have sustained in the 30 years since, despite enormous pressures.

The fact is further and adult education colleges across the country have always been important institutions embedded in their local communities. With the range of courses they offer and the work they undertake, they are vital for social cohesion and for meeting the needs of individuals and communities. They don't only provide training courses for people deemed to be not 'academic'. They often make an important difference for individuals from low-income backgrounds and marginalised groups whose experience of the education system has not connected up successfully to a future of hope and fulfilment. In other words, further and adult education has an important role in bringing about social justice.

1

The Transforming Lives research project and the further education policy context

Education is … a fostering, a nurturing, a cultivating, process. All of these words mean that it implies attention to the conditions of growth.

John Dewey, *Democracy and Education*

Introduction

This quotation from John Dewey's book *Democracy and Education,* (Dewey, 1916, 12) published more than a century ago in the United States, provides a lucid starting point for this book. It invites us all to think again about what the fundamental purposes of education are. It invites us to waft away the ideological fog that often seems to obscure these purposes. Every age presents opportunities and challenges with regards to our ability to realise what it means to be fully human and how we make being fully human accessible to as many people as possible. The previous quotation reminds us that education has a role in this. More than a century after Dewey made this simple and (we might suppose) unquestionable assertion that connects education to democracy itself, it seems extraordinary that the systems and cultures that pervade our schools, colleges and even universities appear to be determined by different and conflicting values and that our attention appears to be directed more towards the conditions by which students are governed to fit into the status quo rather than the conditions of their growth. It would seem that the ideological fog of league tables and inspection, of standards, of funding, accountability and performance, of 'skills' and 'productivity', this fog has been allowed to obscure a simpler, purer human purpose.

This book draws its energy and its purpose from the Transforming Lives research project. The project was commissioned by the University and College Union (UCU – the main college teachers' trade union) over three phases. The project represents another opportunity to affirm the primary purpose of education as proposed previously by Dewey, in this case in relation to further and adult education. As such, it explores the important and often hidden stories of transformative teaching and learning that come from further and adult education, its meaning and impact on students' lives, the lives of their families and their local and wider communities.

The research developed a series of meaningful and powerful case studies from colleges and adult education settings across the country. These case studies illustrate the important work done to offer opportunities and choices to learners from across diverse communities – communities that are enriched and given hope by the power of education. The case studies are of students of different backgrounds and ages whose lives have been changed and also of teachers whose practice supports the shaping of those experiences in creative and meaningful ways to bring those changes about.

The focus then is firmly on perspectives from inside further and adult education. It is vital however that the book examines the way this 'post-school' education is funded because of the ways in which this influences and undermines teachers' educational work. Further and adult education is funded in a distinctive way when compared to primary, secondary and higher education. That doesn't just mean it is underfunded – although, historically, that is undeniable. There are, we would argue, significant drawbacks with the process through which funding for colleges and other providers works. Funding changed at the same time as colleges were incorporated in 1993 and these problems persist. Despite mergers and college closures since then, there are still huge problems. At the end of 2020, one of the key funding agencies announcing that sixty four colleges were in need of 'emergency funding' as a result of the COVID-19 pandemic (Whieldon, 2020). That means we've had more than a quarter of a century to get the funding right. But it isn't right – at least as far as providers are concerned. Research into further education funding (and this is something we will look at in more detail in this chapter) tells us as much. The research evidence tells us there are still fundamental problems. Possibly, this is by design and the instability created and sustained by under-funding is regarded as a useful lever by government. But before we go into more detail about policy and funding, we want to foreground two examples from the research to highlight the kind of human narratives that sit at the heart of this book.

Two case studies

These two examples are a taste of the transformative educational experiences that the book seeks to highlight. In the research some learners' accounts revealed the range of barriers that they overcame on their often-challenging journey into further and adult education. Many of these involved navigating deeply personal and painful issues, for example, abusive relationships, alcohol and drug dependency and mental health issues. The empowerment they gained was linked to accessing further education; was linked to the renewed dignity and self-belief it afforded them.

i) Adam

We met Adam at a prearranged time in a college in the Black Country. We were given a small meeting room at the back of the staff room where we set up our camera and sat waiting. Adam was the first of three people we interviewed that day at the college.

The research uncovered many examples of labelling: cases in which participants felt that they had had markers placed on them by teachers and that this had a very negative impact on their experience of school education. One way of explaining how education can have a negative impact on individuals rather than the positive impact that we would all hope it should have is through the concept of symbolic violence. This concept comes from a French philosopher called Pierre Bourdieu and we explore it fully in Chapter 7. At this point though it is enough to say that symbolic violence in education acts to impose a restrictive and damaging set of expectations and meanings (such as categories or labels) on students. We tend to think of violence as the inflicting of physical pain by one person on another. In education, the older ones of us will recall teachers slapping, caning or giving our classmates the pump or the slipper. Symbolic violence is different because it may not be meted out by a single teacher – although teachers do play a crucial role, instead it can be an effect of structure. So, for example, in a situation in which streaming is used, a student who is habitually put into low groups with little opportunity to move 'upwards' can be regarded as having been labelled. This might be the overall effect of many small decisions by different teaching staff, but unsurprisingly, ultimately it will affect that student's experiences of learning and their sense of themselves as a learner and indeed a human being. This can cause feelings of shame and damage students' hope, confidence and self-worth.

Adam provided a powerful representative example of this. Adam was a 16-year-old who had been excluded from his local school and explained how one reason for this was that he had anger management problems: '[i]n school I was getting angry quite a lot. I was punching walls ... I used to think I was dumb all the time in school. I had no hopes at all ...'. The knock-on effects for Adam's family and home life were significant. His mother described how she received phone calls every day and sometimes had to leave work in order to pick her son up early from school. Adam's sense of being 'dumb' and ignored was, in his mind, connected to teachers' labelling him as coming from a particular estate with a 'reputation': this created negative expectations that meant his identity as a learner was severely compromised:

'I was in a lesson and I was there with my hand up asking for help and there was another person with their hand up asking for help. I'm the naughty one and he was a good lad … So (the teacher) went straight to him and then another person put their hand up and then another person even though I had my hand up. And he kept going round and round until after nine people then he come to me. And that was why I was getting angry … Everyone just looks at you and they think Oh yeah … They judge a book by its cover, and you shouldn't do that.'

In Adam's story, symbolic violence is observed in the way the teacher relates to and interacts with him. It's not physical violence but is nevertheless deeply felt. As with another participant, Anita – who talks about being put 'in a box', this violence takes the form of an ongoing assessment of 'ability' that shapes social interactions between teacher and learner. The educational relationship becomes characterised by a teacher's judgemental position and regard towards the student.

Students described how uplifting it was for someone to value them for who they were and recognise the obstacles they had overcome. Along with this recognition came validation. The learners described how this empowered them and gave them a feeling of self-worth, inspiring them with confidence and hope.

There was another part of Adam's story that came almost a year after the first time we talked with him. We had been in contact with his mum, Kim, as part of the ethics process. We needed Kim's consent because Adam was just 16. We asked Adam if we could talk to his mum about the impact of the move from school to college, (we focus on Kim in Chapter 4). We were sitting in the front room of Adam's house talking to Kim about what had happened when Adam started his course at the college. A shape appeared in the doorway. Adam had been upstairs, had heard our voices and wanted to show us something. Under his arm he had a ring binder. He came over to us and opened the binder. It was filled with handwritten notes and assignments from his course. He leafed through and held it open at a particular page. 'Look at that hand-writing,' he said beaming at us with pride.

In many ways, this incident typified the transformative aspects of Adam's educational experience. It suggested a journey from being an angry and frustrated young man with negative feelings about learning, who, having been excluded from school caused worry and concern at home, to becoming a confident student with a growing belief in his own abilities. This had had a ripple effect in his household and an intergenerational impact, making his parents and extended family proud.

ii) Awor

In 1992, Awor arrived in the UK as a teenager from South Sudan. Sudan is the size of Western Europe and, as the Anglo-Egyptian Condominium was a part of the British Empire until 1956. At the time of Awor's arrival, Sudan was embroiled in one of the longest civil wars on record (1983–2005) and Awor's home, Abyei, lay in oil-rich disputed territory between the North and South. With no English, she struggled to find her way and establish her independence. While she had links within the Southern Sudanese community, a particular set of personal circumstances meant she had to strike out on her own and establish herself independently. Things changed for her when she began studying on an English for Speakers of Other Languages (ESOL) course at a local college in Birmingham.

> 'Going to college was my main goal. There were people there who were willing to help me … I was so happy. I worked as a cleaner at the hostel. That's when … I started my education, despite everything that has happened to me, I have to get to where I want to be. And I have to show those people who want to keep me down, that I can take care of myself. That one day I could be somebody.'

Awor's story is striking because she started from nothing and forged a career with very limited family support.

> 'I had so many obstructions. Health-wise it wasn't good. I had a child when I was 23 – my back was injured during child birth. But I was still determined to get where I wanted to go. I went back to college to do my course. I did English, then I did NVQ in care. I went on placements and socialised with people. That helped with my spoken English. I did my placement in City Hospital. I did NVQ 1, 2 and 3. I also studied at Fircroft College (an adult education college in Birmingham). After that I had a break and worked. I had to support my family at home in Sudan. My mother is elderly now. Then I went back to education. I did my level 5 at Birmingham City University where I did my Health and Social Care. Now I am doing my nursing degree. My dream job is to be a head nurse. I'm not going to stop until I become a qualified nurse.'

What we see here is the straightforward commitment Awor had to supporting herself, her immediate and her extended family while studying. This is what sustained her over a number of years, and enabled her to get to where she wants to be. What drove her was the desire to become a qualified nurse. Twenty years after arriving in the country, she was studying for a degree in nursing and is now a qualified nurse with a specialisation in assisting in operating theatres. At the time of writing, Awor had been working for almost 2 years. 'The most important thing is the drive and the feeling you want to achieve. My daughter is doing accountancy and finance. I brought her up on my own. She has picked up my drive and my focus on education.'

For Awor, college gave her opportunities to improve her standard of living and provide a secure home life for herself and her daughter. Her daughter has just finished a degree in Accountancy and Finance and now works in the legal sector. Awor's determination to overcome multiple obstructions in her health and personal circumstances expressed itself in a progressive cycle of further education over more than a 20-year period. This enabled her to gain employment first in care but then to facilitate the realisation of her dreams and ambitions to become a nurse. Her story illustrates the abundance of aspiration that further and adult education taps into and that can help people in the realisation of their hopes.

Apart from providing an example of individual determination against the odds, Awor's story illustrates how further education can act as a space that facilitates social cohesion in assisting refugees and others to establish themselves in their new lives in this country. Awor's story provides insight into the role of further education in colleges in supporting social cohesion in our super-diverse cities. There are few collective spaces in our society in which adults and young people of widely different ethnic backgrounds can come together as peers and equals to be with each other and learn about each other. Further education is one of those spaces. Yet, once more, this is a social benefit that is widely ignored by government.

Temporality is another important ingredient in the further and adult education offer. What we mean by this is that this education offers the additional time that some students need to learn and achieve qualifications. Further and adult education operates beyond the rigid mapping of age-based assessment that has come to characterise schooling in England and other countries. Another way of seeing this is to recognise that colleges cater for people whose needs are not met by this kind of rigidity. In fact, further and adult education often has to address the damage done to positive learning identities by a rigid set of expectations that students have to achieve a particular level at a particular age, or they are 'failures'. With colleges taking on the majority of young people in the 16–18 age group as well as adults like Awor who want to study vocational courses to improve their income, policy makers need to acknowledge the value of this flexible provision and fund it proportionately.

What is neoliberalism?

A key to understanding the forces that continue to shape further and adult education is offered by the term neoliberalism. We are all currently caught up in a neoliberal era that has exerted a powerful grip on the way recent governments see education. What is neoliberalism? It's best to think of it almost like a historical period. Beckert (2020, 319) describes it as 'the policy paradigm that has shaped the world like no other over the last forty years'.

It is a way of thinking about economy, government policy and how best to run complex organisations in society (including those in the public sector). Neoliberalism is often thought of as an ongoing all-pervasive process, a process of neoliberalisation – typically including the privatisation of public sector organisations and amenities (Davies, 2014).

Under neoliberalisation, organisations are supposed to compete against each other in a 'market-like way'. 'Market-*like*' is right because these are not like any other markets you might be familiar with. For a start, the government is always ready to get involved: to tweak a parameter here and adjust another setting there. In addition, the information that real markets depend on, accurate insights into the performance of the competitors, is absent. In its place, the customers (and for further and adult education we are supposedly thinking here of students and/or their parents) are blinded by a wealth of complex and confusing performance data that has been 'dressed' by each institution to give the best impression. In other words, competition creates the pressure on each organisation (college or provider) to present themselves and their 'performance' in the best possible light. Within this so-called market then, making a judgement about quality is almost impossible. It's like trying to form an opinion by looking at a photo-shopped image. The real picture is underneath it somewhere, but you would be a fool to rely on the manipulated image in making a decision.

A good way of understanding the power of neoliberalism is not to think of it as a set of policies but as a 'commonsense' way of viewing how our modern society works. The idea of something being 'common sense' is of course suspect. It is a term often used by politicians to try and prevent listeners and viewers from subjecting what they are saying to a proper level of critical scrutiny. Like an attitude or mind-set, neoliberalism has coloured and colonised the way we think about the world. We can see that in the economisation of consciousness that is such a feature of the lives of all professionals and indeed the public more widely nowadays. In organisations today, there is a nagging voice that asks continually about the cost of this or that – even when no 'money' is actually changing hands; and there is an accompanying impulse that urges us to put a monetary value on everything.

Fundamental to the neoliberal take on further and adult education is a closed-down view of human beings as cogs in the service of employers and the national economy, a view that sees people as objects to be used. In this mind-set, what is economic, what is efficient starts to inform and even take precedence over political decisions, it starts to define *what is possible*. So, in our global economy, politics has yet to catch up with economics and marketisation has become a transnational force that is insufficiently regulated and consequently able to colonise and disrupt our lifeworld (see Habermas, 2006). At a time when social justice has become a burning issue and the need to address social inequality is more pressing than ever, the neoliberal view of further and adult education as a 'skills provider' shackles colleges and other providers, preventing them from pursuing a much richer and broader mission.

Transformative teaching and learning also belongs in this picture. As the reader will see, the examples we will provide in the book are founded on a view of all people as beings with histories, feelings, needs and potential. Transformative teaching and learning proceeds by opening up the *who* of students and bringing that into the curriculum as the starting point for learning. This books argues that further and adult education often accomplishes this by acknowledging and redressing the damage done by the marketised system of schooling that has become fixated on assessment and on ranking young people by 'ability' in ways that are at worst destructive as they feed directly into social inequality and injustice.

Our argument is that despite policy makers organising further and adult education through the use of bureaucratic systems tied to (ever-shrinking) funding, transformative education is still taking place. If government could only remove some of the constraining paraphernalia of marketisation (the instability off funding year on year, the grotesque level of accountability, the depressingly regular policy interventions that destabilise the curriculum, the centralisation of decisions about courses away from local considerations), then this could become a more widespread phenomenon, indeed, a signature characteristic of further and adult education.

For this to happen, for the life-changing stories that sit at the heart of this book to become more prevalent, we need a change in attitudes and a change to structures of governance (see Chapter 6).

Further education policy and its implications

Post-World War II, a Ministry of Education pamphlet, *Youth's Opportunity: Further Education in County Colleges* (HMSO, 1946) provides an important historical insight into the way further education is and has been perceived by government as well as perceptions on young people. Building on the Education Act of 1944, the pamphlet details the establishment of County Colleges under the auspices of local education authorities to provide further education (seen as part time) for young people between the ages of 16 and 18 years old.

In the introduction, two key perceptions stand out. The first is the relationship of wage-earning work to education:

> Young people need to be kept in touch with the life, the discipline, the teaching and the outlook of an educational institution for some years after they have become wage earners, and that their personal happiness will be increased and their lives made richer by such a contact. (HMSO, 1946, para. 2)

Rather than simply seeing this as an old-fashioned view, we might want to see it as a position that has led to where we are today. What stands out here is how education is seen as offering something important that can't be obtained in the workplace. More striking still is an attitude to young people seen in paragraph 3:

> The country is not likely to forget what it owes to the steadfastness, the enthusiasm and the courage of its young people during the war. The demands of the post-war world will be considerable and will be no less difficult to meet than those of the immediate past and present. (HMSO, 1946, para. 3)

What we see in this then is the expression of a governmental commitment and responsibility towards young people. Perhaps it might read: 'You have been dragged through five + years of a nation being at war. You have been evacuated from cities and handed over to rural communities to live with people you didn't know, you may have returned to see your house had been destroyed. As the country has been at war and this has affected you as our most precious asset, we have a sense of responsibility in looking to design an education system that will look after your interests.'

When we read these sentences, there is a sense of how dated the booklet is in terms of national policy. What we probably shouldn't do is fall into the trap of thinking that people were very different from the way we are today. The social landscape may have been different, and clearly, attitudes and assumptions like these must have shaped young people's lives in a hugely significant way, but that doesn't mean that they didn't feel things (like injustice and/or anger and/or ambition) in the way that young people do today.

Compare the previous sentiments with an extract from the government White Paper published in January 2021:

> This White Paper aims to strengthen links between employers and further education providers. We will place employers at the heart of defining local skills needs and explore a new role for Chambers of Commerce and other business representative organisations working with local colleges and employers. The courses offered by providers will be tailored to meet the skill needs of businesses. We will support their delivery through £1.5 billion of capital funding to improve the condition of further education colleges, a further £291 million to support 16–19-year-olds and £375 million to deliver our contribution to the Plan for Jobs in 2021–22 and start delivering our Lifetime Skills Guarantee. (DfE, 2021, 4)

Both documents originate in a time of upheaval and great social and economic change. But what's immediately striking is the contrast in the way young people feature. The White Paper (entitled *Skills for Jobs: Lifelong Learning for Opportunity and Growth*) has an entirely instrumentalist emphasis. It's not even entirely clear whether the opportunity referenced in the title is an opportunity for students or for businesses and employers. The national economy is the central character of the narrative that threads through the White Paper, the young people merely bit players. Somehow, over the course of 75 years, the focus of further education policy discourse has shifted profoundly from being about the well-being and development of young people to being about their objectified role as contributing to the skills needs of the economy. In addition, there is no longer a trace of the concern for their development and welfare that characterises the 1946 document.

What we're suggesting is that in another seventy years' time, are we not going to look back at today's policy documents with their discourse about skills and employability and react in a (possibly quite unpredictable) way to the commonsense notions underpinning some of the statements? Our guess is that we will. And another guess is that one aspect of the criticism by that reader in the latter half of the twenty first century is that the policy document objectifies young people as though they were disembodied repositories of human capital which it was the job of policy makers and government to fill with 'skills'.

Looking for meaning in stories like those of Adam and Awor is the key task of this book. Our contention is that such stories offer resources of hope for all of us but more than that they are a cultural capital that we need to draw on to understand more fully the purposes of further and adult education. As already outlined however, we have to take account of how these stories are framed by a policy context and policy understandings that are at present seemingly blind and deaf to them. These policy understandings seek to impose that bigger narrative about skills and the economy that damages and undermines the potential of further and adult education to provide this kind of transformative teaching and learning. At this point, it is important then to provide a policy overview and some historical context to the current situation.

Funding, accountability and performance: the FAP apparatus

A key determiner in how further and adult education is experienced by both students and the teachers and other staff in colleges and other providers is the funding, accountability and performance (FAP) apparatus that was put in place at incorporation in 1993. This FAP regime is dynamic in that it is tweaked and adjusted annually to suit emerging government agenda. The principles of the FAP apparatus anchor further and adult education in a marketised system through the first term: funding. While there has been a steady evolution over 25 years, the basic principles of funding are that students are not funded simply as *per capita* (as they are in primary and secondary schools and in universities). Instead, funding starts with recruitment, but there are additional elements of retention and achievement. There are also prescribed elements to courses (for 16–18-year-olds these include, since 2015, a work experience placement (see DfE, 2015) and maths and English). The complexity of funding (consider that most colleges have thousands of students rather than hundreds) requires a huge bureaucracy of accountability: tracking through registers, assessments and online systems to evidence the provider's performance (Coffield, 2008). The metrics that each college/provider generates every year are vital for future funding and for that reason every provider invests heavily in administrators and administrative systems to ensure their performance data is robust.

So far, so reasonable (although if successful achievements were linked to GCSEs, secondary school funding would be cut by a third at a stroke). But the FAP apparatus has significant negative consequences for colleges and other providers, and these have been downplayed and normalised ever since incorporation. Like a beating heart pulsing with performance data, in the way it controls colleges' curricula and funding, funding and performance cannot be ignored. The FAP apparatus is the only game in town and every provider understands the rules and how they need to adapt and respond to whatever is being 'incentivised' by government policy in order to maximise income.

What is the impact of the FAP apparatus?

In 1998, as a part of doctoral research, one of us (Rob) interviewed teachers across a number of colleges in the West Midlands (see Smith, 2007A; Smith, 2007B). Among the stories of what was happening to teaching and learning as a consequence of incorporation and the link (then more solid than now) between funding and students' achievement was one example that sticks in the mind. An experienced teacher talked about marking students' portfolios in the summer and returning in the autumn to find that some of those who had not passed the qualification had now mysteriously passed.

The original exchange went like this:

Joe: The results are probably the worst. In order to get good results, you just pass people. So there are people who never gave any work on the module and er, the lecturer will say, 'Well I don't know how this student passed my module because they never handed in any work.'

Rob: So the lecturer who's teaching the subject discovers that the student has passed?

Joe: Oh yes. Lots of times.

Rob: But they didn't pass them?

Joe: No.
Rob: Who passed them?
Joe: Who knows?
Rob: Is this GNVQ?
Joe: Yes, that's one of the courses.
Rob: Does anyone put their hand up and say?
Joe: Oh yes, we have a good laugh about it.
Rob: Has anyone ever said, 'No'?
Joe: Well, you do. But if you go away on holiday and somebody's passed whom you thought had failed, at the end of the day, you're usually told, 'Well, they haven't passed it yet but they'll probably pass it during the year...' (T)he statistics for the results have no connection with reality at all. (Smith, 2007B, 43–44)

A second example from around 2006 which seems to illustrate a similar phenomenon comes from an experience of initial teacher education for further education teachers. In this example, one student from Rob's tutor group wrote an incident in her reflective journal. As a student literacy teacher, she had attended a faculty meeting at which the head of faculty had criticised the literacy department for not having carried out enough online assessments. In response to this, the head of department insisted that all the staff undertake the online assessment to 'bump the numbers up'. The student was horrified but the demand was framed as a rite of passage: this is what working in further education means.

A final example comes from a conversation only a few years ago. A dedicated English and Functional Skills teacher told me how he had turned up to invigilate the Functional Skills online assessment and several functional skills teachers were present and had their chairs pulled up next to students alongside the computer monitors. His requests that they leave were met with disgruntlement. The same teacher then recounted how after teaching on a portfolio-based course, he returned after the summer break to find that several portfolios he had marked as not having passed had now mysteriously achieved a pass grade.

The fact that almost the exact same story is being told in 1998 and in 2017 is an astonishing indictment not just of the failure of the existing funding regime but of its damaging effects on the meaning of teaching and learning. These examples show how pressures on colleges to push students through at whatever cost are turning further and adult education into a ritual of data production: a financial transaction in which the meaning and value of the student experience has been eroded and made unrecognisable.

What compounds this is that the 'data' that is produced is accepted and presented as 'fact' by government and then used by policy makers to inform policy decisions. There are huge problems with this over-reliance on performative measures in social policy, as any doctoral researcher in the social sciences could point out. In Chapter 2 we look at Campbell's Law that originates in research evidence showing how quantitative indicators become subject to 'corruption pressures' and ultimately, begin to distort and corrupt the actual processes they are supposed to be measuring. But here we can draw on an example from the natural sciences, from physics to be precise. The issue is simply this: does gathering data about educational practices (or any other set of complex social practices) affect the practices being monitored? In other words, does the act of research change the behaviour of thing being researched?

According to the Heisenberg uncertainty principle (Cassidy, 2009), the act of observation does change the behaviour of whatever is being observed. Werner Heisenberg was one of a group of physicists investigating the behaviour of sub-atomic particles called electrons. His work, along with that of Nils Bohr, established that measurement is not transparent and effect-free. Not only is measurement shaped by the apparatus used to measure the phenomenon, but the act of observation affects the phenomenon being observed. To use Karen Barad's term (Barad, 2007), the researcher and the researched are 'entangled': the knowledge producer is entangled in and forms a part of the knowledge produced. Kincheloe summarises the significance of this research from the natural sciences: '[t]he basic idea of Heisenberg's uncertainty principle was that the human observer cannot be removed from any experiment – divergent observers will view the world differently, thus producing uncertainty. Thus, the classic ... notion of objectivity does not exist'. (Kincheloe, 2008, 65–6). There isn't the space to go into the finer points of particle physics here – besides Karen Barad's book (Barad, 2007) does the job so well – but in relation to knowledge production in the social domain, such an insight, that objective judgements are anchored in cultural rather than scientific understandings, raises some big and important questions.

The argument around observation and judgement and whether or not objectivity is possible is hotly debated in the social sciences. Important insights, for example, into the inseparability of observation from existing social relations, have emerged from these debates (see Bratich, 2018) and how observation and assessment/judgement forms part of wider moves towards a surveillance society. The relevance of this to education is specifically tackled by Matt O'Leary's work (2013). The doubt that this thinking casts on the so-called objectivity of judgement has huge consequences for many of the practices associated with quality assurance in education providers.

For a start, the managerialist approach to organising the activities of a complex organisation like a college (see Randle and Brady, 1997) is confounded if the act of measuring is judged to be unreliable. This insight undermines managerialism because it derives its power from measurement. Equally, the current function of the Office for Standards in Education

(Ofsted) is called into question. Until recently, dependent on the grading of observed lessons, Ofsted was publishing market information in the form of whole-institution judgements. The failure to deal with the principle that these judgements can never be objective is one thing, but when we recognise that the judgements are not followed up by any developmental activity, it becomes clear that these measurements serve one key purpose: they are imprecise measurements of performance that are used as information to 'inform' consumer choice, to justify governmental control and to drive the so-called market. Apart from that, in a context in which positivism and scientific thought is so highly valued, it is troubling that government policy is still so stubbornly reliant on such crude forms of measurement – that do not tell anything like the full story.

After more than three decades of marketisation, we can see that the role of the funding, accountability and performance system in education is flawed and actually underpins a massive deterioration in the transparency of systems of enquiry into the educational activity of different institutions. The premium on 'results' lies at the heart of the problem. The relationship between teaching and data is unstable, and in cultural environments in which high success rates are a financial necessity, spoon-feeding and teaching to the test might seem the only option.

Looking at further and adult education policy over the past 25 years and more, one is forced to conclude that successive governments have been dissatisfied with what it does – although we would argue that this dissatisfaction originates in a lack of experience and understanding. There are two aspects that illustrate this. The first, already touched on, is the extraordinary (and unjustifiable) policy interventions that re-organise, restructure and generally disrupt the activities of colleges and the practices of teachers and their students with woeful regularity. Instead of leading to a gradual refinement or a steady sharpening of focus, this incessant tinkering de-stabilises colleges and other providers, reinventing wheels that have been reinvented multiple times before. On each occasion, these policy initiatives are dressed up as a major step forward and always claim to be 'putting the student/parent/employer) at the centre'. Unfortunately, as we shall see later (in Chapter 4), in a context of under-funding, the only way they put students at the centre is by making providers view them primarily in terms of income: effectively they draw a £ sign target on students' backs.

The second example is that, since 2009, as everyone who works in colleges knows, further and adult education in England has been subjected to deep cuts – and these cuts have gone far beyond anything endured by other sectors of education (Paton, 2010). In effect, these cuts have hurt the communities that colleges serve and have penalised college staff. According to a recent report by the Institute of Fiscal Studies (IFS), funding for teaching and learning in adult and further education was chopped by 24% in real terms between 2010/11 and 2015/16. However, the adult skills budget funding, which covers all education for people older than 19, declined by 29% in cash terms in the same period. Despite these cuts, the existing regime of funding and so-called 'accountability (through Ofsted) has continued to enforce colleges' adherence to maintaining high standards of 'quality' through the production of favourable performance data. This systematic under-resourcing means that at the time of writing, 16–19 students in Birmingham are likely to be funded between £1,000–£1,500 less per year when they leave school go on to a local further education college (see Belfield et al, 2018). These cuts need to be viewed in a context in which around 40% of school-leavers transition into further education (Belfield et al, 2018).

Belfield et al (2018, 39) provide an important overview of the percentage of 16- and 17-year-olds taking different education and employment choices which shows how this discriminatory funding system targets a majority of young people, see Figure 1.1.

According to this chart, further education (which here includes sixth form colleges) are the preferred route for the majority of 16- and 17-year-olds and this proportion has increased steadily since incorporation. It seems unfair then that these young people are receiving less funding per head than their peers in schools.

At this point, we need to be clear about the scope of the claims we are making about further and adult education and transformative teaching and learning. This is because this research needs to be contextualised within a broad discourse about education policy and that by its nature, is

Figure 1.1: Percentage of 16- and 17-year-olds taking different education and employment choices

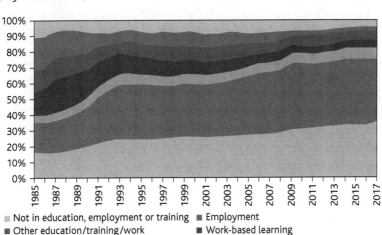

Source: © Institute for Fiscal Studies, www.ifs.org.uk

a politically contested area of work. A mark of this is the extent to which the terms 'transformation', 'transformative education', 'transformational learning', 'transforming lives' and such like are being used (some might say 'colonised') by a range of different voices in the field of education. Most of these voices see education as a social good but clearly there is a risk of the notion of transformation being harnessed to a neoliberal project of uncritical, competitive individualism. Many of these voices share our concern that the enormous potential of colleges to contribute social and economic benefits – often to marginalised groups and through that to help realise social equality and justice, is being squandered.

We are mindful then that transformative teaching and learning as a phrase and concept risks being emptied out of meaning by misuse and/or overuse. Our study then needs to be framed by a broader policy critique of the marketisation imposed by the Further and Higher Education Act (1992), which brought about the incorporation of colleges, since when further education has been viewed in increasingly reductive and instrumentalist terms by successive governments. Different elements combine to create the abstraction of 'the FE sector' that appears to shape policy makers' decisions about further education. The growth of 'datafication' – the production of performance data (a symptom of the grip of the FAP apparatus) and the tendency on the part of government to use this data to inform policy making in an undifferentiated and decontextualised way, is an additional feature.

What this book is not claiming then is that all further and adult education is transformational. Neither are we claiming that the so-called 'FE sector' is inherently or essentially transformational. Instead, this book provides substantial evidence that, despite a funding and policy environment that objectifies students and incentivises a transmission view of teaching and learning, across the broad spectrum of further and adult education, amazing and inspiring stories are being played out. Typically, these are stories in which students have been able to rearticulate a meaningful link between education and their lives. These are stories in which the personal, professional and educational relationships that teachers establish with their students have created the conditions in which hope has flowered and dramatic changes have been made possible.

Contextualising these stories are the colleges and providers: local, historically embedded institutions whose networks and rootedness make them such an important feature of municipal landscapes across the country. These important institutions may have managed (just about) to withstand the wrecking ball of austerity measures and budget cuts, but their vital role in their communities continues to be undermined through the incessant, interventionist policy churn issuing from the Department for Education (DfE)/Business, Innovation and Skills (BIS) (the vulnerability of further education may stem from its being positioned between government departments). The disruptive policy churn corresponds to the election cycle and the movement of ministers from one portfolio to another. The result: successive waves of 'reform', none being given time to 'bed in' properly, amounts to systemic governmental vandalism. Our argument then is that the narratives and the other evidence presented in this book illustrate the stubborn resilience of a set of values and a kind of teaching and learning that has withstood the onslaught of instrumentalist policy. Our argument is that further and adult education is for everyone and has never been just about 'skills'. Our argument is that further and adult education can provide a model for a renewed understanding of lifelong learning in which transformative teaching and learning could be the norm – enabling it to increase exponentially colleges' contributions to the social and economic benefits they already make.

Over the last quarter century, policies that have fostered neoliberalisation with its focus on de- and reregulation, economic competitiveness (both national and institutional) all framed by (so-called) 'free-market' competition have had a significant impact. These policies have disrupted the role and function of colleges and other providers in the ecologies of local communities, employers and local democratic structures and have positioned them instrumentally as sorting houses through which the population is processed in order to provide human capital (Becker, 1993).

Among other things, these policies have tended to consolidate a 'classed' two tier (academic versus vocational) system which, following the funding cuts imposed as part of austerity, has created a system of structural disadvantage (Duckworth and Smith, 2018b). While neoliberal educational policy often pays lip-service to social justice through the discursive vehicle of 'social inclusion' and 'widening participation', behind this promise of social mobility (a term we interrogate in Chapter 5) through educational attainment is a skills discourse that depends upon the objectification of students and their stratification within an intractable structure that perpetuates divisions between 'academic' and 'vocational' pathways.

For more than a third of our young people, the age-staged tyranny of compulsory education presents the main or only opportunity to transcend their family's social background (if that is what we take social mobility to mean). If nothing else, this reaffirms governmental complacency in the face of ongoing social divisions. What remains of the 'social mobility' dimension of the policy rests on a reliance on a short-sighted supply side intervention in the labour market (Keep, 2006) while largely ignoring measures to adjust employer demand. Underpinning the whole approach is an ever-less-convincing fable about economic growth and the classic neoliberal assumption about social benefits accruing from a 'trickle-down' of employers 'wealth creation' activities (Harvey, 2005, 64–5).

Further and adult education is more than this. Further and adult education can and should be a space in which students are able to reimagine not just their role in society and the world but also to reimagine that society and world. The claim that teaching and learning can be transformative has an individual but also a wider collective significance. Policies and structures (and the FAP apparatus figures large here) that constrain that potential are inimical to this broader project. To return to our opening quotation from Dewey, further and adult education should be about fostering, nurturing and cultivating space, a space attuned to the conditions in which individuals can grow.

A note on terminology

The stories that emerged from our research always involved not just the individual participant but a range of people in their social circle including teachers, friends, partners and often other significant people in their lives. While student participants often only made it into colleges with the support and encouragement of allies from this social network, it was then the role of the teachers that stood out. Teachers were active in creating the conditions that made transformation possible, and the part they played was so important that to characterise it as an episode or event that applies to an individual – almost like an epiphany or religious conversion, seems to us to be a narrowing of the relational social process that we want to describe. In order to reflect the dialogical and interactive aspects of the learning experiences we are interested in and the centrality of the teacher's role, we have settled on the term *transformative teaching and learning*.

2

Researching further education and putting a critical embodied research methodology into practice

> My candidate for the most distinctive and praiseworthy human capacity is our ability to trust and to cooperate with other people and in particular to work together so as to improve the future.
>
> Richard Rorty, *Philosophy and Social Hope*

Introduction

Drawing on the thinking of John Dewey (and Ralph Waldo Emerson before him) one powerful argument that emerges from the North American philosopher Richard Rorty's collection of writings in the book *Philosophy and Social Hope* (Rorty, 1999, xiii) is that education can and should connect with hope as a condition of growth, over and above the pursuit of knowledge and 'truth'. This perspective has profound implications for the practice of educational research. It suggests that research that simply seeks to expose the paper-thin inauthenticity produced by the funding, accountability and performance apparatus is not enough as, while that may be valuable, it is only a first step. A further step, which seeks to provide grounds for hope, is also necessary and indeed essential if we are to foster the conditions for change and growth in the future. The Transforming Lives project undertook educational research that attempted both steps.

Following this then, the focus of this chapter will be to provide detailed insights into how we carried out our research for the Transforming Lives project and the way we gathered additional material. The research was distinctive in being funded in phases over a number of years and while some aspects were in place from the beginning (in particular the 'interview' approach) other aspects evolved over time including the theorisation of transformative teaching and learning. The research utilised a mixed methods approach to capture the rich narratives not just of the students but of their teachers, family members, friends, community voices, employers and, in some cases, communities as well. Contextualisation of the college/provider each participant was connected to, as well as of their background, was a key focus. The diversity of the participants necessitated an exploration of their views framed by a broad analysis of the educational landscape both nationally, in respect of policy, and locally in respect of how policy was playing out in their particular setting. Participants engaged with the project because they had a positive story about further and adult education that they wanted to share.

The research methodology itself was informed by affirmative practice that was closely aligned to critical pedagogy (Freire, 1995; Breunig, 2005; see Chapter 7) and extended a number of its underpinning principles. In that sense, taking part in the research reinforced the positive learning identities that the participants talk about having achieved. In addition, the methodological approach we adopted sought to share in a collective imagining of future plans. We drew on participatory methodologies which cohered with our intention to position social justice at the core of the undertaking.

Research aims

The research project that this book originates in had several interconnected aims. A primary aim was to raise public awareness about what further and adult education is actually about in the local and national domains. We aimed to achieve this by disseminating positive stories about students, their teachers and communities, not with a focus on the skills they have gained but instead by foregrounding individuals' personal development and how this often connected to collective change. But why, the reader might ask, is it necessary to raise public consciousness? And what need is there for stories of that kind? There are several possible answers to those questions. But most of these answers find their origin in the instrumentalist view of education whose emergence and consolidation we traced in Chapter 1. You might protest, *but our local college always uses pictures of individual students' successes on their promotional material!*

It seems likely that further education may have different meanings for all of the staff and students who are part of it. But the central vision, the vision that has been promoted forcefully by government and finessed by policymakers over more than a quarter of a century is remarkably consistent. The further education market in all its bureaucratic complexity is premised on a singular vision of what is most important, and it isn't focused on dignity, on a struggle against poverty or inequality of treatment. These aspects are eclipsed by a primary emphasis: that of skills, work and 'employability'.

This is not to deny the importance of labour and the meaning that it can give to human lives. Properly remunerated work that gives dignity and confers respect while enabling workers to feed, clothe and provide shelter for themselves and their families is a universally precious thing. Work that challenges and rewards, that enables growth and development while also contributing to the greater good is something all of us should experience. Unfortunately, the rise of the dominant instrumentalist view of education has coincided with a significant and widening division between jobs that provide all of the previous ideas and another great mass of work that is so badly paid that people need several jobs to provide the minimum for themselves. An increasing number of workers both national and internationally are dependent on low-paid insecure work as part of what has been called 'the precariat' (Standing, 2011).

These inequalities are taken as a given by some. In 2013, campaigning to become London Mayor, Boris Johnson famously dismissed the possibility of economic equality and continued: 'Some measure of inequality is essential' (Watt, 2013). His argument, one that has powerful support, is that inequality is necessary in order to spur hard work. For us, as researchers in further and adult education such a view is deeply problematic as it presupposes that our society depends on the existence of an underclass who are permanently striving to climb out of poverty which some people see as self-inflicted. And here it has to be said that it appears that many policymakers see further and adult education students as primarily belonging to such an underclass. For a vision of our education system and our society that is premised on such views to endure and seem legitimate, it has to be justified by a narrative, a narrative that makes the skills discourse necessary and that overlooks the stories of individuals and focuses instead on a 'bigger' picture. This is the economised view that is fuelled, as we shall see, not just by the instrumentalisation of education but by the objectification of students. At the heart of this, like a spider at the centre of a web, sits the regulatory apparatus or regime that controls funding and sucks in all the data colleges are forced to produce data related to accreditation, attendance, course hours and achievement.

There is a lot to say about how the legitimisation of this instrumentalist purpose is sustained. But the funding, accountability and performance (FAP) regime is the key technology. The FAP mechanism operates through maintaining a watchful eye on colleges and their 'performance', data about students' achievements, students' attendance, students' progress. So much data has to be produced by colleges to satisfy the demands of accountability for funding that it takes a small army of administrators and funding experts in each college to ensure it is produced to meet the different deadlines.

What's remarkable about the centrality of performance data in our current marketised system is that it takes no account of what has come to be known as Campbell's Law, namely that: '[t]he more any quantitative social indicator is used for social decision-making, the more subject it will be to corruption pressures and the more apt it will be to distort and corrupt the social processes it is intended to monitor' (Campbell, 2011, 34). A North American social psychologist, Campbell was interested in how scientific enquiry worked in the latter part of the twentieth century. This most influential of his ideas comes from an article in which through looking at problem solving and evaluation in social systems, he concluded that the approaches taken in many impact assessments were clumsy as a result of the 'dysfunctional effects of performance measures' (Campbell, 2011, 35).

Campbell gives an example that seems highly relevant in the context of the current funding and performance apparatus in education:

> From the experimental program in compensatory education comes a very clear-cut illustration of the principle. In the Texarkana 'performance contracting' experiment ... supplementary teaching for undereducated children was provided by 'contractors' who came to the schools with special teaching machines and individualized instruction. The corruption pressure was high because the contractors were to be paid on the basis of the achievement test score gains of individual pupils. It turned out that the contractors were teaching the answers to specific test items that were to be used on the final play-off testing ... From my own point of view, achievement tests may well be valuable indicators of general school achievement under conditions of normal teaching aimed at general competence. But when test scores become the goal of the teaching process, they both lose their value as indicators of educational status and distort the educational process in undesirable ways. (Campbell, 2011, 35)

Campbell's Law has been borne out by research in and comment on further education throughout the last two decades (for example, O'Leary and Smith, 2012; Smith and O'Leary, 2013; Wolf, 2011). Teaching to the test, grade fabrication, recruiting for progression – these are all phenomena that are effects of structure: the accountability and performance apparatus in effect produces them. That this research has had little impact on changing the funding-driven nature of further and adult education is a testimony to two things: first that central government values the lever of funding in its ongoing desire to shape provision and second that the objectification of students that results is not something that government cares sufficiently about.

Alarmingly though, in educational terms, these effects of so-called assessment backwash are extremely serious. Indeed, we could talk about assessment backwash as threatening the integrity of learning itself. To teach someone to pass an assessment, at its worst can result in the drilling of students on conventions (how to pass, how to achieve a Level 9 and so on), a narrowing of the curriculum (why teach anything that is not going to be assessed?) and rote-learning (memorise answers, it doesn't matter if you don't understand them). The role of the regulator might be key here. But when Ofsted's grading places a heavy emphasis on performance data (as has been the case until very recently), then that is likely to impact significantly on the way teachers respond to pressure to focus on assessment and achievement.

Most teachers in colleges know about the importance of data because they have been forced to spend a lot of their time and energy helping to produce it. While they might be spending time and energy supporting students and preparing interesting teaching sessions instead they spend up to a third of their time registering students, monitoring student progress, recording achievements, chasing student attendance and ensuring the benchmarked proportion of each class passes. The overall effect of this is that the public narrative about further and adult education is dominated by this kind of data. It should be apparent from this argument that our perspective sees further and adult education as locally situated, its value springing mainly from what it contributes in local contexts. It's important to outline how the priority given to quantitative data has helped to construct a distorted picture because it provides a context for our research. In our view, the fetishisation of data, the sovereignty of the spreadsheet has done untold damage to further and adult education: to its potential to bring about positive change and to its meaning at local and national levels.

We wanted to take an alternative route in undertaking our research. We acknowledge that quantitative data can be important in giving an overall picture (as long as the distorting effects of the market are taken into account), but obtaining a nuanced and granular sense of the meaning behind the data requires qualitative data at a local level. Numerical data may signal that there is an issue that needs to be addressed in the education landscape, but only local qualitative research can provide insights into the possible reasons and, even more importantly the possible ways such issues might be addressed effectively.

For those reasons it was vital for us to carry out the research in a way that involved the research participants as partners in meaning making. The point of the research was to share stories about further and adult education as a space in which the social inequalities consolidated by schooling can be reversed and the messages that some people are failures as students can be proved wrong. If we wanted to find stories about students of all ages finding hope, then the research process itself needed to reflect those aims. This stems from the idea that no research is ever 'neutral' or objective (Creswell, 2003; Kincheloe et al, 2017). As we have explained, in response to government and funding policies, colleges have built up cultures and practices that focus on 'measurable' outcomes. These metrics are what sustain the FAP apparatus. Our position on this is not neutral. We believe these outcomes only tell half of the story. Our belief in carrying out this research was that these metrics alone give an inaccurate and slanted view of the enormous importance of further and adult education. We wanted to focus on the social benefits that colleges actively work for, day in and day out that are *not* measured.

How who we are as researchers shaped the research

As teachers and critical educators as well as researchers, throughout the research we continually reflected on what we were doing and how we were doing it. Just like with teaching, research that involves people talking about themselves takes place in a space in which participants make themselves vulnerable. We tackled this through reflective discussion – usually straight after each encounter, although sometimes we would remember particular incidents and or glimpse shafts of illumination when writing about the research and listening back to recordings of a research encounter. The things we learnt from those discussions fed back into the research.

Something that we established very early on though was how important it was to frame what we were doing by talking about our own backgrounds and the role further and adult education had had in them. In qualitative research this idea is called positionality (Merriam et al, 2001; Holmes, 2020). Working out your positionality may be something you undertake for the first time when you become a teacher or when you start masters' or doctoral study. It isn't a superficial or easy process, but one that requires each of us to work through a series of questions around what we do, what we believe and why. Looking inwards, it can mean an intensely personal evaluation of parenting, family trees, educational and other formative experiences. Looking outwards, it can mean an enquiry into how social factors like social class, ethnicity, religion, sexuality and abledness/disability has or hasn't impacted on us. Investigating and then articulating your positionality requires criticality, an intense commitment to looking beyond surface accounts and easily accessible explanations to seek out the sometimes hidden factors that shape who we are (Brookfield, 1995).

The premise for doing that with our research participants applies equally to our relationship with you, the readers: how can we critically research then comment on others' claims to knowledge without declaring our own positioning and trying to communicate that in a transparent way? Positionality is about making who we are visible as a frame for what we then go on to discuss. A statement of positionality helps orientate the reader by giving them a sense of where the voices behind the typescript are coming from. For those reasons, we will briefly outline our own backgrounds in order to frame what follows.

Rob's Journey

I attended a multicultural comprehensive school in Birmingham in the 1970s and followed a conventional middle-class route, doing A levels and then, after a year working in schools in Sudan, I studied English at university did a PGCE and became a secondary English teacher. While in secondary I saw the introduction of the National Curriculum and the Local Management of Schools. I then got a job in a further education college in September 1992 and witnessed the changes brought about by incorporation and neoliberal education policies at first hand. The experience was 'character-building'. The next ten years were characterised by involvement in trade union activity and a long-running contract dispute. My doctorate issued from these experiences as I sought to understand how policy in further education (and more widely) was impacting on teachers' work and the culture of college management and leadership. There was a point in the decade I spent at that college when further education almost killed me. Professionally I was at a very low ebb. I desperately sought to get out and (during the fourth restructuring exercise in as many years) applied for voluntary redundancy. I didn't get that but, fortunately, I finally got a post at another Birmingham college where, after a year, I was managing a large multi-site Access to HE course. There, my belief in the meaning and purpose of further and adult education was restored – not because of anything the college leadership team did but through my contact with staff and students. From there, I strengthened my understanding of further and adult education by taking up a teacher education role at the University of Wolverhampton. This involved circulating around lots of colleges in the West Midlands region supporting students through which I witnessed the ongoing impact of the funding regime and effects of marketisation on teaching and learning.

Vicky's Journey

At sixteen I left behind the local comprehensive school where I'd spend most of the day staring out at the clueless sky. I couldn't wait to be grown up, working and earning. The school bell ringing for the last time, see me and my mates breaking free, as we run through the green gates. Full of laughter and screams, we chase one another across the school fields, egging each other's white shirts. Excited to be leaving the classroom behind, I didn't realise back then that I'd never see some of those kids that I'd grown up with. Our lives would fork in different directions, directions of no return. I swapped my school socks for tights and started my first job on a Youth Training Scheme which paid twenty-five pounds a week; I worked in a couple of local factories before the penny dropped and the monotony set in. I wanted more – didn't know what that more was I wanted more than time passing behind the redbrick that had seen my nana and granddad grind away their years.

Rather than the factory becoming a way of life, it offered me resistance and a determination to challenge being unskilled and without qualifications. Starting at the local further education college was liberating and filled me with endless possibilities. From the college I moved onto training at the hospital for a career as a registered nurse and then a midwife. Independence has always been important to me and having a career that involved caring for others across lifespans was fulfilling and also offered me choices and routes. I worked in the hospital and as a voluntary adult literacy teacher; from here I went onto work for a number of years in further education, and then higher education. My upbringing, along with my relationships with other educators and students, has impacted on me as an adult educator and a researcher. Further education gave me a voice; a voice that is empowering and reaches out to empower others.

In carrying out the research, the narratives of transformative teaching and learning that we wanted to document are a way of articulating some of the hidden benefits and the full value of further and adult education. We wanted to contribute to a historical record of what makes further and adult education unique and to tear the veil of the 'skills' and 'performance' discourse that taints the historical picture produced by the FAP apparatus. The aim was to celebrate these achievements and affirm the positive identities being forged in college classrooms across the nation. But we wanted the celebration to move beyond mere applause and instead to connect the stories fully to the background issues – often rooted in social inequality – that lie behind the successes and achievements. The research necessarily aimed to foreground and to problematise these to document a fuller picture of what further and adult education means and where it is positioned in our social fabric. In capturing this, we sought to provide answers to some broad research questions.

Research questions

- How is further and adult education successful in offering learners the chance to engage in education at multiple stages of life, recognising that their relationships to employment/education are not neat and linear?
- What is special and particular about further and adult education in encouraging social mobility – particularly for students from 'nontraditional' backgrounds – by increasing the range and types of student support available?
- What are the short-term and longer-term impacts on individuals' lives – including on their confidence, resilience and careers?
- What is the wider impact on their families and communities?

The second phase of the research refocused on the role of teachers in transformative teaching and learning and addressed a further set of research questions, as follows:

- What are teachers' understandings of themselves as further and adult education teachers; how do they judge their competence; do they feel in control of their teaching, and do they feel valued in their role?
- How do teachers respond to and overcome challenges and difficulties in teaching in colleges?

When we set out, we hadn't refined a definition of what transformative education was. We knew from our own experiences as teachers and students that further and adult education could provide a space in which some students experience learning positively often with a consequence of catalysing change more widely in their lives. We had also read some of the literature that explores 'transformational' learning (see, for example, Mezirow, 1990, 2000, 2009; Illeris, 2014), but our starting point was the stories of students from local colleges and other providers that we knew. It seemed to us, at the outset, that the transformative experiences detailed in these stories were occurring despite the policy environment, despite a dominant instrumentalist view and despite the way teachers' work has been increasingly throttled by the demands of producing accountability and performance data. From this realisation – which emerged as the research progressed, we formulated a further question:

- How can we improve on the efficacy and appropriateness of the current funding, accountability and performance regime in order to develop a model that supports transformative teaching and learning?

Project methodology

The research utilised a mixed-method approach to capture the rich narratives not just of the students but of their teachers, family members, friends, employers and, in some cases, communities as well. The sample of participants was achieved through a snow-ball sampling method (Parker et al, 2019) which relies on referral and informal networking. The approach to sampling was, at the outset, purposive and opportune (Campbell et al, 2020). We started with contacts through our own professional networks, but we also emailed principals and senior leaders in colleges informing them about the project and asking if they could connect us with any courses that they thought provided examples of transformative education. The email was usually replied to with a member of staff copied in and we arranged research visits from there, forwarding information sheets and consent forms prior to the visit. Once on site, we would typically see and speak with five to six people: a mixture of staff and students. We would try where we could to find links through them to other potential participants – sometimes these were people who had played a significant role in the stories we had listened to.

We drew on participatory research methodologies where the oppressive qualities of the 'researcher' and the 'researched' relationship were challenged. This connected with our intention to foreground social justice at the core of the undertaking and a sense that educational research (like education itself) should have an important role to play in addressing social inequality. As such we strove to convene research discussions in a safe space, a brave space moreover that shared some characteristics with critical pedagogical space.

This open-hearted approach to research was a response to our perception of the dominance of intellectual capital that sees research as having an authoritative 'aura' and views researchers as somehow 'superior'. Both perceptions create a barrier to understanding and participation in meaning making. We are ordinary people and integrity as well as accessibility were important elements in the social relations we tried to establish during the project. Seeing educational research as a formal, exclusive, 'academic' and intellectual activity is problematic. While it is important to strive for integrity, openness and diligence in applying theory to research findings when carrying out research, researchers are human beings who exist and interact with other people in the 'now' of any given social and historical moment.

As such, all research is 'social practice' (Herndl and Nahrwold, 2000). In other words, research should not be divorced from everyday relations or appear to hide behind a 'mystique' that positions researchers as somehow 'special' and authoritative and that can thereby allow them to wrap themselves in a cloak of disinterestedness and objectivity. At its worst this mystique can make participants feel like 'subjects' – as the research is done *to* them rather than *with* them and the meaning extracted and used elsewhere for someone else's benefit.

Our approach was founded on the conviction that, just as education can be experienced as a socially embedded process that is to a greater or lesser degree conditioned by the social forces and structures that shape our society, so can educational research. It was therefore important to us to move beyond a research approach founded on limited and convention-ridden exchanges between people who do not enjoy an equal social footing (Duckworth and Smith, 2019). We wanted to (co)produce a research space that acknowledged our position as researchers. One way of trying to achieve this was to reveal how we got to where we were and involve the participants as much as possible to ascribing meanings to their experiences. This concern also motivated our use of video.

Research conversations (early on we found ourselves interrogating the term 'interviews' because of the connotations it carried of an unequal and unidirectional exchange and distribution of power) were framed to foster and sustain a sense of equality between participants and us. The term 'research conversation' better reflects the egalitarian atmosphere we tried to achieve while conducting the research. For us, it was vital to try to establish a relationship of trust with participants so that they could be active in an ongoing co-construction of knowledge and meaning. We shared our stories of our educational journeys with participants as we acknowledged that these encounters had a social significance above and beyond the 'research' element. These meetings were typically reciprocal and dialogical as stories were exchanged and opinions and feelings shared. As already noted, they were also often affirmative in tone as we talked with participants about how they had '(re)learned to learn' and how this had brought about changes in the ways they felt about themselves and about their future. The questions we as researchers thought it important to ask ourselves when producing this knowledge and disseminating it were: what meanings were being foregrounded? Where were participants being positioned? What impact might dissemination have on their hopes and trajectories and on the precious learner identities that they had constructed?

Participants' experiences of education had in the past frequently involved symbolic violence – a term used by French philosopher Pierre Bourdieu that refers to a way of thinking about how ideology influences people from working class backgrounds to view existing social relations as normal and justified. It is not direct physical violence by an individual or individuals but rather a social force that works through creating and sustaining the impression that social divisions arise from the seemingly 'natural' and inevitable superiority and inferiority of different classes (see Chapter 7 for a more detailed discussion). In this case, the symbolic violence was visited upon them by schooling and sought to position them (and get them to accept their position) at the bottom of an existing social order.

But symbolic violence does not only occur in educational circles. A critical and reflexive research methodology has to be conscious of the potential for research interactions to visit just the same kind of violence of definition and imposed meanings and of *use* on participants and their stories.

Research as social practice

Like other forms of knowledge production, educational research can become an activity that not only grounds itself in existing social hierarchies but also, ultimately, consolidates these. To address this problem, a methodological approach was needed that enacted a sense of research as a 'social practice'. In other words, in undertaking the research activity, we recognised our participation in a set of societal power dynamics that contribute to our current state of inequality and inequity. There was a sense then that the research discussions were social encounters, extended conversations that might have occurred on a bus, in a pub, on a park bench, in someone's front room; they did not take the form of a neutral, detached extraction of information by researchers in white lab coats holding clipboards.

In this project, there was also the strong sense that the encounters did not end after the camera was turned off and the conversations had ended. The research discussions were meeting points and the narratives being shared were ongoing. As people, the researchers were contactable beyond the boundaries of the research discussion. This potentially added the opportunity for developing a longitudinal dimension – through possible follow-up interviews, but that wasn't the primary motivation. Instead, the lack of closure was just one aspect of us researching dynamic phenomena, processes of growth, development and change that were individual and particular. To date, we have organised a return visit with only a handful of participants, but there are myriad avenues that we might pursue in the future.

Life story narratives

The research brought together different aspects from a range of methodologies. For us, life history and biography provided important entry points (Goodson and Sikes, 2001; Duckworth, 2013). As our life stories are closely bound up with further and adult education and its history, this provided a crucial frame of authenticity when meeting and speaking with participants. Telling our stories while asking participants to share their own was an important principle in the collaborative practice of gathering the data. This reciprocity was a crucial aspect of the collaborative approach. Goodley et al, (2004, 167) comment that: 'researching life stories offers opportunities for drawing on our own and others' narratives in ways that can illuminate key theoretical, policy and practice considerations'. Listening to participants' life stories provided insights into what we came to call the transformative impact of further and adult education for them and on their lives; it also illuminated the ripples of impact on family and community. These research conversations were collaborative in the sense that new understandings were generated for everyone involved. For the research team, participants' stories provided important insights into the factors that facilitated transformative education. For participants, these conversations involved participants recounting negative experiences of schooling but from those retellings a shedding of spoilt identities (spoilt for example by the symbolic violence of being labelled) emerged and the affirmation and reclaiming of the new learner identities based on agency and self-respect. The discussions also, more broadly, fostered a growing awareness of social and historical factors that had shaped their experience of education to date (Duckworth and Smith, 2018a) and often involved talk about future plans.

Life histories were used as what Plummer describes as a sensitising 'tool' (2001), that helped give the researchers insights into the participants' world picture but also enabled them to engage with each other's narratives (and ours) and to open up these narratives for discussion and meaning-making. Throughout, we remained highly sensitive to the importance of the language we used as we wanted to explore the issues without echoing language use that might label or stigmatise the participants. That said, the experiences recounted were often lived experiences which demonstrated the forms of inequalities which had impacted on their lives. Occasionally, they were hard to listen to and painful to hear.

The project adhered closely to the British Educational Research Association (BERA) ethical guidelines (2018) and paid particular attention to the ethical issues associated with using a digital platform which included video. Anonymisation was a key consideration in that respect. Keeping research participants anonymous is an important way in which researchers can ensure no harm comes to them. However, in this project, while participants understood that they could remain anonymous, most wanted their real names used – that included teachers as well as students and others. The colleges and providers that were mentioned were anonymised or permission was sought to include names. Often, student participants mentioned particular teachers who had for them created the conditions in which new possibilities for change had appeared in relation to their active participation in and *use* of education. When this happened, we sought out the named teacher and asked them if they were willing to participate. If necessary, we anonymised them.

In this way, recruiting participants to the project often happened organically: starting with the existing professional networks and contacts of the researchers, it gradually spanned out across the UK and indeed beyond. This momentum grew through an ongoing programme of virtual and actual dissemination.

We began presenting data from the project to networks and at local, national and international conferences around the country within 6 months of it starting. This also naturally fed into participation; those listening to presentations about the project were invited to contribute to the project website. We distributed postcards with images of participants and links to the website asking audiences to share their stories of transformative education. At the end of our presentations, conversations were sparked with members of the audience who were waiting to share how the participants' narratives had resonated with their own experience as teachers and/or learners, see Figures 2.1 and 2.2.

The dissemination of the project findings often felt like social events that punctuated the collection of project narratives. These were occasions at which we sought to promote a shared understanding of transformative teaching and learning. At the outset, it hadn't occurred to us that dissemination would generate further data gathering opportunities. But that's what happened. Alongside these face-to-face conference, seminar and workshop appearances, the research was being made publically accessible by digital means as it developed. The next section will look in detail at the project website.

Phase Two. Broadening the reach of the project: website and survey

Phase Two of the research started around 18 months after the first phase. There were two key aspects to this both of which were aimed at broadening the reach of the enquiry. The first aspect involved the website development. The postcard idea from the first phase had suggested how stories from the

Figure 2.1: Project postcard

Figure 2.2: Postcard distributed at dissemination events

project often sparked responses from the audience. Audience members often recognised parts of their own journeys in stories like those of Adam and Awor. They triggered in them a desire to recount their own stories. It was a dialogical exchange that we wanted to foster, and the project website was a way of extending that kind of engagement. The website had started by hosting the videos, but we wanted to make it more interactive so invited viewers of the videos to contribute their own stories. Once these new accounts had been written into the website under a tab labelled: *Share your story*, we were able to tweet the link out to the growing digital audience for the project (for more detail on this see Chapter 3).

The second key aspect of Phase Two was the circulation of two surveys: one for staff and one for students. Why then did we decide to bring a quantitative aspect to the research and use numerical data following our insistence that such data has been and continues to be a part of the problem? One reason connects with the idea of research integrity and trustworthiness. In research, a concern with trustworthiness addresses the need for researchers to demonstrate that the phenomena presented in the research are not fictitious and are checkable. We would expect then that research integrity strengthens the knowledge claims made within the research project. So the survey sought to enhance trustworthiness with a view to situating the narratives within the wider landscape of further and adult education. Were the stories common? Were they the norm? What features did they share? And what could they tell us about the conditions needed to enable more transformative educational experiences?

The switch from talking directly to students, teachers and others about transformative teaching and learning to gathering data remotely via an online survey was a big decision. The main aim was to get a sense of the extent to which the narratives that we had gathered in Phase One were recognisable by further and adult education teachers and students nationally (responses came from Scotland, Northern Ireland, Ireland and Wales as well as England). The surveys used questions that elicited responses against a Likert scale. Survey respondents were asked to familiarise themselves with the existing data on the project website prior to completing the survey. The use of video was key here as we were conscious of the limitations of communicating the concept of transformative teaching and learning using only language and some kind of prescriptive definition.

Two national online surveys – one for staff and one for students – were then developed and distributed using snowball sampling via regional and national networks. In the next two sections we will focus on particular questions – more detail from the surveys can be accessed in Smith and Duckworth (2019).

The teachers' survey

The teachers' survey used items that were developed from the qualitative data such as:

I try to map students' lives onto the curriculum.
I try to develop relations of trust with students.

I try to ensure assessment addresses students' individual needs not just accreditation.

I try to provide emotional support for my students, when necessary.

I try to ensure that my students feel respected and valued.

I try to foster students' autonomy.

In addition to items that originated in our findings from the qualitative data, some items drew on psychological research in education where we saw connections. For example, the last two items in the previous examples map against self-determination theory (Ryan and Deci, 2000; Niemiec et al, 2010) in which psychological theorists foreground the importance of autonomy and competence in teaching and learning environments. These two factors are also linked strongly to students' motivation.

Self-determination theory posits that: 'satisfaction of both autonomy and competence needs is essential to maintain intrinsic motivation' (Niemiec and Ryan, 2009, 135). With most of our individual work prior to the project drawing on sociological ideas and theories, why did we choose to adopt this cross-disciplinary approach? We did so for a number of reasons. The first of these connects with the cross-disciplinary nature of the concept of transformative learning identified by Mezirow (2009). Mezirow incorporates strong elements of individual psychological features in his understanding of transformative educational experiences. But we also took this approach because we believe the seeming mutual exclusivity of sociological and psychological disciplines and rigid boundaries between them (Basil Bernstein (1971) would call this 'insulation' and 'classification') have become entrenched and, some would argue, politicised in ways that are unhelpful and constraining, not least in educational research.

We proceeded then on the basis that psychological notions like 'mindset' (Dweck, 2006) are capable of providing insights into teaching and learning (at the level of the individual) which can sit alongside and interact with ideas about the impact of social class (Willis, 1977) or race and gender (Gillborn, 2008; Davis, 2001) or other sociological perspectives. For that reason, we believed that establishing the (complementary) psychological basis for our formulation of transformative teaching and learning (however tentative) could add weight to the research. We are mindful that some psychological perspectives dominate in the field of education and of how these connect with neoliberal orthodoxies of individual choice and responsibility, and we examine some of these limitations in Chapter 7.

That said, there are some important overlaps between psychological and sociological perspectives. For example, Niemiec and Ryan's work (2009) on intrinsic motivation is interesting because it suggests that the introduction of what they call 'controlling conditions', close supervision and monitoring and evaluations undermines 'the sense of relatedness between teachers and students' and displaces the 'natural' feelings of 'joy, enthusiasm and interest' that students should experience in educational activity with experiences of 'anxiety, boredom or alienation' (134). In addition they state:

> The more that teachers' satisfaction of autonomy is undermined, the less enthusiasm and creative energy they can bring to their teaching endeavours ... the pressures toward specified outcomes found today in so many educational settings promote teachers' reliance on extrinsically focused strategies that crowd out more effective, interesting and inspiring teaching practices that would otherwise be implemented. (Niemiec and Ryan, 2009, 140)

This insight resonates strongly with our research data. In many ways this speaks to the picture from existing research of education environments that are funding-driven, data-fixated and disfigured by managerialist cultures. The factors that feed into self-determination theory are related to the social conditions experienced by students and teachers and connect in particular to a feature of teacher/student relations that can be called 'care' (Noddings, 2005). This also fits with a view of teaching as being more than understanding 'how the brain works': – some kind of technical exercise that assumes that universal physiological qualities can usefully be seen as over-riding the myriad other variables that affect students' learning (see Chapter 7 for discussion).

The cross-disciplinary approach we adopted in Phase Two of the project also resonates with work in mental health research. A report published by the British Psychological Society in 2018 takes a position in relation to mental ill health and psychological conditions that moves away from the pathologisation of individuals and treatment of them through medicalisation. Instead, it proposes an interdisciplinary understanding of 'the behaviour and experience of persons within their social and relational environments rather than (just through) the (mal)functioning of bodies' (Johnstone and Boyle, 2018, 37). We find echoes of project participants' narratives of transformative education in Johnstone and Boyle's suggested use of 'the construction, or co-construction, of personal narratives (that can) open up the possibility for different, nondiagnostic stories of strength and survival' (192). This is part of a new way of seeing and working with people in the field of mental health using what the authors call a *Power Threat Meaning Framework*. Taking these recent movements in the field of psychology into account, we see the psychological aspect of the survey design as an additional feature that can help in the construction of a broad and unifying conceptualisation of transformative teaching and learning.

The teacher survey garnered 730 responses. Respondents were asked to indicate their age against a range of categories and responded as follows: 21–34 (14%), 35–44 (23%), 45–54 (34%) and 55 and over (29%).

Figure 2.3: Geographical location of respondents to staff survey

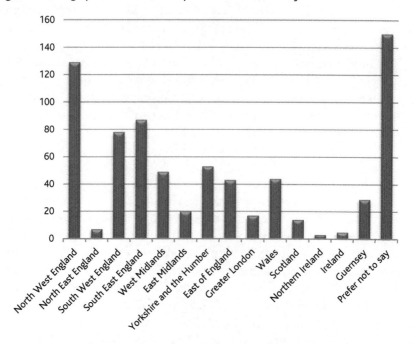

Seventy-two per cent of respondents were on full-time contracts. In terms of the number of years' experience teaching in further education the data were as follows: 0–5 years (20%), 5–10 years (20%), 10–15 years (24%), 15–20 years (19%) and over 20 years (17%). 72% of respondents were teachers, the rest were senior leaders, managers and others. Importantly, while a large majority of respondents were working in colleges, 19% were working in training providers and other further education institutions. The staff survey respondents came from across the country as can be seen in Figure 2.3.

One of the issues with accessing a large sample was the importance of permission of access. There were colleges whose senior leaders were only too happy to circulate the survey link. We heard nothing back from other colleges. Given the general funding-driven rather than values-driven context of further education, this may not be surprising. However patchy the take-up of the survey, we were able to gather views from across the country.

The previous bar chart shows that survey respondents were working in colleges from all regions and countries of the UK and included small numbers from Guernsey and Ireland as well. A significant number indicated that they preferred not to say which region/college they were working in. This is an index of the extent to which respondents might have felt vulnerable about sharing their views about their practice. This vulnerability is a clear indicator of i) teachers' lack of job security in the current accountability and performance environment and ii) the 'high-stakes' market cultures within which the voices of teachers are discouraged and even deprecated and silenced. This then connects with the claims we are making about transformative education that we have already touched on. It also presages the way we develop and refine our definition through reference to the following project data.

The distribution also connects to the way in which the sample was generated. As well as circulating the survey link through emails to college principals, professional networks, social media and the project website were used. It would be remiss not to acknowledge that while the project has been welcomed broadly by people working in further education and by people whose work is connected in other ways (such as HE researchers in the field), another, more suspicious reaction has also surfaced. For us, this connects to a healthy scepticism about the instrumentalist discourses that have attached to further education over the last quarter century. Generally speaking, these discourses promote an abstracted view of further education as a problem-free 'black-box' panacea for employers' (and the nation's) skills needs. It is easy to see how the tag of 'transformation' might feature as a magical signifier in an instrumentalist lexicon. So, the scepticism of some people about the project is understandable and might be seen to feed off a fatigue with the effects of marketisation on language. The tendency to use overblown and exaggerated terms in making claims about the impact of further education is (by now) an established feature of marketised language use. Think of the advertisements for the local college in your town/city/borough; is it not claiming that it can:

> 'Maximise your potential'
– or otherwise that:
>> 'Your future starts here!'
– or demanding that you:
>> 'Follow your dreams!'?

While all of these may be sincerely meant and may even be grounded in the stories of real students, the critical reader cannot but be concerned that the underpinning and overriding impulse behind such slogans is a commercial one.

It is within this linguistic context that asking teachers and students to complete a survey about transformative teaching and learning (notwithstanding the invitation to browse through the project website) might be expected to elicit a polarised response: any respondent might be expected to already hold a positive view of the concept before completing the survey. In that sense, the survey might be accused of acting as an echo

Figure 2.4: 'To what extent does course funding impact on your freedom to meet your learners' needs?'

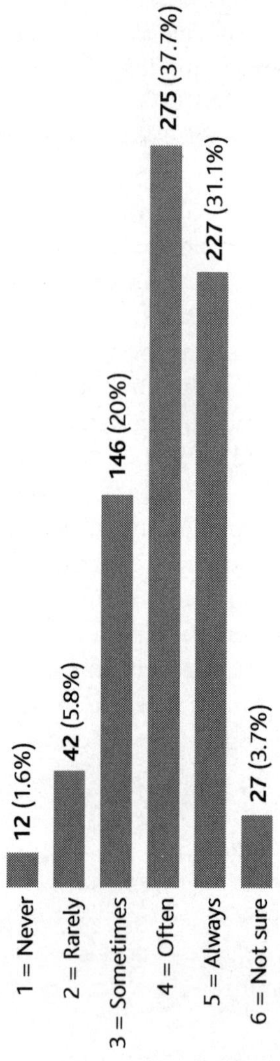

1 = Never   **12** (1.6%)

2 = Rarely   **42** (5.8%)

3 = Sometimes   **146** (20%)

4 = Often   **275** (37.7%)

5 = Always   **227** (31.1%)

6 = Not sure   **27** (3.7%)

Multi-answer: Percentage of respondents who selected each answer option (e.g. 100% would indicate that all this question's respondents chose that option)

chamber which serves to amplify a set of pre-existing views and opinions. There are no easy responses to such a charge, but we would counter that any research that seeks the views of a large number of people through surveys has to be framed by the understanding that participants' responses are not dialogical: what questions and concepts mean can't be checked by the respondents. As such, their existing understandings (both of the concepts and of what they think the researchers want to hear) cannot be explored. Within that frame of uncertainty, we will present and comment on some of the survey data we gathered.

There are two questions we will focus on in relation to the teacher respondents. The first question asked teachers to indicate the extent to which they perceived course funding to impact on their freedom to deliver aspects of their role. Findings are shown below each item (number of teachers shown under the bars), see Figure 2.4.

Shockingly, around two thirds believed that course funding 'always' or 'often' impacted on their freedom to meet students' needs. Despite this, the perceived impact of course funding on teachers' freedom had no effect on the extent to which they tried to foster positive student-teacher relationships or a sense of belonging in the classroom. This suggests that while restrictions caused by course funding constrained teachers, they still strove to incorporate these positive practices into their teaching.

The second question – related to the first – asked respondents to indicate 'the extent to which course funding impacted on their freedom to support students to achieve their aspirations', see Figure 2.5.

In the responses to this question, once more course funding can be seen as a constraint rather than a facilitating factor. Only around 10% of respondents thought that funding never or rarely impacted on their freedom to support students to achieve their aspirations.

These responses illustrate something powerful about the FAP regime. The system of funding that drives provision in colleges has become the 'tail that wags the dog'. The teachers are able to identify the students' needs and have the ability to meet those needs. But funding provides an obstacle to this. Funding requires them to do something other: to meet the needs of the institution in order to ensure funding is garnered over and above meeting student needs. But the idea that the funding also distorts teachers' abilities to help students achieve their aspirations is perhaps an even grimmer finding: it undermines the idea that students are consumers who 'choose' the course they want to do and the career they want to follow. Instead, it suggests that their aspirations are secondary. This would fit with the instrumentalist 'skills' agenda, suggesting further that a funding system that incentivises some routes and courses over others incentivises providers to steer students to enrol onto those courses, *whether they aspire to or not*! In other words, if their future is to

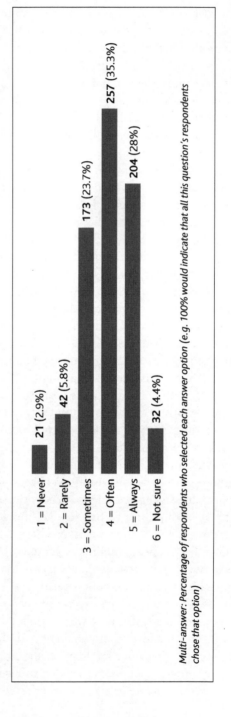

Figure 2.5: 'To what extent does course funding impact on your freedom to support students to achieve their aspirations?'

1 = Never — 21 (2.9%)
2 = Rarely — 42 (5.8%)
3 = Sometimes — 173 (23.7%)
4 = Often — 257 (35.3%)
5 = Always — 204 (28%)
6 = Not sure — 32 (4.4%)

Multi-answer: Percentage of respondents who selected each answer option (e.g. 100% would indicate that all this question's respondents chose that option)

start here, it is a future mapped out by someone else. Rather than following their own dreams, they find themselves a pawn in someone else's grand design.

These findings are so shocking, to someone who knows little about further and adult education, they might seem incredible. But ask any further education teacher and they will tell you that this has become the grotesque norm.

The students' survey

The student survey garnered 630 responses almost equally divided between male and female students. The age range of respondents was from 14–16-year-olds (24%) through to 35+ (15%) but the majority of respondents were aged 17–19 (40%). The majority of respondents (81%) were full time students. Responses also came from colleges across the country as can be seen in the chart in Figure 2.6.

Our student survey sought to identify the kind of educational experiences that students valued in further and adult education. Once again, our idea here was to supplement our sociologically grounded data with data from the psychological domain. Using and adapting validated items from other psychological surveys (for example, Beauchamp et al, 2010), our survey

Figure 2.6: Geographical location of colleges of survey respondents (students)

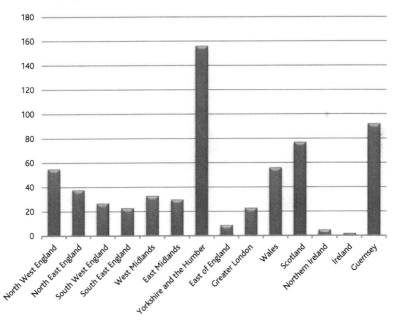

set out to explore the extent to which respondents felt they experienced autonomy, 'competence', feelings of relatedness and behavioural and emotional engagement at college. The notion of engagement is often used in policy discourse to describe 'successful' teaching and learning. Here, we are moving beyond the label to redefine it as a state that is not (only) inherent in the students and is not (only) something that the teacher should be 'accountable' for, rather it is an effect of the social conditions of teaching and learning and a product of the relationship between student and teacher. Engagement implies a particular caring kind of educational relationship.

The survey data provides a wealth of evidence to support the view that the survey respondents had a positive experience of further and adult education. Over three quarters (76.36%) of students reported having positive learning experiences 'often' or 'always'. This can be interpreted as providing evidence of the distinctive and potentially transformative educational experience offered by colleges, particularly if viewed alongside the qualitative evidence that saw many feeling the need to reclaim spoilt identities caused by deficit labelling at school.

Students reported feeling that they had autonomy at college and felt competent at college to the same extent (76.36%); for statements rated on a scale of 1–5 in which a higher score indicated higher autonomy/competence, the average score was 3.76 (in between 'somewhat true' and 'often true'). Using the same scale, the average score for the extent to which they related to other people at college was 4.00 ('often true'). The mean score for feelings of relatedness with teachers was particularly high (4.31, in between 'often true' and 'very true'), showing that students felt that teachers cared about them and were friendly towards them. This connects with important findings from the qualitative data. Students aged 35 years and over were also more likely to believe that their fundamental psychological needs for autonomy, competence and relatedness were being met.

One important finding related to prior educational experiences in school. In the field of medicine, there is a word: *iatrogenic*. The definition of this word given in the Shorter Oxford English Dictionary is '(Of a disease, symptom and so on) induced unintentionally by a physician's treatment, examination, and so on)' (Brown, 1993, 1,300). The example of usage given is: *The epidemic in iatrogenic deaths in asthmatic children* – which comes from a 1971 article in the British Medical Bulletin. The word is part of the vocabulary of the health professions and signals a recognition that healthcare is a dynamic field in which some treatments have a (very) negative impact on some patients whatever the intention.

In our view, we need a similar word to describe the negative impact of schooling on some students. Certainly, the pattern in our data of participants talking about how they left school feeling as though education had been *done* to them and they had been judged to be not good enough, stupid and/or that they would never amount to much was so prevalent a phenomenon that it warrants a name. While in the case of iatrogeny, the disease is caused by the treatment or intervention of the health professional, for project participants the labelling they experienced was one aspect of the broader systematisation of schooling including formative and summative assessment. The negative self-view of themselves as unable to learn that some project participants emerged with, had a cumulative impact that combined relational aspects with individual teachers and 'formal' aspects represented by the grades and marks attached to them through assessment. To capture the systematic qualities of this negative damage suggests the need to identify the schooling rather than the teacher(s) as the issue. The word that we might then want to attach to the phenomenon that teachers in further and adult education have to address as an initial and ongoing aspect of the pedagogy is *scholagenic* – a negative set of traits in students induced unintentionally by schooling.

There were no differences for this scholagenic factor in the scores of male and female students, or between the various age groups for this question. But the responses showed that roughly a third of student respondents felt that they had endured negative labelling by teachers at school. Once more, this highlights the distinctive contribution colleges and other providers make in having to address the (often negative) prior educational experiences of the students who walk through their doors.

Another linked finding related to self-confidence as a learner. Against a series of factors, respondents were asked to what extent these were important when they started college. Against the factor: feeling that you were no good at learning, responses looked like this (illustrated in Figure 2.7).

The data shows that the issue of self-confidence and the self-image associated with oneself as a learner is a prominent characteristic of students on arrival in further and adult education. This connects with the restorative aspects of transformative education foregrounded in our qualitative data. Put another way, we can say that there is an important integral feature in the work of further education teachers. A first challenge that sits outside particular course curricula is the need to focus students on the reconstruction of positive learner identities. For this question, female students scored higher than males suggesting that there is a gendered dimension to the prevalence of spoilt learning identities.

In addition to the response rate for the survey, we acknowledge that there are limitations to this quantitative aspect of the study. One of these is that it is not possible to generalise from the survey findings as the samples were not random and cannot be claimed to be representative of all teachers or students in the sector. That's another way of saying: the research data will not allow for definitive statements like: '[a]ll transformative teaching and

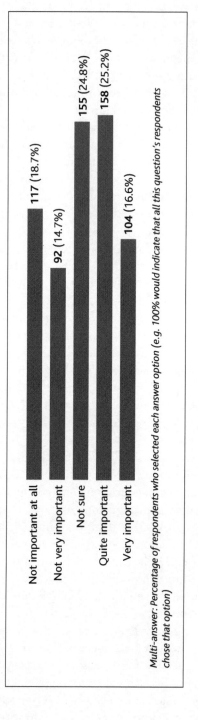

Figure 2.7: 'To what extent were the following factors important when you started college? Feeling you were no good at learning'

Multi-answer: Percentage of respondents who selected each answer option (e.g. 100% would indicate that all this question's respondents chose that option)

learning looks like X'. As we shall explore in Chapter 7, we don't think in any case that that is a helpful way of thinking about transformative education. That said, we think the addition of the use of validated items from existing psychological surveys adds substance to an emerging conceptualisation of what transformative teaching and learning is. But these reservations and caveats are a symptom of our sense that transformative teaching and learning is a *becoming* process. To return to the Rorty quotation that started this chapter, its meaning lies in the trusting and collaborative relationships that are produced by teachers and students as they work together towards a new future. In Chapter 3, we will explore further our use of digital technologies as an important aspect of the project.

3

Using digital technologies in social justice research

> What can we do to make the world, a better, more human place?
> John Holloway, *Change the World Without Taking Power*

Introduction

John Holloway's book *Change the World Without Taking Power* (Holloway, 2002, 11) presents the reader with a picture of the world in which our humanness, what it means to be human, is yet to be realised. Holloway's message is grounded in Marxist thinking and is premised on the idea that there is a not-yet-ness in the way human societies operate in our current world order. In other words, his thinking galvanises us into looking to the future and acting to bring about change in response to the realisation that the world as it is, is a denial of human potential.

The advent of the internet and the exponential growth in communication and the sharing of information afforded by digital technologies mean that the current age offers the possibility of change in human history as dramatic as anything brought about by the Industrial Revolution. But, just as in the 1760s Matthew Boulton could not have predicted the impact of harnessing steam power in his factory in Soho, Birmingham, in the same way, it is difficult to foresee the ultimate impact of this digital revolution that currently envelopes us. We can see how it is transforming commerce and the way many of us live; we can see how it is being used to gather vast quantities of data which may or may not be used for the benefit of human beings; we have witnessed how it is being used to misinform and to provoke anger, outrage and hatred. In the context of educational research, in what positive, unifying and solidarity-orientated ways can digital technologies be used?

So far, we have looked at the origins of the Transforming Lives project and how it was born out of a determination to focus on a further and adult education agenda that was not distorted by an overly instrumentalist view of the purpose of education. One consequence of this instrumentalist view is that it has had the effect of alienating many teachers by imposing a meaning on their work that demotivates them. It also transforms their relations with students in negative ways: by attaching a monetary value to each student.

In this way, it can lead to objectification that sees students either in terms of financial gain or as history – and identity-less receptacles to be trained up in the skills needed in future for the national economy. Another distortion, that this time affects students, is the reductive focus on assessment and achievement driven by the current funding and performance regime that changes the complex, socially nuanced, human process of teaching and learning into a scripted 'bums on seats' knowledge-delivery system, much as though students were empty vessels that can simply be filled with knowledge and skills.

The digitisation of knowledge production is an important structuring component of the funding, accountability and performance apparatus. The current FAP infrastructure enables the gathering of national data by a central body that can then use it to shape provision. In our view, this has had mainly reductive and deleterious effects. But digital developments and the internet can also be used to facilitate positive knowledge production practices and in this chapter we will focus on the way the Transforming Lives project used digital technology: video recording and editing, a project website, social media platforms (in this case Twitter and YouTube), combining these to share the research data and to broaden the impact but also to extend the project's reach. Even in the space of the 5 years that the project has been running, digital technology has changed, and its significance continues to shape our lives unpredictably. According to some commentators, modern technology within our capitalist society is accelerating work rates and productivity in damaging ways (see Noys, 2013 and Virilio, 2006). That technology (for example laptops and Wi-Fi) enables an intensification of work was certainly borne out for many during the lockdowns due to the COVID-19 pandemic of 2020/21, during which teachers worked from home and the boundary between home and work life became increasingly blurred.

Early on in the project, we made the decision to use digital technologies but wanted them to act as an extension of the methodology and to be underpinned by the values of the research. The principal idea in this is the making accessible of individual narratives to a wider audience to establish a collective understanding of transformative teaching and learning and to challenge the prevailing instrumentalist purposes of further and adult education. We will begin to apply theory in this chapter to explore the use of digital technology through the Lefebvrian concepts of 'the present' and 'presence' and Edward Soja's concept of the 'thirdspace' (1996) and use these ideas to help us to understand how the project has attempted to engage in a specific kind of knowledge production. This will involve exploring how the use of digital technology can enhance the democratic and participatory aspects of data gathering and dissemination. The ethical considerations that arise when using digital technologies will also be discussed, foregrounding the importance of maintaining the dignity of the participants.

As we saw in Chapter 1, further and adult education in England comprises a broad range of courses and educational experiences for 16–18 school leavers but also for adults who are returning to learn. As we have also outlined, marketisation with its funding regime and its fixation on performance metrics has led to a linear, systematised mode of knowledge production (governed by the FAP regime) that colleges and other providers are forced to comply with – designed and functioning to facilitate arm's-length control by central government. Working against the grain of this, our research project chose to adopt a more organic form of knowledge production: to utilise digital media to foreground the narratives of students, teachers and their communities with a focus on the individual and wider social and community benefits of learning. Our use of digital media in this was intended to work as a de-centred way of sharing the research across a myriad of accessible digital platforms. Also, unlike the knowledge production regime enforced by marketisation, our sharing of data was drawn from a democratised methodology grounded in a dialogical approach – inviting as it did its audience to comment and contribute. Finally, it's also worth noting that the methodology, centred as it was on human experiences of learning and teaching, was exploratory and didn't seek to nail down a precise and exact definition of transformative education.

As we steadily carried out our research visits and accumulated videos of our research discussions, we published edited videos via the project website. The aim was to provide a nuanced, textured and critical picture: a picture we would argue that creatively represents perspectives that, in their granular, irreducibly qualitative nature are typically ignored as 'too complex' and contextual within marketised settings. These personal accounts are viewed as emotive and 'subjective' in a policy environment that relies (and insists) instead on numbers and the pretence that numerical and quantitative data is more objective, accurate and reliable.

As a project that sought methodologically to bring values and approaches from critical pedagogy (Luke and Gore, 1992; Kincheloe, 2008) to research practice, we viewed the cycle of research as enhancing the agency of the participants by foregrounding their stories and offering an alternative set of narratives that crossed institutional boundaries and challenged reductive discourses about the further education 'sector'.

In an environment in which knowledge (often characterised as 'evidence' or 'fact') is used to justify policy decisions, knowledge production – in other words, carrying out research, writing about it, drawing conclusions from the data and publicising findings – needs to be demystified. Criticality when it comes to information that will be used to shape policy has an important role to play in our society in helping to rectify poor decisions. Criticality in knowledge production is key because it plays an important role in helping to bring about social justice (– a contested concept, as we shall see in Chapter 5). In contrast to the highly constrained and performative knowledge production practices that the incorporation of colleges ushered in with its over-reliance on at-a-glance performance 'metrics', this project sought to collect *counter-metric narratives* in video form: stories told in the voices of students and teachers and others that fall outside of what is deemed to be measurable.

The Transforming Lives project was founded on the principle that the market data that colleges (and teachers) spend so much time and monetary resource generating ultimately has not contributed to righting social injustice through further education in the way they should. Instead, as part of the machinery of neoliberal governance – the complex practices of performance data production that are then fed back to funders, the government and the public as part of the competitive 'market' structure – they have strengthened an instrumentalist and 'classed' view of further and adult education. As an alternative, the project provided a collaborative and democratic space for the sharing and celebration of participants' stories in which their voices were validated. The website was the key facilitating factor in this. The following sections will focus on the project's creative use of digital tools to enrich the research through the establishment of a discursive *forum:* an online space in which further education teachers can tell their stories, discuss their practice and voice their concerns and a virtual space in which ideas and narratives related to transformative education can be shared. The chapter concludes by theorising the connection between a digital research methodology and critical pedagogy where we outline a democratic and dialogical approach to knowledge production that goes against the grain of current neoliberal knowledge production practices and discourses.

Videography

As we detailed in Chapter 2, our research discussions drew on life history and biographical approaches. Typically, we met in either an empty classroom or office. But we also met in the front rooms of participants' houses, in cafeterias and, on one occasion, in Oldham, in an Indian restaurant. The two of us would sit with the participant and the video camera set up so that it didn't sit between us and the participant. It was important that the video camera didn't prevent us from establishing an informal atmosphere and in most cases, once we'd started, it was forgotten.

We mainly used a digital single lens reflex (SLR) camera on a tripod to record the research conversations. Occasionally, we used a mobile phone instead. These videos then became the medium for presenting participants' narrative voices. The immediacy of video and its ability to communicate participants' stories as told by them was one reason for this choice of medium. It's possible to describe the character of a research participant, the excitement in their voice as they speak about how the way they view the world has changed, or how after learning to read, they voted for the first time. It's possible to give a reader a sense of their strength and the bitter educational experiences they may have been through prior to the episodes they see as having been transformative. But the use of video bypasses the need for such descriptions and can convey such nuance unencumbered by the mediation of language (and our ability to use it). Also, just as the funding and performance apparatus that dominates education in England has an over-reliance on numbers which often fail to tell the whole story, in the same way, we need to be wary of the assumption that printed words on a page can seamlessly communicate all aspects of a research conversation.

Our decisions in taking this approach were governed by a concern to avoid transforming the project participants into passive research subjects. We were keen to move beyond the kind of imposition of meanings sometimes made with participants' stories that is rendered largely invisible when snippets of transcript are presented on a page. A key finding of the research related to participants' experience of symbolic violence in their educational histories (Duckworth and Smith, 2018B, 2019) in which some were positioned in deficit terms as learners and labelled as 'thick'. The critical and reflexive research methodology that we sought to utilise was conscious of the potential for our research interactions to embody symbolic violence in the same way. Editing raw video footage required us to ask ourselves continually what meanings we were reinforcing and imposing. The videos were structured using thematic captions which acted as a framework for initial analysis. We also shared all videos with participants prior to publication and asked for their comments, bringing a collaborative dimension at this stage of the research.

Contextualisation was a vital part of this as well. As best we could, we framed each video account with a social context. In order to understand participants' narratives, the viewer needed background information, sometimes about geographical location, other times related to the participant's background. In using video as part of ethnographic research, Pink (2007) suggests that visual knowledge should be presented in a contextualised way as forming part of a broader picture rather than simply being translated into written knowledge during analysis.

By maintaining reflexivity in the participant/researcher relationship, we positioned ourselves as co-producers of meaning. While it is true that we were still responsible for the editing process, participants' approval was sought in each case for the final video. In some cases, additional edits were made at their request. This was not surprising as many of the narratives were of an intensely personal nature. Indeed, the project provided participants with the opportunity to voice their experiences in education and to talk about the impact of these in the personal and public domains of their lives.

We converted video data to a format that could be embedded into visual or multimedia presentations while also uploading videos to YouTube. Digitisation facilitated posting and sharing across the academic and public domains. The emphasis throughout was on keeping a background consciousness of the dignity of participants as people able to tell their own stories. The research allowed us to understand participants' lifeworlds, their situated practices and lived local realities. Some of our participants went on to develop their own digital literacies.

The rapid advancement of digital modes of communicating and interacting has opened up new ways of being and of subjectification. Tik Tok, Instagram, Twitter and a host of games that allow for participants in different countries to play together in vividly imagined virtual worlds have in recent years enabled the construction of new identities and their accessibility through mobile phones meaning everyone with a phone can explore the opportunities. These virtual avenues might be important testing grounds for identity construction and can and should be viewed as a resource in educational settings. As Beetham and Oliver state:

> In a digital age, learners need to practise and experiment with different ways of enacting their identities, and adopt subject positions through different social technologies and media. These opportunities can only be supported by academic staff who are themselves engaged in digital practices and questioning their own relationships with knowledge. (Beetham and Oliver, 2010, 167)

But the digitalisation of data does not necessarily make it more comprehensive or more 'accurate'. The research conversation is a further place in which subjectification happens, in which research participants represent themselves and are known. The stories they want to share about themselves are an important aspect of that subjectification and there can be slippage in the space between research and public space.

An example of this comes from our experience of video recording the research conversations with project participants. It is important to acknowledge that however hard we tried as researchers to create an informal setting, switching the video camera on and off somehow changed the atmosphere. It seemed unconsciously to affect how we interacted as researchers with participants as well as how they interacted with us. It was an additional and modifying 'presence' throughout. While many participants were comfortable with the use of videoing on phones and with the notion of a lens capturing images, still the camera sometimes seemed to interpose itself between us. A consequence of this was that often, the moment the interview ended, and the camera was switched off, some participants would then seem to relax, and the sense of suspended formality would trigger new comments and rich, important insights. A number of participants at this point related an experience or perspective that we wished we had recorded as part of their narrative. On at least one occasion, we switched the camera back on and asked for the story to be repeated. On other occasions, the data was off the record and while relevant, was judged to be too personal to be included.

This also underlines how interviewing as a technique can never capture 'the whole story'. People's lives and experiences are so multifarious and rich that verbal interaction that cycles around predetermined topics has only a small chance of intersecting with potential seams of relevant 'data'. Furthermore, the relevance or significance of an experience may emerge (for the participant) for the first time in the interaction. Or an experience might be significant for the participant who nevertheless finds it difficult to explain why. The participants' control of what they wanted to disclose and talk about was respected, as we as researchers remained mindful of not exploiting the conversations in a voyeuristic way. In one sense, it is vital as researchers to 'let go': if the right affective environment is achieved, the research conversations will take on their own organic rhythm and flow.

The retelling of the participants' narratives was not without difficulties and emotional challenges. The difficulty for us was feeling at times impotent as details surfaced within the telling that spoke of deprivation, poverty and struggle. As comparatively privileged academics, we were sharing experiences with people who had often come from (or were still in) very different circumstances. The space produced by the research conversations was reflexive and placed a strong emphasis on 'affect' (see Chapter 7 for an explanation of this). That meant the 'feel' of the discussions was important, always informal and sometimes emotional. There were tears – on both sides, as well as laughter, excitement, pride, sympathy and even anger.

Maintaining a respectful and caring relationship was paramount with participants who talked about freeing themselves from drug dependency, abusive relationships, spending time in prison, episodes of clinical depression and similar experiences. This required a careful and judicious editing of the data that we thought appropriate to include. Very personal and sensitive information (for example, details of drug dependency or of family trauma) while often very significant were omitted to preserve participants' dignity and where there was a potential for impact on other family members.

The project website

The use of a digital platform to present and disseminate the research responds to the rapid development of new technologies which impact on people's experiences of space and time. Within this context, the project utilised a research methodology with the reach and power to engage, inspire, change and connect. This meant taking account of a non-linear approach to accessing and navigating information sources; the constant and instant online communication and connectivity that enables a sharing of information and culture (see for example, Prensky, 2001).

Figure 3.1: Project website landing page

The website was the central digital resource for the project, see Figure 3.1. The aim of hosting the narratives on a website was to catalyse a virtually enhanced engagement with the project audience. But, another motivation for using the website was to constitute what Soja calls a 'thirdspace' (Soja, 1996); that is, a space in which further and adult education could be represented differently. The idea here is that these narratives of transformative education can be seen as constituting a reimagined further and adult education, co-constructed through a dialogical interaction with practitioners and students. Key here is the idea that the project offers an alternative meaning, an imagining as *more than* the quantitatively defined abstract space that current further education policy discourse promotes and consolidates.

Furthermore, this digital third space looks beneath the skills discourse and speaks back to a collectively imagined 'version' of further and adult education that effectively objectifies students. Instead, it insists on a sovereignty of meaning in personal stories of finding purpose and dignity in education. It refutes the subordination of these narratives to a neo-imperial fantasy of economic competitiveness and 'productivity' within a global economic model that is so clearly orientated towards the achievement of something other than social justice and the alleviation of human suffering. As such, it seeks to challenge the powerful discourses around 'economy' that retain all of the unfathomable and mysterious unreason of a dangerous, world-wide religious cult and that have sustained the social order across the world for the last quarter century.

The interactive dimension offered by the website extended the influence of the project and constructed new and alternative meanings in the public domain. It also facilitated engagement with policy makers and led to additional opportunities for public dissemination and speaking back and to the development of policy. Each post on the website linked to a video of one of the participant's narratives. We then used the project's Twitter handle to share the post via social media.

The project participants spanned different generations: the youngest being 16, the oldest in her fifties. A number of participants in our study lacked digital literacy skills and the project became a platform for them to develop these. For example, some learners set up accounts in order to watch their videos, or set up Twitter accounts and engaged with an online community for the first time as a result of participating in the project. In this case, digitally mediated research, drawing on technologies such as laptops, tablet computers and smartphones, provided access to and engagement with research across social media networks and at times and locations that were convenient to the social media users.

Our use of digital tools was geared towards facilitating the expression of stories of the individual caught up in 'the everyday' (Lefebvre, 2014) and hidden by the corporate college narratives engendered by marketisation. Participants' sense that they belonged to a dispersed community that they could connect with through the project made possible a broadening of individual horizons. These project narratives present a human picture of lived experience grounded in social reality. In addition, they are orientated towards future development for the individuals concerned but also for further and adult education itself.

As we will explain, we felt the nature of the narratives we were gathering demanded that we step outside of the rush and tumult of 'the present' and into a space of reflection in which we aimed to summon up a greater level of 'presence' (Lefebvre, 2004). French theorist Henri Lefebvre uses the terms 'presence' counterposed against 'the present' to critique '*le quotidien*' or everyday life (Lefebvre, 2004) which he sees as ideologically imbued with the marketised relations that pass themselves off as 'natural' in capitalism. In contrast with the present which for him is 'a fact and an effect of commerce', in 'presence', '[t]here is dialogue, the use of time, speech and action ... presence situates itself in the poetic: value, creation, situation in the world and not only in the relations of exchange' (Lefebvre, 2004, 47).

The research was reflexive inasmuch as it recognised its own potential impact as social interaction. That consciousness made it important for us to draw on our understanding of critical pedagogy and to attempt to produce an egalitarian space for research conversations to take place in. In this space, we attempted to level hierarchical positions; informality fostered a 'feel' of participants being on an equal footing with us as researchers.

As a 'thirdspace' in which narratives documenting and celebrating transformative education are shared, the website does not only host information or act as a repository, instead it acts as an informal space for the interaction of teachers from different colleges across the country and beyond. The use of digital media here became a way of addressing: 'the realisation that it is space now more than time that hides things from us, that the demystification of spatiality and its veiled instrumentality of power is the key to making practical, political and theoretical sense of the contemporary era' (Soja, 1989, 61). Soja here is commenting on how history is more and more accessible to us but space (as seen for example in the relation between local and national perspectives) is becoming increasingly important in our understanding of how power works. If we accept Soja's claims about spatiality, then the internet is a crucial development with the potential to reveal 'the hidden' and to spread locally produced knowledge across networks at previously unimaginable speeds. Examples from consumerism and our increasing awareness of the origin of different products and the living and working conditions of those people who help to produce them, show how the internet can reveal the relations that sustain our standard of life and prop up global inequality.

In its celebration of local stories and voices, the project disrupts the generalised notion of an 'FE sector' that disguises the huge breadth in socio-economic contexts in which adult and further education happens across the country. At an ideological level, one effect of the generalisation of an 'FE sector' in policy discourse, is that it encourages the imagining of further and adult education as homogeneously whole. This is certainly how policy makers view it and project policies onto it. In fact, further and adult education exist within local ecologies and the imposition of centrally prescribed policy directives is likely to be inappropriate and to have unforeseen consequences. This 'sectoral' discourse has a broader and more insidious effect as it presents as a given an instrumental and economised skills purpose for colleges and providers in ways that override longer term social benefits. Where these two purposes are in tension, there is a likelihood that the social justice purposing that is articulated (more or less) by most providers will be marginalised and or undermined and the granular level of individual narratives are lost. When that happens, further and adult education is in danger of becoming a structural force for the replication of inequality and thereby social injustice.

The website became a way of resetting this kind of homogeneous perspective. The dissemination of the research in the local, national and international domain through the website can be viewed as crossing spaces and boundaries in an attempt at consciousness-raising orientated to what further and adult education can and should be as it engages learners and communities in the development of knowledge that can inspire hope and work towards social justice.

Figure 3.2: The Project YouTube Channel

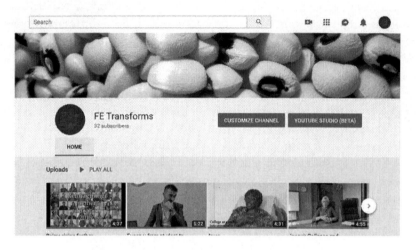

While it is curated by the researchers, both students and teachers are free to contribute their narratives. The website thus becomes an attempt to assert what is relevant and what is meaningful in the work carried out in further education settings. These are not just 'stories from below' that only present the lived experience of practitioners, learners and others; instead they include commentaries about wider policy, funding and artefacts focusing on specific perspectives (for example, women and transformative learning or employers' perspectives). In that sense then, the website is an attempt to create a space that makes dialogue possible between conflicting views on the purposes, meanings, achievements and problems of further and adult education.

We were excited to see how some videos became stimulus materials for teachers that generated further narratives for an online project audience. One example of this was Adam's video. Adam (whose story we shared in Chapter 1) was a student who had been excluded from school for anger management issues that seemed rooted in a frustration at being labelled. At college, he (re) discovered a positive learning identity. Another project participant, a teacher who ran classes similar to those Adam attended, used his video as stimulus material. The students in her class recognised different aspects of Adam's account and were able to relate this to their own educational experiences in a constructive way. One of the students produced a piece of writing that illustrates this empathy and the beginnings of reflection. This was shared on the project website (see Figure 3.3).

Broadly, the project-dedicated website provided a platform to share, validate and celebrate the narratives of learners. The research approach itself became a part of the affirmative practice that aided the transformative

Figure 3.3: The use of stories of transformative education in classroom settings

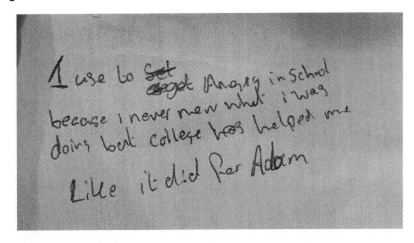

teaching and learning that participants had often experienced, a vehicle for positive subjectification.

Social media

The project made extensive use of Twitter (@FEtransforms). Linked to website content in the form of videos but also text-based participant contributions, tweets helped us develop the sense of a new space of communication in which participants' experiences could be shared and affirmed. The use of Twitter helped establish and build an audience for the research and required an investment of time: at least half an hour or an hour every evening and weekend. This took account of participants and communities more widely going online at various times and in various spaces, for example, on trains, in meeting rooms, at conferences as well as at home, in the kitchen or in front of the telly, see Figure 3.4.

The 140-character limit (for the first 18 months of the project) of the Twitter format led to additional developments in our creative use of media. We established a standard format of providing a headline about a new participant with a link to the video underneath. But we felt more variety was needed so we also produced collages of photos of participants from stills exported from the video data. These were used to link to the reports produced at different stages of the project. In addition, we used free websites to make GIFs (short animated sequences of images) that functioned in the same way as the collages: providing an artefact to attract a larger audience.

Finally, we also organised the video data in different ways. While the majority of videos present individual narratives, we developed a number that drew snippets from across the dataset to create themed videos. For example,

Figure 3.4: Twitter project homepage

a video was produced that focused on the transformative educational experience of women; another video focused on adult literacy. These were essentially a reframing of the data. Sometimes they included new segments from the research discussions, sometimes, they were a montage of extracts from videos that had already been published. The targeting of specific events, like International Women's Day, made a real difference to the impact of these tweets that magnified the interactive potential of the data. In this digitised and accessible form, the project data was able to reach across geographic borders reasserting a particular meaning for adult and further education that has been obscured by the nihilist objectification of the neoliberal project.

Concluding thoughts

As this chapter has shown, the website acted as the beating, digital heart, of the project. Not all research utilises a website but in this case, a digital platform enabled us to reach out octopus-like to an imagined project audience. Emanating from it, in addition to the Twitter feed and the YouTube channel, themed blog posts were produced for different organisations and websites. Eighteen months into the project, a conference was convened, bringing together many of the participants as well as HE academics and further and adult education practitioners, policy-makers and others. The focus of the conference was to reimagine further education through the lens of transformative teaching and learning.

In this way, all the different aspects of the project acted together to assert a heterogeneous picture of the research in context. The intention was to challenge and disrupt the 'abstract' and dominated space crafted by neoliberal policy making by producing a kind of space geared towards the acknowledgement and appreciation of differences, a space in which there is no hidden commercial relationship between participants and in which equality can be taken as an assumed starting point. In the work of Lefebvre (1991), this kind of space is called 'differential space'. In this space, the individual transformative narratives are sovereign. They are not narratives that tell the story of the inner workings of a 'sector', rather they are stories about how people's lives have been changed by a social (and political) process in which they have shrugged off their spoilt learner identities and rediscovered an ability to learn, harnessing this to agency and change and hope for the future.

An alternative way of viewing the project is to see it as an exercise in dynamic meaning-making: we used a website and videos of the research conversations as tools to communicate a message about the power of further and adult education to the public (Duckworth and Smith, 2018e). The project harnesses the powerful democratic potential of digital media to communicate information, narratives and values to an increasingly digitally adept public. The stories of the participants are inspirational in the messages of hope they communicate. As such, they can provide a resource and a roadmap for others who face similar challenging circumstances. The voices (often silenced in the public domain) are role models and a source of social capital that reaches across landscapes.

Our research has illustrated how digital technologies can offer a way of communicating a reimagination of further and adult education: one that is infused with emancipatory power. The use of the website, YouTube channel and social media in conjunction with each other allows for a breaching of the boundaries that divide scholarly and local communities. Traditional research cultures may have resistant attitudes to digital technologies; however, we would argue that digital literacy and practices are a necessary part of research training to meet the needs of participants in the twenty-first century. Certainly, failing to use them amounts to missing an important opportunity to share data and involve the research audience in meaning making and knowledge production.

The research attempted throughout to realise an ethic of respect for the individual participants and their communities. This is perhaps the key difference between research which can claim to be socially just, and research undertaken within other frameworks and paradigms where, although there may be a focus on social justice, the research itself falls into the position of using approaches and processes which reinforce participants' passivity. We would argue that digital technologies are not neutral tools – they can produce spaces where stories can be reclaimed that unsettle the hegemony of inequality and objectification.

The research was a collective process and in challenging the neoliberal commonsense view of further and adult education, it was of course political (Carr and Kemmis, 1986). For further education teachers, the digital aspect of the project offers an alternative locus of belonging. It breaks down the walled citadels of incorporated colleges and insists that the rewards of everyday human interaction, personal development and a concern for social justice, rewards that give meaning to the work of so many are a real, important and unifying force. Through harnessing digital technologies, the project sought to create a new shared understanding of transformative education that offers an exciting and hope-filled alternative; an alternative that speaks to John Holloway's injunction that we can and should act to try and make the world a better and a more human place; an alternative that can contribute to the resources of hope that are vital in our post-pandemic, post-austerity fragmented 'nation'.

4

Stories of transformative teaching and learning

(E)ducation reform brings about change in 'our subjective existence and our relations one with another' ... This is the struggle over the teacher's soul. Thus, I am concerned with a sense of who teachers are in relations with students and colleagues.

Stephen Ball, 'The Teacher's Soul and the Terrors of Performativity'

Introduction

The quotation above from Stephen Ball's famous article 'The Teacher's Soul and the Terrors of Performativity' (Ball, 2003, 217) is apposite because it indicates that the structures and policies that have resulted in the two versions of further and adult education that we talked about in Chapter 1 are having an impact across education as a whole. Published in 2003, it also illustrates the longevity and adaptability of the 'zombie hegemony' of neoliberalism, that while bereft of new ideas and limping on despite the financial crisis of 2008/09, continues to exercise a damaging influence on a generation of teachers and the histories of our educational institutions. Indeed, the tracks, traces and scars of isomorphic funding, accountability and performance apparatus are visible in health, social work, the criminal justice system and indeed in every area of the public sector that has been subjected to neoliberalisation. In relation to education, Ball uses an eschatological metaphor suggestive of an ongoing conflict between good and evil. The struggle over the teacher's souls suggests a context of divine judgement, salvation and damnation but also, breaking out of this restrictive binarism, of the possibility of redemption. As a frame for the stories of transformative teaching and learning that we present in this chapter, this redemptive potential is entirely appropriate. Ball's article argues that educational structures and policies position teachers in a particular way, as 'technicians' whose function is to service the delivery of prepackaged commodified educational products. Contingent on this, those same structures and policies position students as consumers and debase professional educational relationships by contaminating and undermining them through commerce.

What's remarkable then is that despite an educational landscape dominated by funding, accountability and performance regimes, the other version of further and adult education: the version that focuses on personal development, on growth, on hope and transformation is still evident. That it still exists is also evidence that neoliberalisation like any hegemony is not totalising; it could never swallow and extinguish established and resistant cultural ideas completely. The Transforming Lives project focuses on presenting stories that illustrate how the struggle for the soul of the teacher continues and that despite the terrors of performativity, in classrooms across the country and in the relationships between teachers and students, the reductive and destructive funding, accountability and performance apparatus has not succeeded in redefining the purposes of further and adult education entirely.

This chapter will present the voices of research participants from further and adult education settings as they have recounted their experiences to us but also, where relevant, will include the voices of parents and employers that sometimes assume great importance within these narratives. These stories communicate the triumph of individuals over difficult circumstances and illustrate how transformative educational experiences have a positive ripple effect into families and communities. We will explore how important the project participants' past experiences were in shaping their journeys into further and adult education and beyond.

Childhood experiences of being poor, struggling at school and not achieving, being subjected to (physical and symbolic) violence leaves many students desperate with low self-esteem and low confidence both in childhood and adulthood. As already touched on, scholagenic experiences are a recurring feature in the research conversations we were involved in. It is astonishing that this aspect our current education system goes unrecognised. But this lack of recognition is symptomatic of the obsession in recent government's current approach to schooling with assessment, the classification of students by 'ability' that pays scant regard to the impact on individuals of such judgements.

For school leavers at 16, further education colleges are where this damage has to be addressed if learning is to (re)commence and students' potential to be re-energised. For adults, re-entry into educational spaces might be in a college, in local authority provision or via organisations like the Workers' Educational Association. At its best, further and adult education sees teachers striving to support students to (re)connect their educational experiences to their lives in meaningful ways. This chapter will provide examples of that. Furthermore, we will highlight how teachers' practice incorporates keeping the destructive cultures and corporate mind-sets spawned by the funding, accountability and performance apparatus at bay, in order to produce a particular kind of educational space and so as not to allow these negative influences to disrupt and undermine students' learning, confidence and self-belief.

Sometimes, after many years, both young people who have taken exams at 16 and adults returning to education need critical spaces to support and empower them to reassert their agency as learners, no matter what their trajectory so far. As a result of often painful histories, many of the project participants had low self-esteem and experienced feelings of failure when they began their courses. Working as part of a collective with the teacher and their peers was a way for the participants to see themselves differently as individuals, to question their positioning in unbalanced power relationships that have marginalised them, and to act to transform their experience.

In this chapter, we share some project participants' stories – but we encourage the reader to watch the videos of the participants that are all viewable on the project website. As outlined in the previous chapter, their words, spoken by them convey meanings that we can only hint at by transcribing them onto the page. For this book, these written snippets from the research interviews are being used to formulate an argument about transformative educational experiences. A key theme of that argument is that further and adult education offers a space of renewed engagement with educational experiences through which individuals experience affirmation, a sense of greater agency and, crucially, feel supported to look to the future with hope. We develop the argument through mapping it across existing theory on learning and 'transformation' in Chapter 7.

Transformative teaching and learning as a lifeline of hope

Schools are sites where identities and futures are formed, and the Transforming Lives project traced the sometimes-detrimental impact of that. Rather than being sites that offer an egalitarian model where everyone is on an equal footing, schools are often experienced as sites of marginalisation, social exclusion and labelling by teachers and peers, our research revealed. For some participants this was experienced as a kind of violence. While corporal punishment was made illegal in British schools in 1987 (Shepherd, 2012), it would be fanciful to believe that it did not continue to be expressed in other ways. In Chapter 7, we explain and explore the concept of symbolic violence that originates in the work of Pierre Bourdieu (1994) but here, it is enough to say that symbolic violence, as seen for example in labelling, imposes a negative identity onto students that, through low expectations and unsympathetic interactions can have long-term consequences on a young person's educational experiences and outcomes. Symbolic violence can leave bruises that don't show and don't go.

For many of the project participants, schools were sites in which they experienced symbolic violence, and this had a huge impact on their learning experience, how they defined themselves and their subsequent trajectories. For them, the experiences of education as transformative that are documented in our research often involved a revisiting and a revisioning of the learning identities created in primary and secondary education that were spoilt by the labelling process which targeted them as they struggled with educational achievement – a struggle that often originated in social factors like their cultural and family background and sometimes poverty.

Anita is an adult project participant from the North East of England, a region that has experienced significant unemployment and poverty as a consequence of de-industrialisation: the loss of heavy industry including ship-building steel and the closure of mines in the 1980s. Anita provides an example of someone who was regarded as a failure at school (in this case because of undiagnosed dyslexia) and who carried this label with her throughout her adult life until she returned to learning. She told us in frank terms about her negative experiences at school:

'I've always been told I was thick. Always been told I was stupid ... The teachers at school assumed I was born to fail. Dyslexia ... had (only) just been identified. So you were thick, you were stupid and if your parents didn't even have any faith in you, you're not going to have any faith in yourself.'

Anita's dyslexia was not addressed at school as identification and support for that disability was not routinely available at that time. She felt stigmatised as a result. However, she gradually accumulated a body of experience in her working life that signalled she had strong administrative, organisational and interpersonal abilities. Encouragement by her partner and a chance opportunity to stand in as a project manager led to her questioning the judgements about her ability from school that had hung over her like a rain cloud throughout her adulthood. Eventually, she built up enough confidence to resume her education by enrolling on an Access to Higher Education (HE) course. Anita's tutors helped to consolidate her growing sense that she had something to offer. 'In eighteen months, I'll be a qualified social worker. My tutors are the ones that got me here ... They encouraged me. They never once doubted me. They made me grow ... They are the first people, apart from my partner who ever had any faith in me.'

Her story shows us how further and adult education can offer opportunities that build confidence in learning environments with an affirmative culture. She emphasises the importance of her partner's 'faith' in her and, importantly, her teachers' support. These factors facilitate the development of new knowledge and a new learner identity. We think it's vital not to separate out the teaching from the learning in any analysis of these transformative experiences. The two are interdependent and symbiotic. Transformative educational environments offer a dialogical experience that involves students in learning interactions with teachers and other students. These commonly draw on students reviewing and sharing understandings of who they are and on their prior learning experiences as a basis for moving forward.

Anita's transformative educational experiences have meant new responsibilities and a renewed self-belief that have allowed her to pursue a career as a social worker:

'I am actually going back, doing something and not just sitting in a cakey shop ... now I have my bits of paper, I have my confidence, I have my voice and I have a future. That's what education has given me: a life, a new life, a better life. It just opens up a whole new world and a whole new you. Suddenly, people are seeing you as you really are and not in the box that they have put you in.'

The concept of the 'subject as an effect of power' – which comes from Foucault (1982) can help us understand the impact of transformative teaching and learning. This can be a tricky concept to understand as we are conditioned to thinking of ourselves as self-determining individuals. However, as soon as we move into different spaces with unfamiliar people and unfamiliar surroundings (perhaps in a college for the first time or in a different country) we are likely to become aware that we are seen in different ways that we may not particularly like. We are all affected by this subjectification but it's only when this is consistently negative that we might become aware of it and feel the need to question it. Anyone who has faced discrimination simply for being who they are, has experienced 'the subject as an effect of power'. On the flipside, people who keep a close social circle limited to other people of similar backgrounds, values and expectations may not understand the concept at all – particularly if their social attributes (for example their class, gender, sexuality or race) habitually advantage them. The previous passage shows how Anita's transformative learning experience has impacted on her identity as a 'subject'. Here the subject is not just how we regard ourselves but maps across to how the person we are features within the different power networks that we connect to. It's how people see us and how they interact with us. This isn't just about self-esteem but involves a sense of social standing and status as we interact with others in wider society.

A corollary of this is that transformative educational experiences also herald changes within existing social networks and the connection to new and different social networks. Anita talks about how her Access to HE course has literally changed the way she interacts with people she might previously not have felt able to talk to with confidence:

'I can now talk to people that I've never felt I could talk to: the doctor, the clinician. But now I have my bits of paper ..., I have can talk and

I have valid points to make. And I have a voice. If it wasn't for college, I wouldn't have that voice.'

Here Anita provides a compelling picture for an alternative view of social mobility. Further education has enabled her to continue being who she is but has changed her social footing; it has brought about a transformation in how she relates to people in the outside world and *how she expects them to relate back to her.* She is also clearly aware of the symbolic meaning and power of her qualifications. These 'pieces of paper' have a symbolic value that people respond to, they have impacted on her as a subject, on the way people look at her. This suggests she has sharpened her critical awareness of the way the world works. Anita's account is important in the way it emphasises how her life experience, including suffering bereavements and moving away from abusive relationships fed into her choice of career as a social worker. It seems appropriate to use the term 'vocation' to describe her enthusiasm and commitment to this career. In choosing it, she is drawing on her existing experiential capital and potentially, through her work, affirming her own journey as she interacts with people in her work.

'I now want to be that person where I can say: "Come to me: I can help. I can give you the tools and as much support as you need to get you to a better place." Whether that's out of an abusive relationship, whether it's parenting skills, whether it's education; so you can have a better job, so you can have a better life for you, your kids, your family. I have moved, maybe not physically but mentally, emotionally and I've grown.'

When we met her, Anita was ebullient, and she radiated contentment and warmth. Her description of her 'growth' during her course is striking here. She sees her mental and emotional change as inseparable from her learning. In effect, she *feels* her learning. We must not underestimate the embodied nature of transformative teaching and learning. It can mean people feeling different and more confident in themselves. This can play a vital role in what happens next for them. In addition to providing evidence about the impact of her experience on the self as subject, Anita also talks about how her learning journey brought about a change of expectations in her family:

'Through that, I've been able to inspire my kids. One's at Manchester University ... he's in his final year. My daughter wants to go to Oxford to do Medicine. My oldest one has gone into the building trade and is doing fantastically well. He's gone into the management side. He would never have done that but he saw that I could do it. "If mum can do it, I can do it." I like to think I have inspired them.'

Where transformative education happens, there is this ripple effect, a dividend of significant social benefits that is unmeasured and unacknowledged by the blinkered funding and performance apparatus. This dividend extends from the individual to their families as parents become role models for their children. But it also extends beyond that and into the communities in which they live. A concrete example of this comes from Anita as she talks about how, since returning to further education, she has actively persuaded others to do the same:

> 'I love people … There isn't anyone that I have met who hasn't got some good in them, something you can bring out and something you can nurture. There's a girl that I met … she's just started her foundation degree in Health and Social Care. I persuaded her to do access … I met her in a pub, she was in bad place. She started coming in for a chat. I encouraged her. Over a period of time she did the progression course … Another one that I've recommended: a young lad in the village … I absolutely badgered him. He was a good kid going to waste. He's a hard worker. He just needed direction. He saw the resources that they've got (in college) and he was in his element. He signed up there and then. He's settled … it's lovely to see.'

In this passage, we see Anita becoming an advocate for further and adult education in informal social spaces within her community. There are several points to make here. First, it seems unlikely that the two people she talks about would have returned to education without her intervention. Her intervention provides an illustration of how further education that is embedded in communities is less likely to have an issue with accessing so-called 'hard to reach' students and communities. In addition, her interventions reveal the hollowness of notions of marketing and public relations that underpin the commodification of further education in these neoliberal times and that may be governed by commercial interests rather than the care and concern informing Anita's actions. Word of mouth, the most reliable and time-honoured means of finding out from a trusted source about how good something is, will not be replaced by an advertisement on the side of a bus any time soon.

We cannot emphasise enough how Anita's story is not about 'escaping' from her background and her community. Rather, it is about the realisation of existing potential that was somehow squandered by her schooling. We are distinguishing here between 'schooling' and education. 'Schooling' is the institutionalised process of education, informed by parental background, wealth and geography that shapes a young person's life on their journey to becoming an active member of our society. The fact that there is an increasing number of parents who choose to home educate their children (Carvalho and Skipper, 2019) illustrates how education doesn't have to include schools.

It is also indicative of a growing awareness of the scholagenic impacts that our current schooling system has on some young people that parents are actively seeking to shield their children from.

Some project participants had only a very patchy experience of going to school. David, a participant from an English traveller background, attended the adult literacy classes in a charitable organisation in the north-west of England. He arrived with his family, his wife steering a pushchair. David talked about how being unable to read and write made it difficult to navigate everyday social encounters:

> 'When you can't read and write out there, it's really hard. And it's scary. Now I can actually read and write and sign my own name. When I go to the doctor I can sign a note ... You need education to learn about everything that's going on outside.'

The fear that David speaks about in this passage stems not just from an inability to decipher a given text but the uncertainty that comes from not knowing when you might next be called on to do so. Finding yourself in a social situation in which you are called upon to read, but are unable to is awkward and is likely to compound feelings of inadequacy and even anger as being 'put on the spot'. David's reasons for not being able to read and write originated in his childhood and in coming from a marginalised ethnic minority group:

> 'I had a bit of a bad childhood ... I didn't really have help while I was at school. I'm an English gypsy so I was raised in a travelling family. So it was quite hard. I never went to school; I went to work instead. There's a lot of people in the travelling community, mostly with the boys they don't read and write, a lot of them don't. It's normally down to the women to do that kind of thing, the reading and writing of letters and things. Like the gas and the electric bills and all that. They normally sort all that out. The men normally go to work. (At) about eight I went to work. Started working with my dad, till I was about fifteen or sixteen.'

David's narrative contrasts strongly with Anita's. Like her, his re-entry into educational spaces was as an adult but rather than steering him towards a specific career, in this case, it was about improving his literacy skills and enabling him to interact with others through reading and writing tasks that many of us might regard as quite ordinary. For David though, these everyday 'literacy events' (Barton et al, 2000) held the key to a different future. For example, he stressed how learning to read would enable him to get his driving licence. This in turn opened up additional employment possibilities.

That said, the primary motivation David had for learning was connected to his role as a father. Being able to read and write was a way of ensuring his children had more choices than he had and thereby meant breaking an intergenerational pattern of poverty. David talked about wanting to be able to read bedtime stories to his 4-year-old daughter:

> 'I've got a bit more confidence, I never had much confidence. I couldn't read at all. Now I've started picking up words. It feels great. My little girl, she used to read stories to me and I couldn't read stories back to her. But now I can actually read back. It feels brilliant. It's only from coming here that I've got that … You can do these things, you've just got to want to do it.'

For David then, an effective way of tackling his literacy issue was to focus on habitual practices with a finite number of texts, so that these could be revisited in a safe environment. The 'literacy events' of reading bedtimes stories offered him the perfect opportunity. Children have favourite stories and enjoy hearing them repeatedly. Once again identity and where education positions us in our interactions with others is a strong focus. It's personal development and change that connects to social mobility but it's experienced within the family. The overlap and interconnectedness of adult and family literacy is striking here. Tackling his inability to read and write was also a catalyst for David to take part in our democratic processes.

> 'I never voted in my life ever. I sat down and read the thing that came through the letterbox and I thought "Yeah I'll give that a go." And I voted for the first time. I'd never ever voted before and you need to vote. Everyone needs to vote. Now I can actually read and write and sign my own name. When I go to the doctor, I can sign a note … You need education to know what's going on outside: the politics and all that. I'd never voted in my life, ever. I read the thing that came through the letterbox and I voted for the first time.'

While David had moved away from his traveller background, the impact of participation in adult education had clearly had a multi-faceted impact on him in the community that he and his family are now a part of. For David, learning to read triggered the beginnings of a political awareness. Not only did his re-entry into education give him confidence in a range of everyday social situations, crucially, it also gave him access to our current democratic practices (however jaded a view one might have of them). The social benefits here of growing autonomy, enhanced parenting skills and a newfound willingness to participate in the democratic processes which should be a distinctive and important aspect of public cohesion are hugely significant. However, yet again they fall outside 'what counts' according to the current FAP regime.

Restorative education: addressing students' prior educational experiences and psychological needs

Further and adult education can often be a critical space to support and empower learners (and indeed teachers against the dominant discourse) to take agency, no matter what their trajectory so far. On starting again in further and adult education settings, for a number of the participants there was a strong feeling that they would be judged and labelled by others in a way that mirrored their experiences at school. Working as part of a collective with the teacher and their peers was a way for the participants to see themselves differently as individuals, to question the 'subject' positions that had marginalised them, and to act to transform their lives.

Active involvement in decision-making and a learning dialogue for these participants meant experiencing an educational environment free from fear and stigma. The sharing of experience between the teacher, participants and other students, led to a dialogue framed within a social praxis that included reflection and action (Macedo, 1994). For David and Jade (stories to follow), whose courses took place in community settings, the blurring of informal and formal boundaries allowed for a spill-over of this kind of social interaction outside the classroom. This inclusive approach to education with its democratic features and community-centredness was for many of the project participants the antithesis of what they had previously experienced.

The research sought to explore the qualities of the relationship between the teacher and the student as central to the process of transformative teaching and learning. The narratives in our study reveal the contradictions, complexities and ambivalences of their daily lives and how they tried to make sense of them from their structural positioning as students with minimal dominant social capital, in a society based on inequality of opportunity and choice. Transformative teaching and learning can be seen as the interactive process whereby they re-discovered agency in educational experiences to enable themselves to harness the symbolic capital of educational qualifications to an imagined future.

The challenge for teachers and policy makers is therefore to establish the social and educational conditions in which students are empowered to grow their agency within the field of further and adult education. This has implications for curriculum and for funding. The curriculum needs to connect at an important level with learners' lives and experiences. The funding has to support small-step progression. Some project participants were facilitated by colleges to take a series of short courses over an extended period, a pathway that ultimately led to full engagement with a mainstream qualification. This involved by-passing the straight-jacket created by the FAP apparatus and often depended on non-government funding. We will now illustrate the immanent power of further and adult education to undo the scholagenic damage done by schooling and/or limited and low-paid employment prospects, drawing on data from conversations with two more project participants.

Access to HE courses have a long tradition of welcoming adults who have been out of education for some time and who often have few qualifications. Over the course of 1 year (full-time) or 2 years (part-time), bespoke courses prepare students for HE courses in a range of different fields. At a college in the North of England, Claire found in her Access to HE course a new world in which for the first time she was listened to and was able also to find her own voice. This led to her seeing the world from a fresh perspective and to positioning herself differently within it. This change in her view of herself in relation to the world was an integral outcome of her success as a student.

We met Claire at the Northern College which, at the time of writing is one of the small remaining number of adult residential colleges in the country, a college whose continued existence appears to be under threat (Staufenberg, 2021).

'You start to look at things more politically because you start noticing those messages that you get on social media, on the news. And you start to question things and you start to question other people. That in itself is empowering as well. And I'm really big on equality for women … which I suppose I'd thought about it but not necessarily been able to make those connections … and not been able to challenge that in a productive way.'

The previous passage from our discussion with Claire resonates strongly with Freirean principles of 'conscientisation' – in which students acquire an awareness of structural inequality in society and their struggle within that (Freire, 1995). This awareness provided Claire with the opportunity to challenge the subject position she felt had been imposed on her and to break its grip and impact in the private domain of her family. Claire went on to complete her course and ultimately, became a teacher in the same college where she first began her re-engagement with education. This enabled her to realise for others the transformative educational experiences that had helped her change her own life.

Claire provided a range of evidence about the different conditions that work together as constituent parts in environments that foster transformative teaching and learning. One key aspect of a learning environment of this kind is the way in which the curriculum relates to the learners' biographies. For Claire, this was as simple as being accepted for who she was:

'My self-esteem and confidence wasn't what it was when I was eighteen. (Now) I'm comfortable in my own skin. And that's something to do with equality. And people at Northern College accepting you for you ... And just that right to speak without being interrupted. I found that, like, so powerful. And being really listened to as well.'

Here, Claire describes the power she experienced by not feeling awkward or out-of-place and by simply being listened to. There is a strand of educational research (about Higher Education) that looks at students' feeling of 'belonging' (for example Thomas, 2012; Ahmed, 2007). In this case, Claire associates this sense of affirmation in the educational space co-produced with the Access to HE teachers. She went on to say how she used to long to return to the classroom in order to experience those feelings of wholeness and worth every week. This research illustrates how teachers, researchers and research participants can collaborate to create alternatives for encouraging self-expression and discovery in education. Our vision of education is that the system as it stands is fuelling social inequality. More attention needs to be given to marginalised individuals and populations through the deployment of curricular innovations that both enhance and promote literacy development and personal self-esteem. Further and adult education is a perfect vehicle for achieving such a goal (Duckworth and Smith, 2017a).

Claire's account illustrates another important attribute of transformative education. Central in this was the sense that participants had of not being 'judged' and of being accepted for 'who you are' – overturning the negative judgements, the labelling and being designated 'thick' or as coming from a particular family or estate that we have already touched on. In contrast, learning environments which enable transformative learning to take place are founded on an ethos of egalitarianism – usually explicitly. People's background, thoughts and views are accepted and foregrounded as important areas of interest and importance in the curriculum and as a basis from which to move forward.

Claire's story revealed how further education courses can be pathways to overcoming and moving on from problematic and painful domestic issues and histories. Claire talked of feeling 'empowered' by her course. Empowerment for her did not mean a teacher somehow 'giving power' to her or the other students; rather, it was the sense that she had of growth and an increased ability to act in her own capacity.

The participants described how the telling of their personal stories was empowering in the classroom; their stories and how they led to this new educational experience was a capital for resistance against the barriers they had faced. They described having their eyes opened to 'a whole new world' by returning to education and improving their confidence and skills.

Parenthood, challenging intergenerational poverty and the 'ripple effect'

Research from across the world has identified how family background influences young people's educational trajectories (see for example Buchmann and Diprete, 2006). Working-class parents just like middle-class parents desire to help their children, but may lack the social and cultural resources to become involved in a way that will influence their children's educational pathways. The project's longitudinal dimension enabled us to build up evidence of the impact of further and adult education in challenging cycles of intergenerational inequality and contributing to the achievement of social justice with its powerful individual, social, economic and health benefits.

As already touched on in Anita's story, a key theme that emerges from the study is the notion of the 'ripple effect'. In further and adult education, dominated and governed by the FAP regime (see for example Smith, 2015; Smith and O'Leary, 2013), the ripple effect can be described as one of many *counter-metrics*: the unmeasured and therefore widely unrecognised social benefits that fall outside a neoliberal purview but nevertheless have significant positive personal, social and economic impacts beyond the achievement of a qualification by a single individual and the enhancement of productivity that supposedly results from that.

Addressing the impact of intergenerational poverty is obviously more important in areas where there is poverty. It's important at this point for the reader to remember that the Transforming Lives project commenced after 6 years of so-called 'austerity'. As outlined in Chapter 1, the cuts to public expenditure which, as well as other things, resulted in a huge rise in homelessness in UK cities, also impacted enormously on the ability of further and adult education providers to combat social inequality. Our research found that these colleges and other providers offer a significant safety net for students from backgrounds affected by poverty. In effect, colleges are picking up and alleviating the detrimental social effects of recent government decisions to cut public expenditure. College teachers are having to address issues associated with this newly acquired role on a day-to-day basis. Poverty and its effects reach right inside further and adult education classrooms and impact on students' ability to learn.

Any discussion about education being a key to social mobility needs to take account of how some parts of our education system shoulder the burden of addressing issues associated with poverty more than others. We would suggest that colleges, whose demographic disproportionately includes young people and adults coming from backgrounds such as these, should be funded to reflect that fact. The 'ripple effect' of transformative education illustrates why. According to our research, despite the cut-backs imposed by a government policy of austerity, the pay-back from investment in further and adult education if transformative teaching and learning is enabled is incalculably significant. We will now present three accounts to illustrate the power of this 'ripple effect'.

Jade is a young mother who attends the same adult literacy classes run on a local high street by a charitable trust as David. She is motivated by motherhood, her confidence as someone who can learn has increased as a result of attending classes and she has learnt new literacies (Barton et al, 2007; Street, 1990). Together, these accomplishments have inspired her to plan for the future and she has become determined to be the best possible role model for her son.

> 'It gives me confidence. It makes me feel better. It makes me feel more like I can go and get what I need to achieve and … be who I want to be. I just want to be like … someone with a job. Have money. I want to be able to treat my son. I used to get holidays when I was younger and it was exciting and I want to be able to treat my son to stuff like that. At the moment I can't really do that and it's making me feel like I can do it. I can do it … I want to give him the best childhood that he could have and that's by me doing what I want to do as well … I've been through times of depression but I've always tried to stay positive … I've been at the lowest place in life … My son brought me out of it. Children look up to their parents and I want him to look up to me … It's for my son. It's all about him really. What he's had in his life up to now is crap. He deserves a lot more. Kids are innocent and pure and they are the way they are taught.'

This passage illustrates the centrality of motherhood as a motivational force for Jade as an adult learner. Rather than a focus on the production of a neoliberal vision of human economic potential signified by human capital, Jade's literacy classes engage with her existing emotional capital (see Reay, 1998, 2000) as a way of opening up possibilities for educational success. Once again we see evidence of the power of changing subject positioning: the way other people view the participant – as a key motivation for revisiting education. Jade is profoundly motivated by the desire to be able to enjoy ordinary things with her child. Echoing David's account of wanting to be the father who reads to his child at bed-time, here emotional capital includes the need to be a good mother and provide educational care (O'Brien, 2007). In Jade's case, it also extended to her circle of friends. Like Anita, Jade was determined to introduce one friend (with experience of mental health issues and also a mother) to the literacy classes as a way of helping her out of a cycle of depression and deprivation:

> 'I'm always saying to people … Like my friend, she's had her kids took off her, and she's suicidal, I don't like seeing her like that – it breaks

my heart, looking at her. I try and help her as much as I can and get her on the parenting course or the literacy course. Just to get her to stop thinking. Or to get her mind onto something else. I'm always speaking about courses that my friend could go on because she's just so low and I think she deserves a lot more than she's ever had in her life – to build up a bit more, because she thinks very lowly of herself.'

Jade expressed a sense of being comfortable, feeling welcomed and belonging in her literacy classes. The locality of this small adult education provider was an important consideration here, as it was clear that Jade might not have felt comfortable travelling on the bus to a college campus. Being able to learn in a room above a shop on the High Street made the opportunity more attractive. The educational space here was transformative in the way it sought to connect her current aspirations for herself and her son with a future lifecourse trajectory. Reay (1998, 2000) suggests that an investment of emotional energy in education by working class mothers can sometimes deplete their own emotional well-being. However, in Jade and Anita's cases, rather than depletion, we see invigoration: motherhood seems to have acted as a catalyst to the women accessing education and through that hope as it opened new possible trajectories in life and work, and in helping their children to succeed.

Dean: a transformative apprenticeship

Work-based learning is a component of the further and adult education portfolio that would seem to connect most closely to the 'skills' and productivity discourse that currently dominates policy in this area. But even here, some of the principles underpinning transformative education that we have so far touched on can be seen to have relevance. The structures underpinning apprenticeships have changed several times over the last two decades. The latest iteration of this kind of training programme positions employers in 'the driving seat' (DfE, 2016: 1) and introduced a levy from large companies. Employers were involved as regards content, design and the focus of new standards. A government pledge in 2015 to increase apprenticeship numbers to 3,000,000 (BIS, 2015) suggested the centrality of this resuscitated programme in government plans to improve the instrumentalist drive of policy following 5 years of austerity.

The way the new apprenticeships programmes configured arrangements for on-the-job training and off-the-job training (two key features of the new programme) reveals a great deal about how the government continues to privilege the interests of private business over those of publicly funded organisations. For the off-the-job training, provided by colleges and private training providers, the existing funding, accountability and performance regime that has proven so damaging to further education provision was used. This demands huge amounts of accountability paperwork and is structured by a complex series of funding bands – that enable the government to incentivise some skills areas over others in an established pattern of destabilising irregularity.

The employers, on the other hand, tasked with providing on-the-job training, were not made subject to *any* quality regulation. Research by Cui and Smith (2020) and Brockmann and Smith (forthcoming) reveal that these arrangements have created the conditions in which three very different models of apprenticeship are able to operate: apprenticeship as the development of experts in an industry-wide community of practice, apprenticeship as staff development and apprenticeship as income stream. Clearly, the last model of these three is an objectifying and exploitative one. The first, on the other hand, is what Fuller and Unwin (2003) would term 'expansive' and involves close cooperation and understanding between employers and training providers to dovetail the on-the-job and off-the-job elements of apprenticeship. In the Transforming Lives research we were fortunate to encounter an employer who had adopted this approach and who had established a constructive partnership with a local college and the construction teaching team. It was through the college that we met Dean.

Dean offered an insight into how an environment that fosters transformative teaching and learning could meet an employer's needs and also enable personal and professional development. In Dean's case, his employer liaised closely with the college to ensure a construction curriculum that was appropriate. But the employer relied absolutely on the expertise and the affirmative approaches adopted by the college teaching staff. For Dean, attending college also meant overcoming the significant barrier of a lack of self-confidence:

'Given the opportunity to further myself, that's a no brainer. But then coming to college, that first day, I was like: I'm not sure I can do this … It's changed me. I can do things. I am capable … The first day I started I had no computer skills … Now I feel like I've got a bit of respect. It's definitely life-changing … Even with the kids, I went to parents' evening … I ended up chatting (to the teacher) more about me than about (my daughter) … I've been promoted to be site manager. It's been an amazing turnaround.'

Simon, the managing director of a construction company and Dean's employer, talked about the importance of 'growing' his own talent. By this he meant positioning learning at the heart of his company with an eye on its long-term prospects. Although Dean had no qualifications and had worked as a labourer up to that point, Simon supported him in taking on the apprenticeship. This involved Simon in developing a holistic educational experience with a local college that blurred the boundaries between learning spaces and the workplace. Simon effectively entered into a partnership with the college that provided the off-the-job training aspect of the apprenticeship. Frequent visits and communication between Simon and the college construction tutors was a feature of the partnership as the Simon wanted the college-led element to dovetail with the on-the-job training that was provided by the firm.

Dean's apprenticeship programme was dependent on Simon's personal commitment as an employer to his employees. Simon saw construction as a vocation and a career with opportunities for personal growth and the development of skills and knowledge:

'I've built a five-year course – when people say an apprenticeship, (normally) it's two years. I've been absolutely saddened by the attitude of the industry where it is encouraged and rewarded to collect as many apprentices as you can, massive intake then after two years, you take an eighteen-year old and you say: I'm sorry there's no future with us … The driving force for us is, you pass and do your apprenticeship with us and you are guaranteed a career. That's part of the deal … you work hard for me, you work hard for the business and we will look after you and we will guarantee you a framework.'

Within Simon's contribution there is an explicit criticism of some other employers' attitudes to the (current) apprenticeship programme and indeed, evidence is emerging that the new scheme is not fulfilling expectations (Richmond, 2018; Cui and Smith, 2020). This passage provides insight into how a funding-driven environment in the worst cases can lead to the exploitation of students as a source of income. This is strong evidence of the flawed nature of the way funding is used in a drive to improve 'productivity' that is dominated by supplying skills. It's also an indictment of the way further and adult education is funded through the funding accountability and performance apparatus. In the case of apprenticeship programmes, the exploitation is on the part of big employers rather than training providers and colleges. Simon's non-exploitative approach is distinctive and, in the transformative experience on offer through the bespoke model of apprenticeship he organised through partnership with a local college, he seeks to connect the success of his company with the personal development of employees. In his case, there is space alongside the employer for the learner and the teacher on the 'driving seat' and his is an enabling rather than a dominant role.

In Dean's case, we can see that further and adult education once more is not simply about the individual student making their way. But, just as with Anita, it involves the connected commitment of others. As Dean's employer, Simon provided a vital foundation of care and that, along with the expertise, experience and support of Dean's college teachers, helped in the realisation of his story. Partnership across and between different institutions each with its own balance sheet and financial needs is possible and is essential if apprenticeship programmes are to create the appropriate social conditions for transformative teaching and learning. Huddlestone and Laczik (2019, 20) suggest that: 'If employers are to be engaged, then it is suggested that what is expected of them is de-scaled, structured and prioritised in such a way that what they can offer is relevant, realistic and adds value'. Simon's contribution is all of these and this stems from his involvement being underpinned by values that connect the needs of his firm to the interests of his employees.

At the heart of transformative teaching and learning lies an affirmation of the kind of relationship between teacher and learner and the activity of learning and a commitment to these. Positioning the educational (or training) experience as something that is done *to* the trainee/student rather than *with* them overlooks and reduces even dismisses the significance of their participation and agency. Dean's story illustrates how in what might appear to be the most clearly skills-orientated training programme, transformative teaching and learning still takes place and still has a huge impact.

Dean's story illustrates how in training as in education an emotional commitment and a relationship of care on the part of the different stakeholders play a vital role. It's interesting how vocational education and training and apprenticeships are somehow more vulnerable to perceptions (by policy makers and others) that conviction, belief, affective and intellectual commitment are less important. Dean's example offers a totally different perspective and begs the question: How can an apprenticeship function without having at its heart the apprentice's sense that this is something that is not being done to them but done with them – and that it offers the opportunity for personal change and development that can feed into their life going forward?

To see work-based learning in any other way, most of all to see it simply as the behaviourist delivery of a set of skills to fulfil an employers' needs, is to objectify the student: to do teaching and learning *to* them rather than *with* them.

Transformative teaching and learning and the teacher's role

The role of teachers in transformative education cannot be over-emphasised. Market discourses of 'falling standards' (Hansard, 2018) perpetuated largely by Ofsted (for example Ofsted, 2020, Ofsted, 2018) and government rhetoric have created a trend towards the devaluation of teachers, despite evidence of a hugely expanded workload. Stephen Ball's (2003) perspectives that in general teachers under marketised systems are being reduced to 'technicians' who deliver curricula rather in the way that a robot might, is one of many critiques. Literature that focuses on further education in particular speaks of the 'de-professionalisation' (Yarrow and Esland, 1998, 11) and even 'proletarianisation' (Randle and Brady, 1997, 134) of further education teachers.

Data from the teacher survey we carried out as part of the project can be interpreted as supporting a view that over the 25 years since incorporation, teachers' conditions have worsened, and their work has intensified. As previously mentioned, there were 730 responses to the teachers' survey. Importantly, while a large majority of respondents were working in colleges, 19% were working in training providers and other further and adult education institutions. Similarly to the student survey, the staff survey respondents came from across the country. The survey data is useful inasmuch as it provides a contextual frame for the research discussions we had with teachers in colleges and providers across the country. In this section we pick out and comment on some key aspects related to teachers and teaching.

The survey data showed that 41% of respondents are in classrooms teaching 24 or more hours per week. It is a staple of managerialist discourses in further education to deny that increasing a teachers' weekly contact time will result in a decline in 'quality' which may explain these high figures. This rationale can be seen as dominating further education settings for the last quarter century. We consider it an appropriate time to evaluate this supposedly 'commonsense' view which has worked to generally increase teachers' contact time in further education. In the current context, while there are no nationally recognised upper limits on contact time in colleges, it has been left to the teaching unions to call out excessive hours, usually on the basis of the health and safety of members. The enforcement of local negotiation by teachers' trade unions in colleges can mean that teachers' working conditions and the working week of individuals depends on the relative power of local branches. Consequently, that can mean that in a financially insecure college with a bullish management, college teachers are forced to take on additional hours in the name of 'efficiency'. This doesn't only mean that working in colleges is less attractive, we contend that it has damaging consequences for the conditions which make transformative education possible – as we will outline.

While secondary school teachers are reported as teaching between 20 and 21 hours per week (Sellen, 2016, 18), our sample suggests that a much higher total of teaching hours per week is common in respondents' colleges.

Figure 4.1: Hours spent teaching per week (full-time teachers only; n = 350)

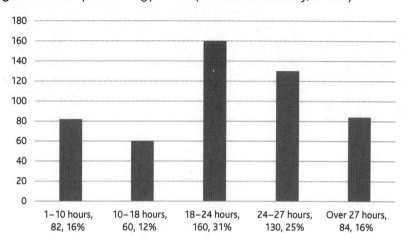

At the upper end of this, 16% of respondents reported teaching more than 27 hours per week. Anyone who has taught full time knows that a weekly workload of that number of hours for longer than a few weeks is likely to lead to health problems. In the context of this chapter, when viewed alongside other factors, we would argue that such a workload considerably reduces teachers' ability to facilitate transformative educational experiences. The following figure gives an indication of the amount of time per week respondents were spending on administrative tasks.

The following bar chart is suggestive of a broader context in which the administrative work of teachers is also high. While teachers may be key in creating the conditions in which transformative learning takes place, college senior leaders and managers are responsible for creating the social conditions in which teachers work. But they in turn are constrained by FAP apparatus: the external pressures of accountability for quality assurance, of Ofsted and the funding agencies. How these pressures are mediated as part of a culture that is supportive of teachers' efforts to do more than simply spoon-feed students for assessment purposes is all-important. Taken together, Figures 4.1 and 4.2 illustrate how the market environment brought about by the Further and Higher Education Act has led to heavy workloads and conditions in which the kinds of educational relationship that underpin transformative education are unlikely to thrive.

The incorporation of colleges brought about by the Further and Higher Education Act (1992) plays a key role in facilitating the conditions that have contributed to this situation. Incorporation meant colleges coming out from under the control and direction of local authorities. Their funding from then on came from a different (centralised) body and they had to produce data to justify how much they could 'earn'. As well as these effects, incorporation also

Figure 4.2: Hours spent working on administrative tasks per week (full-time staff only)

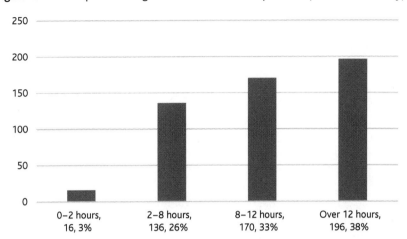

created the conditions in which the division between managers and teachers was accentuated. It allowed colleges to act independently in determining the terms and conditions of teachers – very like the more recent academisation of schools. Perhaps most importantly, it changed the structures and cultures of governance (see Chapter 6), increasing the representation of employers and fostering a business culture to oversee college finances and, in the longer term, the implementation of the government's neoliberalising and instrumentalist view of the purpose of further and adult education (Lucas and Crowther, 2016).

1993, when incorporation took effect, presaged a national contracts dispute in colleges and led to a worsening of terms and conditions for teachers (see Smith, 2015). But arguably an equally significant milestone is represented by the Lingfield Report (Lingfield, 2012) that, in an effort to justify the removal of public funding from the Institute for Learning, revoked the need for a teaching qualification for further education teachers that had been mandatory since 2007. This was something, it was argued, that could be left to the discretion of college principals and presumably, 'the market'. How it is possible to remove a regulatory requirement for college teachers to be qualified educators (with, as we have seen, potentially unlimited hours) and continue with an (Ofsted) inspection regime focused on 'standards' and the 'quality' of outcomes is a question that has yet to be answered. If the answer ever comes, it is unlikely to make any sense.

Our research indicates that teachers do not have a merely 'technical' or extraneous role in transformative teaching and learning. According to our research data, the teacher's role is vital in creating the social conditions and establishing the strong relational ties through which transformative education takes place (Duckworth and Smith, 2017b). As a starting point, these teachers understand that in some cases it has taken enormous courage on the part of many students to cross the threshold onto college premises. An initial focus of teachers' work is to create a safe learning environment, to establish trust and build and sustain confidence. The teachers form affective bonds and these bonds arise from an awareness of the historical positioning of the learners and their communities and how their location has shaped their trajectories (Duckworth and Smith, 2018d).

One teacher participant, Judith, an Access to HE teacher in the North East, was conscious of the importance of her teaching work in a region with historically high levels of unemployment and job losses that dated back to the closure of heavy industry and a significant number of coal mines.

> 'For me transformational teaching is teaching that makes a difference. Whether it's people enjoying the lesson … or sometimes … people have come in and they've been very quiet and haven't had much confidence. You'll see them five or ten years later and they'll say I'm a primary school teacher now or I'm a social worker or I'm doing my master's degree, I'm doing my PhD. And you think: Wow what a difference!'

Apart from recognising that her work is often at the start and often catalyses a much longer process, sometimes over many years, what's interesting about the description is that Judith sees the transformative potential as immanent in the students. Once more we see in this description the limits of the funding and performance regime that claims to reward learning and progress through annual performance metrics. The teacher's perspective we see here is founded on a far longer timeline. In addition, Judith sees this transformative process as a collective phenomenon and as having social as well as individual origins:

> 'People feel once they get to their twenties or thirties, Oh I didn't get stuck in at school or I'm not clever enough or I'm never going to do anything. And it only takes one person in a friendship group to go and do something like an Access Course and go on and do well and then their friends want to come on as well.'

Judith here signals how the impact of the Access to HE course on an individual often leads to the recruitment of others from that individual's social network. Judith identifies some important ingredients in the formation of dialogical caring relationships with the learners. Additionally, although not specifically named, is the respect she has for them as people. Once more the egalitarian nature of transformative teaching and learning comes across powerfully:

> 'We try to get to know the students as people and be part of their journey … A lot of people think they're not academic when actually,

they are … They're so used to thinking of all the things they can't do, we've got to focus on what they can do … By the time they finish they realise that they can do the same as those people they thought were better than them because they had a degree or they are a doctor. I've had people say to me: … "I've learned how to phone up and complain if I'm not happy about something. I've learnt to say, I disagree with that". At the end of the day they are empowered and they have more confidence.'

Getting to know students and seeing themselves as 'a part of students' lives' involves supporting students and being interested in them as people outside the classroom. The survey evidence supports this perspective and gives a vantage point on a kind of educational space and interaction that is not accounted for in existing metrics. Figure 4.3 gives a picture of the amount of time respondents spend per week supporting students outside of classroom time.

Within colleges, acting in accordance with the managerialist performance-centred regime, this time is not counted as so-called 'contact' time, but our research shows that these informal supportive interactions underpin the kind of educational relationships that make transformative educational experiences possible. Typically, they take place in pockets of elastic time. Pastoral care doesn't operate by appointment and unlike timetabled lessons it doesn't end when a bell rings or the hands on the clock reach a certain hour. It may involve providing additional support for students to complete classroom work, but our data suggests that it spills over into helping individuals manage bigger personal issues (for example, housing, travel, relationships, food,

Figure 4.3: Hours spent supporting students outside class per week (full-time staff only)

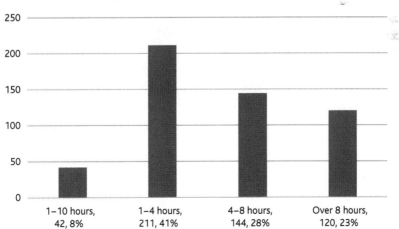

money): issues that sit outside the taught curriculum but, if they are not resolved, make learning difficult or impossible to achieve.

Eugene

Eugene's story is illustrative of how having experience of further education and not being successful at school can be an important asset for teachers. At the time we met him, Eugene was a member of the teacher education team at the college where he worked. He had left school with no GCSEs before going on to develop an interest in sports at his local college starting with a Level 1 (pre-GCSE) course. From there, he gradually worked his way from course to course until he gained entrance to university. Interestingly though, Eugene identified his transformative educational experience as happening when he was studying for a degree. For Eugene, up until one particular incident that he describes, education had only been about getting a qualification, it wasn't something that he was personally invested in. Eugene's transformative experience happened in the third year of his Sports Science degree. Once more, it was a teacher that created the conditions for the change. This teacher he describes as 'inspirational':

> 'I think she then made another change in me just kind of ... from going there to get the course done for the sake of getting a qualification to actually wanting to learn and develop. I think it's one of the reasons I'm teaching as well because of the impact she had on me.'

Unlike many of the stories we gathered in the research, the teacher in this case wasn't just empathetic but earned his respect through her strictness. He found her teaching sessions difficult as he had dyslexia and she used a technique in which any student could be asked to write on the white board.

> 'Everything in the classroom you had to do ... So she used to come round the classroom if there was a question on the board it'd be "There, take the pen. You go in and write on the board" and "What do you think?" Because my English weren't the greatest and I weren't the most confident person still, at the time it really really unsettled me and I found her lessons at the time ... I didn't enjoy them.'

Eugene's lack of confidence in writing led to a confrontation. He was picked to present to the class and so skipped the session. He then felt he had to talk it through with the teacher. 'So I went into her office and I said I just feel uncomfortable in your lessons because I don't like to be picked out, be picked on ... and it was basically she says, '"Tough ... if you want to develop you need to step outside your comfort zone."' One interpretation of the incident as recounted foregrounds the nuanced shift of meaning between being 'picked out' and 'picked on' in educational space. Eugene suggested to the teacher that to ask him to participate felt like being picked on. He seems here to be signalling the existence of a threshold: a point at which he as a student moved from being someone who was unwillingly involved in class participation to a new and different relation with the teacher and the other students. Getting over that threshold, one we might describe as being when the student takes charge of their learning, is something only the student is able to do as it is an act of will. But the teacher's role is to help the student navigate the pathway to that moment. Although Eugene admitted that at the time, he found this response difficult to accept, in the longer term its impact was significant.

> 'I think it's only now I look back and she had such a massive impact on me. She kind of changed my mind-set in terms of learning and exploring things and doing things for myself. It was kind of like the teacher set the stuff in there, they planted the seeds and then it was kind of like things always stuck in my mind and it just grew and it was kind of like I wanted to take control for myself after. It was unbelievable.'

We might argue that a teacher insisting on a student moving out of their 'comfort zone', and the effectiveness of this as a strategy for motivating and establishing the conditions in which learning can take place are high risk. Whether that kind of challenge would work with all students is questionable and the teacher's professional judgement would seem to have played a vital role. Clearly though, for Eugene, this was a pivotal incident and he connected it to the way the teacher related to him and knew him. These were aspects that he carried forward into his own practice as a teacher:

> 'For me I think the most important thing it's probably the relationship with the student and I think that's because of my own journey ... I have sat down and I've gone through my own journey myself on lots of occasions with the students ... and even if it's stuff on the outside as well so if they've got problems on the outside of college, you know talk to them about that whatever it may be even if it's got nothing to do with college. It doesn't have to be just college and college work but looking or watching out for the person as an individual holistically.'

Concluding comments

As with Adam and Awor, the stories of Anita, David, Dean, Jade and Claire are all individual. While they can be described as having a transformative aspect, the precise nature of the transformation is inflected for each of them by individual circumstances. Their journeys are unique. Across a spectrum, the transformative aspects extend from Anita's unexpectedly positive experience of learning that undoes the damage wrought by schooling to Claire's experience that results in a remarkable change of perspective on her position in the world and how the world works. Both then lead to change and growth in their lives and to different employment opportunities. Their stories simply cannot be reduced to them gaining new 'skills' or increasing their 'employability'.

Some key ideas associated with transformative teaching and learning have emerged in this chapter: that it frequently has a restorative aspect, addressing the damage done to individuals by our current system of schooling and that transformative educational experiences involve students in some way finding themselves (again) in learning. In addition, we have identified some of the benefits: not only do these experiences lead to qualifications gained and personal development, but the ripple effect means that these benefits spread beyond the individual to impact positively on families and wider communities. Sadly, as these benefits remain unmeasured and fall outside the crude and prescriptive metrics that fuel the FAP apparatus that has deformed further and adult education for so long, they remain unacknowledged. The concern here is that this lack of acknowledgement brings with it a failure to recognise that the FAP regime undermines the pedagogy that supports transformative teaching and learning and also the social and educational conditions that foster it.

Judith and Eugene's stories offer different takes on the teachers' perspective of transformative teaching and learning. Both highlight how transformative experiences are not instant but often gradual, sometimes taking years to unfold. During this time, which overlays the guillotine-like annual FAP cycle, the teacher's 'watching out for' the student is what provides cohesion and contributes to the 'journey'. The holistic aspects of this care extend beyond classroom walls and the teacher's role is so much more than that of a 'technician' or a curriculum delivery agent. Through care and the nurturing of hope, the teacher is positioned instead as a person who is a part of the student's life. Judith and Eugene's stories also illustrate how the everyday of teaching in further and adult education offers opportunities to resist the gravitational pull of the FAP Deathstar through positioning human, caring relationships at the heart of the educational experience. While the attrition of performance targets and a zombie skills discourse continue to dispirit and alienate, it is in these local relationships that the teacher's soul continues to strive and thrive.

5

Transformative teaching and learning and social justice

(W)e need to acknowledge the teleological character of education —
the fact that education always raises the question of its purpose.
Gert Biesta, 'What is education for?
On good education, teacher judgement, and
educational professionalism'

Introduction

Gert Biesta's article 'What is education for? On good education, teacher judgement, and educational professionalism' (Biesta, 2015, 84) argues that teachers' judgement is an important aspect of their professionalism but that this needs to be inflected by a stronger focus on the purposes of education and by a discussion about what constitutes a 'good' education. Biesta writes here and elsewhere (for example Biesta, 2010) that the three key purposes of education are qualification, socialisation and subjectification but each of these he sees as playing a contributory role in an end goal: he uses the Greek word *telos*.

This move to foreground purpose has huge consequences in any discussion about further and adult education. What this does is force us to scrutinise the instrumentalist emphasis of skills-orientated discourses that objectify students (and teachers) and to ask how they align with less narrow purposes that we might expect a 'good' education to be orientated towards achieving. Because this narrowness is an issue: how, we might ask does (only) meeting local skills needs and economic, nationally boundaried goals of central government connect with broader global perspectives – that enable us to address, for example, ecological issues, climate warming or social justice? Because in our view, a neglected but nevertheless fundamental purpose or telos of further and adult education is social justice. And while this goal, this purpose of addressing social inequality and injustice has clear local dimensions, as we will see in Chapter 7, the links between critical pedagogy and transformative education mean that educational purposes that are confined by a national agenda and limited by national economic imperatives become deeply questionable. In today's internet-connected and unified-through-climate world, such purposes are simply insufficient. Today, more than ever before, concerns with social justice traverse borders. Social justice knows no national boundaries.

So far in our argument, we have focused on how further and adult education can play a part in transforming the lives of the students from all backgrounds who access it. Starting at the locus of the individual, transformative teaching and learning is a powerful force for change, but, as we have outlined, the social benefits do not stop at the individual, instead they can radiate out to family, friends and communities. To want to ring-fence the transformative potential of these experiences, to confine it to the individual, to stop at the local community seems like a strange idea indeed. Ultimately, transformative teaching and learning is not just about addressing the damage done by our current divisive system of schooling or even just about helping those that have 'fallen behind' to 'catch up'. To view transformative teaching and learning in that way is to see it as a remedial technology for an education system that is otherwise without fault. Our view of transformative education is that its logic and motive force has to question and carry through to the beliefs, practices and structures that lead to the need for it in the first place. To that extent, the ultimate aim of transformative teaching and learning is to bring about transformation in education and wider society.

Under New Labour governments (1997–2010), social justice was presented as an integral aspect of the purpose of further education. The influential Kennedy report, *Learning Works* (Kennedy, 1997) foregrounded widening participation in further education and accented its social benefits. The value that New Labour attached to further education can be seen in whole a series of lifelong learning policies, Green and White Papers. For example, *The Learning Age* (DfEE, 1998) and *The Moser Report* (DfES, 1999) heralded the introduction of the Skills for Life initiative: a suite of adult education programmes and signalled significant investment. *Success for All* (DES, 2002) was another policy document that reaffirmed a commitment to the diversity of further education providers and demonstrated an understanding of the range of social benefits provided by colleges.

There was in addition, however, an underpinning economic drive to New Labour policies that through so-called 'Third Way' thinking, sought to combine the marketisation of public assets with a commitment for social justice and equality. At the time, the incompatibility of these aims was obscured by alarming talk of globalisation, global competition and 'skills for jobs' that positioned the so-called 'knowledge economy' as vital for the national interest. In reality, the significant additional investments like Skills for Life to one side, New Labour policy continued the market-orientated neoliberalising trajectory of the preceding Conservative governments. New Labour valued further education more (compared to what came after) but its stewardship was limited by viewing further education primarily in terms of the production of human capital.

Interestingly, *Learning Works* identified the potentially detrimental effects of the business culture that had taken hold in colleges and this was picked up again in the Wolf Report (2011), but the funding and performance apparatus has only ever been tweaked in response to these critiques. Since the replacement of New Labour by the Conservative-led Coalition government in 2010, social justice has no longer been a priority or purpose of further and adult education. That colleges offer second-chance education as an important means of addressing the major structural injustices that perpetuate inequity has been disregarded. Instead, an instrumentalist agenda within a marketised system has been the focus.

So far we have focused on the some of the conditions that make transformative education possible and outlined how the FAP apparatus works against these. A distinctive feature of transformative teaching and learning as we are describing it is that it has a restorative aspect: working to undo the negative prior educational experiences of learners who in many cases have been judged and written off by a rigidly linear school system that assesses individuals against a normative, age-staged matrix of 'learning progression'. But if transformative teaching and learning is to be imagined as an engine of social justice then clearly, it can't be approached as an unintended by-product of further and adult education. Rather, the underpinning administrative and policy structures need to be adapted and re-orientated to 'maximise' the potential of further and adult education to contribute to socially just aims. We live in a world of great complexity in which social inequalities have become increasingly evident, both within local communities at a micro level and between the global north and south from a macro perspective. Living in 'liquid' and uncertain times (Bauman, 2001), in which the impact of the 2008/09 banking crash still resonates locally and internationally (Dorling, 2011; Peters et al, 2015; Henehan, 2020), and now further shaken by a global epidemic, political upheaval and its consequences are likely to inform centralised policy making for at least another decade. Indeed, as Keddie has stated: 'Amid this climate of uncertainty, what is certain is that we must continue to engage in an ongoing monitoring and critical examination of our presumptions for understanding and approaching matters of justice' (Keddie, 2012, 277).

Arguably, we are at a pivotal moment where abundant evidence of social inequality and widespread demands for social justice require more than a rhetorical response. Inequality in the distribution of resources, and in particular inequality tied to social class and race remain bound to the cycle of inequity across and within communities. This evidence of injustice requires us to direct our focus, energy and resources as a society in general and as educationalists in particular to generate genuine and sustained social and educational change that meets the needs of all.

The Transforming Lives research positions further and adult education at the heart of the debate in England. Our contention is that further and adult education providers are a national resource that is currently being squandered. We argue for recognition of a need for much more inclusive processes that respect differences and in the curriculum, for pedagogy and assessment systems that reverse the current reductive drive that can often diminish rather than empower learners.

The instrumentalist view of further and adult education that has dominated policy making for the last quarter century has limited colleges' ability to function in a broader way that addresses localised social and economic needs. Despite this, further and adult education maintains its unique position in the education system. The historical and socially embedded nature of the colleges across the nation and the breadth of its functions are what gives it its strength and the learners hope. These colleges, often with their roots in local industry and with a history closely linked to the socio-economic circumstances of the people and areas in which they are situated, have established relationships with communities, employers, students and local authorities all of which positions them as potential key players in tackling social inequality and addressing issues of social justice in real and sustained ways.

Before looking at how further and adult education connects to social justice and the role of transformative teaching and learning in this, we need first to clarify the meaning of social justice.

What do we mean by social justice?

Our commitment to social justice has been driven by moral and ethical beliefs, and that commitment is reflected in our research. Inequalities are evident in the trajectory of children and adults through the educational system. As educators, a consciousness of the role of educational institutions in the perpetuation of injustices and oppression was a dawning realisation for both of us. Having worked and taught in schools, colleges and universities, this is something that Rob has seen playing out not just within the institutions themselves but in the wider social structures and patterns of thought that they are a part of. For both Rob and Vicky, the need to act to address this issue is an important part of the background consciousness of everyday practice. But more than that, we would argue that the oppressed need consciously to become part of the resolution of injustices brought about through structural inequality and symbolic violence.

It is important to recognise that social justice is a contested and a politicised concept. One school of thought sees social justice through the lens of the 'choices' that individuals make that then connect to life chances. As an example, this is the view of the 'Centre for Social Justice' and is apparent in many of its publications (including a recent one that proposes the expansion of grammar schools to improve social mobility – see CSJ, 2016). This view appears to rest on an acceptance that inequality in our society is inevitable (or even necessary) and seeks to blame individuals for the level of poverty and injustice they experience. It also seems to deliberately ignore some fundamental points about social inequality – namely that people do not choose which community or family they are born into and, as such, have no power to shape the level of capital they can access as children. It also has wider ramifications when addressing issues of global inequality.

An opposing view of social justice sees inequity as an effect of social structures and systems and is founded on the principle that these can and should be challenged. Barry (1989) sees social justice as resting on the idea of redistributing the goods and benefits in society as a response to inequality. Gewirtz (1998) provides an explicitly educational focus and builds on this, arguing for an approach in which a distributive element addresses individual inequity and injustice but that this is supplemented with a relational element.

This relational dimension is important as it allows us to focus on power. Gewirtz's two dimensions (distributive and relational) problematise structures and hierarchies of power, wealth and privilege. In relation to transformative education, this is important as it suggests that transformation may start with the individual effectively accessing educational resource but for the concept to embrace its fullest meaning, this individual engagement (re)opens the possibility of change in social understandings of the purposes of education. Gewirtz proposes a framework for critiquing education policy, asking the question: How, to what extent and why do education policies support, interrupt or subvert:

1. Exploitative relationships (capitalist, patriarchal, racist, heterosexist, disablist and so on) within and beyond educational institutions?
2. Processes of marginalisation and inclusion within and beyond the education system?
3. The promotion of relationships based on recognition, respect, care and mutuality or produce powerlessness (for education workers and students)?
4. Practices of cultural imperialism? And which cultural differences should be affirmed, which should be universalised and which rejected?
5. Violent practices within and beyond the education system? (Gewirtz, 1998, 482).

This framework resonates powerfully with the participant narratives we have so far explored as it foregrounds the importance of care in pedagogy, but also, as we shall outline in the next section, it allows us to see how categories like social class and exploitation have been allowed to damage further and adult education through the FAP apparatus and as a consequence of (unintended?) policy.

Transformative teaching and learning and social class

The vocational/academic divide has become so entrenched in our education system as to almost seem 'natural'. This would not be a problem if this divide did not carry with it a sense of value and esteem attaching mainly to one side. In ways that are not reflected in other countries in Europe, vocational qualifications in England are saddled with negative perceptions of students' 'ability' and as a result, vocational qualifications are stigmatised. Any parent of secondary aged children can vouch for this when they hear 'BTEC' being used as a term that means second-rate or poor quality.

This divide has become increasingly important in further education since incorporation. One reason is that many General Further Education (GFE) colleges in 1993 combined academic and vocational provision, often under one roof. This structural feature served to downplay and even erode the divide. To cite an example from my own (Rob's) experience, in the early 1990s Matthew Boulton College in the centre of Birmingham ran a good variety of A level classes in the same building as General National Vocational Qualifications (GNVQs). The A level provision was widely regarded as being one of the best in the city. In the same building, a podiatry degree ran two floors below an accountancy qualification (AAT) and the nationally recognised legal executive qualification. A stone's throw away, a dental technician's qualification could be taken down the corridor from engineering.

In a powerful example of how marketisation works to produce and harden distinction (and in this case, inequality), incorporation typically undid this harmonious juxtapositioning. Sixth form provision has characteristically been located in separate buildings often with the reasoning that there is a need to create a 'distinctive feel' for the students. In one West Midlands college, the new build site located the A level students on the top floor alongside the principal's suite of rooms. Until recently when colleges have been encouraged to start providing more HE courses, a sense built up that academic courses didn't really belong in further education at all. Increasingly, as illustrated in Chapter 1 and the 2021 White Paper, further education has been viewed as about employability, skills and work all grounded in a vocational emphasis. It is from these things that a strong sense arises that further education is being 'classed': it is conceived of as space for young people and adults from working class backgrounds.

The strength and rigidity of the academic/vocational divide has long been recognised as a serious structural flaw in England's education system. As with the division between arts and sciences (a relatively new structural feature that is perpetuated *within* academic qualifications), what Bernstein calls 'classification' and the 'insulation' (2000) between vocational and academic routes, when over-zealously applied, can stifle innovative cross-fertilisation between disciplines. Worse still, when reified as a structural feature in which one route is given a higher status than the other, it can become a way of labelling individual students and thereby limiting their potential.

We need to remember that part of New Labour's contribution was an attempt (alas ultimately unsuccessful) to bridge the so-called academic/vocational divide. The 2005 White Paper, *14–19 Education and Skills* (DES, 2005) laid out significant reforms to 'break ... down the artificial barriers between academic and vocational education' (DES, 2005, 3) through the introduction of a new 16–19 diploma. Arguably, a similar impulse motivated the introduction of GNVQs. Unfortunately for further education students, neither managed to get a foothold in the marketised landscape: GNVQs were dogged by questions about their rigour and status with employers; the 16–19 Diploma (a flagship 'bridging' qualification in England) was wound up by Michael Gove as Education Secretary under the Coalition government.

What's deeply concerning is that the steady entrenchment of the academic/vocational divide appears to relate to an increasing objectification of further education students. Vincent and Ball (2007) highlight that traditional middle-class students are often advantaged through their family support system, while so-called 'nontraditional' working-class students may not find the opportunity to develop and prepare themselves with educational dispositions and capital that can support academic development and success. This is worrying because of the evidence that social class is the determiner *par excellence* of academic achievement (see, for example, Lupton et al, 2009; Dorling, 2011; Wilkinson and Pickett, 2010). It follows that within a system that accords higher status to academic routes, further education appears to be being positioned as education and training for working class students. From that perspective, the under-allocation of financial resource to colleges during austerity takes on the character of an attack against a particular section of our society.

The view of traditional Marxist theorists like Bowles and Gintis (1976) is that education is a mechanism shaped above all to ensure the replication of the existing social order (see also deMarrais and LeCompte, 1995; Bourdieu and Passeron, 2013). These views see schooling as a 'production process' in which students are alienated by the curriculum and enjoyment, personal development or a connection of educational experiences to personal plans for the future are deemed irrelevant. The structure of social relations in education, they write: 'not only inures the student to the discipline of the workplace, but develops the types of personal demeanour, modes of self-presentation, self-image, and social class identifications which are the crucial ingredients of job adequacy' (Bowles and Gintis, 1976, 131). This description is likely to resonate strongly with readers familiar with the further education curriculum in England, particularly for the 16–18 age group. It aligns with the introduction of a compulsory experience of work for this age group in 2015 (DfE, 2015) chiming as it does with the skills discourse that sees further education almost exclusively in terms of the production of human capital for employers (see Becker, 1993).

As a further example, the *Post-16 Skills Plan* (BIS, 2016), justifies the latest reforms to vocational qualifications in this way:

> Forecasts suggest greater demand for higher-level technical and specialist skills in the future. Greater international competition and faster technological change will put many roles that exist today at risk. We need young people and adults to have the skills and knowledge that better equip them for employment in the 21st century, in order to meet the demands of the future.
>
> Weaknesses in the UK's skills base have contributed to its long-standing productivity gap with France, Germany and the United States. It performs poorly on intermediate professional and technical skills, and is forecast to fall from 22nd to 28th out of 33 Organization for Economic Co-operation and Development (OECD) countries for intermediate skills by 2020. (BIS, 2016, 10)

As well as articulating an instrumentalist purpose for further education, these documents are notable for their apparent rejection of the substantial body of interdisciplinary empirical and theoretical literature that has established the relationship between social class and educational achievement (for example, Ball, 2005). This leads the government in *Fixing the Foundations*, for example, to conceptualise the improvement of school outcomes as a technical process that can be achieved through the application of new techniques, methods or formulae to teaching:

> teaching quality is the most significant factor driving school outcomes … The government will also encourage greater use of evidence on 'what works' – there remains significant scope for schools to make better use of evidence, such as from the Education Endowment Foundation. (Department for Business Innovation and Skills, 2015, 23)

It isn't difficult to see how this conflicts with our understanding of transformative teaching and learning. What is missing here is any understanding of how the social background of students impacts on attainment. This approach is the same approach that has underpinned the FAP apparatus since its inception. It is premised on an almost exclusive focus on the quality and accountability of teachers and the competition between colleges to achieve regulatory 'benchmarks' of performance.

This assertion of one set of values to the exclusion of others represents what Bourdieu and Passeron (2013) call 'symbolic violence' against further education students. We will develop a fuller theorisation of how this works as a 'triple-lock' in Chapter 7. Here, in relation to social class, we can see how the interaction between a skills discourse, the designation that further education is for vocational learning and the 'classing' of further education students as exclusively vocational, with all the negative baggage that unfortunately entails, all work together against the kind of teaching and learning experiences we are characterising as transformative. Where transformative teaching and learning has the potential to liberate students from negative labels and expectations, the narrow instrumentalist scope projected onto further education by policy makers and successive governments works against this. The project data provides a body evidence that shows how further and adult education can reverse the stunting of individual educational potential that is the unfortunate effect of this dehumanising view. Social class doesn't have to be a barrier to transformative education. The empowerment that project participants regained by accessing further and adult education was linked to the renewed dignity and self-belief it afforded them. But where government thinking enforces the binarism of the academic/vocational divide and leads to such rigid structuration, it is left to colleges and their staff working against the grain of policy to guard and protect student interests.

Transformative teaching and learning and ethnicity

Alongside the issue of social class, the Transforming Lives research revealed important insights into how through transformative teaching and learning, further and adult education providers are able to challenge social inequality in the field of diversity generally and ethnicity in particular. The research identified that colleges offer a critical space in which individuals, their families and communities can challenge such inequality.

These providers offer educational experiences that are different from those offered in schools because they are more likely to recruit a diverse population of students from across a city or town. Prior to incorporation colleges had well-established sites in local communities which enabled people to access educational opportunities more easily. While incorporation brought new-build single-site colleges and Area Reviews often resulted in the closure of such community-based courses, there are signs that colleges are once more opening sites like these in order to make further and adult education accessible once more. What has been learnt is that students from some backgrounds are less likely to travel; so local premises are essential.

A well-established effect of the housing market in the UK is the way it tends to promote the consolidation of residential areas that are ethnically and socio-economically homogeneous (Glynn, 2005). The phenomenon of 'white flight' means that housing in some of our 'inner city' areas and particular districts within towns become a patchwork of neighbourhoods peopled by specific ethnic minority communities. The arrival of new ethnic groups also has a tendency to lead to them being placed in already densely populated areas, sometimes characterised by poor housing stock (Daley, 1998).

For one project participant, Chaima, this tendency meant that her experience of primary and secondary education in Oldham was in schools with a 90%+ population of Bengali background children. For that reason, it was only when she attended college that Chaima got to socialise and make friends with young people from other ethnic groups.

Chaima's experience of schooling ended in disillusion and low-level qualifications. Entering further education however, Chaima rediscovered her learning identity and, with the support of teachers who believed in her, worked steadily until she gained entry to HE. College provided a space where she met people from different backgrounds and, very importantly, learnt about cultures outside that of the Bangladeshi community:

'When I came into college, it was very diverse. I had people in my class that were white, I had people in my class that were black, people in my class that were Chinese … It was nice to be inside that classroom … A lot of them are still my friends to this day. I learnt about them and their community and they learnt about me and my community as well … It eliminates that ignorance.'

Chaima went on to achieve academic success and to pursue her ambition to teach. Working abroad as well as in England, her aim is to become a headteacher. Her comments highlight the often-overlooked role of further and adult education colleges in providing integrated social spaces that have the potential to foster social (and ethnic) cohesion in our super-diverse urban centres. This resonates with Bally Kaur's work (Kaur, 2021) in which she sees the provision of (often informal) educational spaces as crucial for some groups to explore 'in-between' cultural identities. In Bally's research, these 'spaces of cultural hybridity' enabled the female Muslim participants to experiment with an identity that was both rooted in the culture at home, but which also engaged with and deployed features of white British culture. In doing this they were able to forge identities that enabled them to shape fulfilling lives and careers. In these examples, relationships with specific teachers, educational spaces and in particular the informal margins of these spaces were crucial. Chaima's comments also reveal that for some students, the further education classroom can be a first experience of participating in socially diverse space. As such it can provide an important model for socialisation for the multi-ethnic society that England has become.

A theorisation of transformative teaching and learning should not restrict itself to students' reorientation of an individual learning identity. The broader curriculum, who students learn alongside, the informal relations that underpin the learning experience, the perspectives taken on wider society and the purposes of education, the kind of space and the voices allowed within it – all of these are important elements of a broader transformative experience – particularly one that sees the wider transformation of society as an important goal. Our study illustrates that students' histories, while always social, merit closer attention on the part of educators to the details that contribute to significant differences in their ways of being and the choices/ or lack of choices they have.

There are important overlaps between ethnicity and social class that are often overlooked. Where the housing market has led to racially divided neighbourhoods, students may feel rooted in their geographical communities and this may tie them to a particular positioning in social space (Bourdieu, 1994). Chaima's account illustrates how further education space can break down these boundaries. Like Chaima, other project participants described the difficulties they encountered when trying to move outside their familiar space, and for many that included walking through the doors of the local college. But once they had crossed the threshold, further and adult education colleges offered them opportunities to review themselves as learners and negotiate an educational route that could improve their lives. An openness to diversity formed part of the experience. Arguably, the further and adult education classroom is one of the few spaces in our society where this kind of diversity can be experienced as a norm. In the scope it offers for finding out about other cultures and ways of seeing the world, this diversity provides an important frame for transformative teaching and learning.

A second example that illustrates the impact of transformative education for students from different backgrounds can be seen in Rithenella's account. Rithenella, coming from a mixed heritage, looked-after background provides insights into how the influence of social class and ethnicity can negatively inform the expectations of significant others in the lives of young people. She talked about how she returned to education as an adult, retaking her GCSE English and maths and then joining an Access to HE course at her local college.

'I come from a looked after background with all the labels that are attached to that. I grew up believing I was thick, I was stupid. I wasn't allowed books when I was little. The carer told me that the reason I wasn't allowed books was that I was only ever going to be a cleaner. I spent my entire life believing I was thick. I left school with no GCSEs. I was in my 30s when I took my first GCSE ... All the jobs I was doing were dead-end jobs. I did foster for a few years and that's what made me think: I want to be a social worker ... This course is the best thing that I ever did: it changed my mind-set, how I used to think about myself and everything that I carried for years and years.

Rithenella describes how her journey involved rejecting the spoilt identities that had been thrust upon her, by her carer, but then followed presumably by her teachers. Her inspirational account is again illustrative of the idea that transformative learning often involves the student pushing against others' view of who they are and what they are capable of. It can also involve challenging the views they hold of themselves. Rithenella's 'looked after' background signals that she is likely to have had a disrupted experience of school and government publications acknowledge that the attainment of looked after children is well below that of the young people. According to Ofsted: 'in 2007, 13% of looked after children achieved five or more A★ to C grades at GCSE compared with 62% of all 16-year-olds, and 64% gained at least one GCSE compared with 99% of all 16-year-olds' (Ofsted, 2008, 95). Interestingly, the kind of approach that is recommended to meet the needs of looked after children, with its emphasis on care, ongoing pastoral support and its holistic approach echoes our view of transformative teaching and learning. For example, from a list of nine key qualities that characterise 'effective practice', three have particular relevance (DfCSF, 2009, 5):

- Making it a priority to know the young people well and to build strong relationships.
- Actively extending the horizons of each young person.
- Planning for future transitions.

Rithenella's re-enchantment with education began with her retaking GCSE maths and English and then enrolling onto an Access to HE course. This provided a transformative environment which led to the realisation of her dream to go to university to study to be a social worker.

> '(At university) I worked my derrière off. It's been great. I had this mind-set that university wasn't for me, that people were from a different class. I went with this idea that it wasn't for me. But it was a real eye opener. It's such a mix. Nobody is better than anyone else … I'm always looking to improve as I didn't get any qualifications when I was younger.'

As with Claire, the transformative aspect of Rithenella's experiences involves a change in 'subjectness'. There are reflexive changes, the emergence of new views of oneself, but also a change in the way others are viewed and a sense that the ways others view one have also changed. There is also a strong sense of a new perspective on wider society that has a pleasing egalitarian slant: *nobody is better than anyone else.*

In transformative teaching and learning, the principle of the individual and their identities as the starting point combines with an egalitarian ideal to inform any educational discussion about diversity. At the very least it requires us to take the issues of social class, race, gender, sexual orientation and dis/ability seriously as protected characteristics and to address these in the educational spaces in which teaching and learning happens.

Guy is a participant who originally came from the Democratic Republic of Congo where he had gained a masters' in marketing. He came to England in 2014. Starting at his local college with no plan of what he wanted to do in terms of a career and with his first language being French, his initial driver was to develop his English skills. Like Awor, he was able to join an ESOL class and found the atmosphere supportive. He described how learning a new language and being confident in it was a 'very big challenge'. For Guy, these ESOL classes provided a route in to connecting his existing educational experience with potential employment in England. Learning English developed his confidence and skills and enabled him to progress to an Access to HE course.

Guy's rapid progress in English was founded on the strong relationships he formed with his teachers:

> 'The first person that I met here was Steve. Steve G__. I love that guy. He's a lovely person. He's a caring person ... He has very good direction that he can give you. I could not speak English last year. I'm still learning. But this year I am doing all my assignments in English.'

Returning to education in England as an adult was also driven by Guy's ideals about what society should be like. His strong communitarian values, originating in direct experience, also informed the educational route he wished to pursue. He asserted that: 'the most important thing in society is that we should be counselling our children, the new generation, the youth ... if those people can be advised and get counselling, they will not come to a stage whereby they commit crime'.

These ideas influenced Guy's decision to pursue criminology at degree level. He chose this route as he really wants to contribute to society by working with and supporting young people across communities to strive and flourish. Returning to education is a way of Guy giving back to society from an empowered position. From having enjoyed a meaningful, professional career in his home country, it is through developing his English he was able to find hope and a pathway that aligned to his core values. Refugees like Guy, bring a wealth of skills from their countries of origin. Further education in his case provided an enabling environment where he can utilise and develop his potential.

Transformative teaching and learning, planned futures and 'social mobility'

Social mobility is an ambiguous concept inasmuch as on the one hand, it signals that our society affords individuals upward trajectories from lower levels of the social hierarchy of wealth and privilege while on the other, examples often seem to be used to justify the continuation of the existing social hierarchy. For that reason, social mobility has an ambiguous relation with social justice as it presupposes and accepts as a given the conditions in which 'mobility' is necessary. The assumption that legitimises social mobility is that individuals are capable of lifting themselves out of the conditions into which they were born. In that sense, the concept is allied to the myth of meritocracy (Young, 1958; Sandel, 2021), that people can achieve whatever goals they set themselves if they have 'talent' and work hard. The stories we presented in Chapters 4 and 5 suggest a much more complex picture than that. While those narratives focused on individuals, in every case there was a collective or social dimension to the transformations – whether this came through a teacher's intervention, the support of a partner, an employer or a friend.

Our research has thrown up examples in which colleges provide free breakfasts and/or other food for students who are arriving at college hungry. Funding students' bus passes is another common intervention. These are examples of colleges dealing with student poverty and the fall-out from the extensive budgetary cuts endured by a range of public services following the austerity measures imposed by the coalition government (2010–15). Arguably, colleges addressing this level of student need is not what is meant when education is talked of as being an engine of social mobility. However, most of these interventions are about meeting basic needs as a pre-requisite to learning taking place.

As identified by Hanley (2007) in her personal memoir and social history of estates, children who live on estates and attend the local school receive a council estate education where 'you can't ever hope to reach your potential; it's just that very idea of having lots of potential to fulfil that isn't presented.' Access or lack of access to different capitals (social, economic, cultural) can empower or disempower students and this relates as much to the social class as to the ethnic background of students. The discourse around social mobility is interesting here as its apparent focus on the individual escaping an area/social class background/pathologised family or culture suggests that the abandonment of one's origins is a positive benefit of education.

A key finding in the Social Mobility Commission's 2019 report, *The adult skills gap: Is falling investment in UK adults stalling social mobility?* is that the spend on adult skills in the UK is 'half the EU average'. In addition, the report finds that current policies and systems aren't always successful at meeting need: 'The poorest adults with the lowest qualifications are the least likely to access training – despite being the group who would benefit most' (Social Mobility Commission, 2019, 8).

There are geographical as well as demographic aspects to this. Coming from certain areas in a city, town or village may make re-accessing educational experiences less likely. But this is exacerbated if prior educational experiences have been negative. Adult and further education providers are well-placed to meet these needs, where they are supported to open local and community provision. Small-scale, local provision can then do the vital work of overturning the effects of the negative educational experiences that otherwise continue to mark people's lives irreversibly. During our research, however, a decade of cuts to further and adult education budgets was having a clear impact in forcing the closure of this type of local, community-based provision.

The definition of social mobility generated by the all-party parliamentary group on social mobility is worded in the following way: 'essentially, social mobility is the extent to which where you end up, in terms of income or social class, is not determined by where you started' (APGSM, 2012). As already mentioned then, the assumption is of an existing social hierarchy. Unlike our conceptualisation of transformative teaching and learning, social mobility does not appear to be premised on the possibility of collective social change. Rather, it appears to assume that inequality is a 'fact of life': inevitable. The two project participants that we will focus on in this section each illustrate some important truths about how transformative education connects with social mobility in its positive impact on people's lives.

To explore the relationship between transformative teaching and learning and social mobility we will discuss Marie's story. Marie arrived at college after leaving a violent partner. As with many of the adults we talked to, Marie found reading and writing hard at first and struggled with her confidence. She had grown up on an estate outside Manchester, a daughter and sister in a large family. In our conversation with her, she touched on many familiar themes. She talked about how she went back into education after a negative experience of school. A course run by a local college ignited a passion for learning. This might have been an adult education class run by a charity like that attended by David and Jade or an organisation like the Workers' Educational Association, but it just so happened that in Marie's case it was an outreach programme run by a college.

She also talked about the power education had given her and her family to make choices in life. Further education brought about a turning point in her life when she became 'hooked' after starting a literacy course at the local college rather than take up another low-paid job opportunity. Through this, further education became the medium and the space framing a transformative experience and brought about a big change in the opportunities and the educational and lifecourse trajectories of her family. Marie had strong opinions about the value of education:

'I don't care if (my son) stays in education till he's thirty years old.
I want him educated because education gives you power and that's
what I want my children to have. I want them to be able to make
choices. Definitely, I want them to be able to … you know … say,
"Well actually I don't want to do that, I want to do that. And I want to
go and live there, I don't want to stay there and live there. And I want
to have a car and I want to do this." Just choices … I want them to be
able to go to Costa and get a coffee. Something I could never do …
that's what education will give him: choices.'

The passage speaks of personal transformation and the ripple effect of this
into the family. Significantly though, it also speaks of the poverty and lack
of opportunity that characterised Marie's life prior to her re-encounter with
education. There are echoes here of Jade's story, a desire for ordinary things
that are special while at the same time seemingly everyday. There was a sense
in Marie's story that these things were out of reach in her life prior to this
re-entry into education. Her emphasis on the range of opportunities on
offer for her children also speaks to her sense of positionality and a rekindled
sense of agency to act in and on the world.

Determined to improve her reading and writing, Marie grasped at
education as a life-line that provided a pathway for her towards a career in
nursing. The starting point was the discovery that she loved learning and,
for a variety of reasons, had never been able to build on that love during
her schooling. Through further education, she wanted to challenge the
intergenerational poverty of her background. In the following passage,
we once more see many of the ingredients of transformative teaching and
learning which again move beyond the social mobility of a single individual
escaping and abandoning who they are and where they are from:

'Through learning to read and write, I now see life differently. Now
when my children bring homework home I'm right onto it. I sit down
with them and we go through their work together. For example, my
son Andrew is only eight and he has 20 spellings a week to learn. This
week he had words such as exhibition, examination and electrocution.
Before returning to education I would never have been able to help him
with words like this, so the chances are he would not have learnt them.
He would have gone to school, had his spelling test. Maybe he got 4
or 5 out of 20, if he was lucky, felt a bit daft in front of the children
who had got most of them right and slowly but surely before you know
it, it's a knock-on effect, history is repeating itself. But because I can
now sit down with Andrew and help him with his homework he gets
marks like 17 out of 20, which to me is pretty amazing. I really feel
that in my case because I'm all my children have, if I'd not returned

to education the chances are that my children would have ended up experiencing difficulties in their education. I'm not saying that they won't but if they do, like I did, I can now help them.'

Our research clearly highlights how educational journeys empower people by increasing their chances of getting jobs, staying healthy and participating fully in society (Duckworth and Smith, 2019). But more than improving the life chances of the family, Marie's transformative experience of further education has changed the way she sees the world. For women who are marginalised and often silenced, transformative educational experiences offer the tools which can enable them to transform their lives (Duckworth, 2013).

It's important to note that Marie – who is now a staff nurse – still lives on the same estate she grew up on. For Marie then, social mobility has not been about abandoning her background or turning her back on the community that she comes from. Instead, she can be seen as an example and role-model to other residents as she bring dignity and hope to the community. For us, this is a vital reshaping of the concept of social mobility which positions transformative education as a catalyst that, while enabling social mobility and the acquisition of skills and knowledge is not about changing fundamental aspects of a student's identity. Marie is still the same person; it is her financial and economic security and her perspective on the world that has changed. For our participants, social mobility doesn't have to or always mean moving away from one (poor) area to a more affluent one. According to our research then, transformative educational experiences transcend the individualised limitations that attach to social mobility. According to the OECD (2017), improving the education of people from all social strata contributes higher levels of productivity but in Marie's case it also enhances social cohesion within her community: through enhancing the agency of the individual, it benefits the family and, beyond that the home community.

The role of further and adult education in facilitating students' access to university could be taken as one measure of its importance as an engine for social mobility (not *the* measure, Dean's story among others testifies to that). According to Smith et al, (2015, 10), between 2007/08 and 2011/12 the rate of entrants in HE from further education colleges remained stable at around 33%. Funding arrangements for studying at university have changed considerably since the New Labour government set a target of 50% of young people entering HE. With this move towards the 'massification' of HE (Leach, 2013), tuition fees have been introduced to address the issue of funding this expansion. For students from further education backgrounds (in particular, adults), these fees are an additional and critical stumbling block. Despite New Labour's concerted drive (1997–2010) to increase the participation rates of under-represented groups in HE, there remain significant gaps in the participation rates of people from some socio-economic backgrounds. Indeed, although the proportion of students from poor backgrounds attending university has increased significantly over time, the chasm in the HE participation rate between richer and poorer students remains glaring (Crawford et al, 2016).

While it is concerning that the same instrumentalist discourse that has dogged further education for the last quarter century is now being heard in the corridors of universities (Williamson, 2021), HE still has a huge potential for improving students' life chances and income levels. The Institute for Fiscal Studies' 2016 report: *Family background and university success: differences in Higher Education access and outcomes in England* highlights how graduates are much more likely to be in work and earn considerably more on average than non-graduates. In comparison, non-graduates are twice as likely as graduates to be experiencing unemployment 10 years after leaving compulsory education. The benefits of attaining a degree are also gendered: while there is a male graduate to non-graduate pay gap of £8,000 per year, the female graduate to non-graduate pay gap is £9,000 per year.

The reach of further and adult education colleges and their ability to connect with people from poorly represented social groups means that the impact of the service they offer is proportionately greater than schools and VIth form colleges. The research data again and again highlighted this reach and the centrality of access to HE courses in enabling transformative educational experiences for a host of students from different backgrounds. Routes offered by colleges into university are obviously hugely significant when viewed through the lens of social mobility. As a key engine for enhancing the social mobility of the most economically disadvantaged sections of our population, further education colleges' involvement is crucial in providing access to university level study.

Jacqui, an assistant principal at a college in the West Midlands, draws strongly on her own (negative) experiences of education as an important way of getting through to some students. In talking about some of the vital work that colleges do but that is often overlooked and unfunded, Jacqui highlighted working with gang members and young people who have not thrived in the environment of school. She describes how it always helps when she tells them 'I was expelled at school twice and it didn't stop me'. Her approach centres on sharing her story of her own learning journey with the students and acknowledging the importance of that. Jacqui sees informal relationships outside of the classroom as a way of 'earthing' the learning:

> 'The first thing you do with students is you take them out and you break down all those barriers. So you see each other as people first. Breaking down barriers, talking to them as people … You talk to them: I have been there and I have felt what you feel. But this is how you get on. Do you not want to be something? Do you not want to be someone? Because you can be anything. And when you tell them that and they start to believe you.'

In this passage we see familiar themes: the egalitarian approach, the use of biography and taking students' experiences seriously by positioning them as the starting point. But this is quickly followed by a forward-looking reimagining of the future. From there, her classes became spaces in which students were offered routes to move out of vicious circles of apathy and hopelessness.

Jacqui has worked with two of the notorious gangs of Birmingham and she describes how, all housed in the same class, they were reluctant to settle into the classroom and brought anger and suspicion into the environment. Jacqui's approach was to insist on establishing an egalitarian, two-way, mutually respectful relationship. She achieved this through a combination of reciprocity and passion. As a starter, she told them: '[h]ere's my story I went into teaching because I was like you: I hated teachers. I didn't want to be told what to do. Nobody's better than anybody else here.' She explains the impact of telling her students that: 'And that's it! I think if you've got that attitude, they will do anything. Also, if you're passionate about your subject. So it's about getting them enthused, whereas at school they felt little and nothing.' In this way, Jacqui was able to challenge their behaviour not by shouting and demanding conformity from her position of power as a teacher, but from a position of humility, care and importantly by sharing her story as a means to show them that she was not 'different' but had had her own struggles and through education was able to flourish and take back the power of hope. We hear from Jacqui again in Chapter 6.

Mental health and well-being

Apart from the economic benefit for individuals in gaining qualifications and entering employment or beginning a new career, the benefits of further and adult education extend into mental health, social cohesion, family learning and learning for young people excluded from mainstream. In addition to those aspects already covered, further and adult education providers contribute strongly to the mental health and well-being of the communities they serve. It is no accident that GPs are increasingly opting for 'social prescription' and prescribing educational courses for people who feel isolated and whose well-being is suffering as a result. Further and adult education is well placed to address some of the social challenges arising from an educational system that often seems overly competitive and focused on individual advancement rather than functioning as a public service whose purpose is to benefit society more widely. For people who have endured mental ill health, further and adult education offers educational space that can indeed be transformative.

We have identified elsewhere (Duckworth and Smith, 2018d) how adult education can provide an empowering environment for learners to challenge symbolic and physical violence which can often trigger mental health episodes. As highlighted by the WHO (2000):

Women in developed and developing countries alike are almost twice as likely as men to experience depression. Another two of the leading causes of disease burden estimated for the year 2020, namely violence and self-inflicted injuries, have special relevance for women's mental health. (WHO, 2000, 5)

Further and adult education is shown to be beneficial in the positive effect it can have on mental health and well-being. Indeed, as Duckworth (2013) documents, deprivation and poverty are strongly linked to the prevalence of mental ill-health in communities. Clearly, adult education courses for young and older adults offer further opportunities to re-engage with education; they can contribute to personal development, including the development of so-called 'soft skills' such as confidence (a valued outcome in Barton et al's 2007 study) as well as economic, social and health related benefits. The Learning and Work Institute's Report (2018, 20) highlights how 'insecure and poor-quality employment is associated with an increased risk of our physical and/or mental health worsening, from conditions caused by work that in turn lead to absence due to illness, and worklessness'. Further education courses for adults returning to learn offer an opportunity to acquire the tools needed to run their own lives, to reclaim agency and self-respect in their journey from learning into (often more fulfilling) work. The research brought to light narratives about women's educational journeys which suggested a tipping point can be reached in people's lives when a combination of external circumstances can seem to create insurmountable obstacles to the realisation of hope.

Nyomi was another project participant that we met in the North East of England. A mother with a young daughter, her story was one that involved completing a Diploma in Youth Work but then finding, as a result of local authority cuts and the nation-wide reduction of funding for youth services, that there were no jobs in that area of work. This, coupled with her responsibility as a carer for her partner, isolated her and had a negative impact on her mental health.

'I kind of spiralled into quite a bad depression. I got pregnant, had my daughter and luckily my daughter gave us a little bit of a boost, so I went and got help for my depression ... It was the Health Visitor that spoke to us and tried to get us to get a little bit of motivation and to go back out into the world and try again.'

For Nyomi, being on benefits carried a social stigma. She talked about the way she and her partner were 'looked down on' by neighbours while they were unemployed and on benefits. Nyomi's hopes for the future and plans were affected by the economic and employment conditions of the local area added to complex personal and family circumstances. Enrolling on an Access to HE course and having support for her dyslexia provided Nyomi with an opportunity to experience transformative teaching and learning. Nyomi talked about the ripple effects of her further education and the benefits for her family. In particular, further education offered hope as the parent of a child with a health condition:

'I became a mam of somebody with a health condition. That was who I was. I wasn't who I had been. As soon as I got depression I went on a downward spiral. I found it very difficult going out … I had spent the last four years extremely depressed because of the way my life was panning out. I didn't think … I didn't see myself in education again. And it's hard when you come from living and not having a job and you know that you should be working … and nobody employing you … The only thing I could do to give my daughter some kind of life was to do the Access Course. It's been amazing … I came off anti-depressants which I'd been on for quite some time. I made friends with people. And I haven't really spoken to a lot of people in years. It really does change your life. It's allowed me to get back out … Within two months I was a completely different person.'

Once more the transformative aspects of Nyomi's narrative have a strong social dimension. They are not just about learning skills and/or subject knowledge. They are more about Nyomi repositioning herself as an active woman, mother and, ultimately a professional (she went on to study a degree in podiatry). In this case, Nyomi's story is bound up in the economic and political history of the region. She came from one of the pit villages which lost all its employment after the Coal Board (backed by the government of the time) closed mines across the country in the 1980s. In a context in which the impact of circumstances like these are felt by individuals on a social and physical level, local colleges open doors that offer people hope. Nyomi's further education did not involve her signing up for a 'retraining package' – important as such initiatives might be – rather, it was accessed informally, almost as a form of social prescription. Nevertheless, its impact has clearly been massive and has resulted in renewed hope within the family unit.

'I went from being in the house all the time or going to hospital appointments with my daughter to having something to look forward to. It (also) changed my partner into a more confident person. We were both in quite a bad situation when we were depressed because he was depressed too – but his was more to do with his health. So giving him some extra responsibility … he changed completely. Two years ago, he would never have gone back to college because he just didn't have that confidence. So he hid away from a lot of things.'

Nyomi's narrative illustrates how colleges can offer a route out of despair and how this positive impact can feed into and improve family situations. Clearly, her renewed hope is likely to impact on the dynamics of the family and on her daughter's well-being. Nyomi's empowerment as a student also fed into her confidence and the value she felt in her role as a mother and partner.

There are echoes of her story across other narratives in the research. As we saw in Chapter 4, Jade also experienced mental health issues and spoke about supporting her friend through her depression. It is important not to underestimate the affective dimension of the learning experience that both Nyomi and Jade describe. Bourdieu's concept of 'habitus' (Bourdieu, 1994) is useful here. The meanings of habit and habituation that habitus carries within it may be connected to established social patterns of being and acting in the world, but these patterns are also bodily, they connect with how we feel. In this case, feelings of acceptance within a classroom that enables transformative educational experiences lead to rekindled agency. Both Jade and Nyomi's accounts communicate strongly a habitus associated with poverty and unemployment. For both, there was a relationship between these aspects of their lives and their mental well-being. The seeming intractability of their circumstances resulted in depression. This feeling of being trapped and locked into a pattern of life was broken by further and adult education and by experiences of transformative teaching and learning.

Both women were also motivated by hopes for their children. Their re-engagement with education and their new-found determination moves beyond being 'resilient' – an over-used label (like 'the deserving poor' see Diprose, 2015) that contains within it an implicit justification of the necessity of austerity measures. Both women were hopeful for their future and were happy that their further education meant they could be important role models for their children. However, the role of transformative teaching and learning in this, once more, is inaccessible to the kind of measurement that yields funding for colleges. In this, transformative education makes an invisible and uncounted contribution to social benefits that will only come into view in the future. And this lack of recognition is a failure of the current funding and performance apparatus that needs addressing urgently.

Pippa, another adult student that we talked to in the north-west of England, describes how 'It's all been a challenge but I'm somebody now'. Pippa's journey through returning to education started when she left school with a handful of O Levels and went into nursing. Nursing, however, she found tough. In her nursing employment she wore her 'heart on her sleeve', had a nervous breakdown and began drinking and experiencing panic attacks. This led to a period of unemployment which ended when she had what she called 'a light-bulb moment' and joined a northern adult residential college to start the level three course in teaching adults.

Arriving at the college she says that: 'I've never been so scared in my life. I really mean that. My legs were like jelly'. We forget this fear, its physicality: how it is bodily experienced. Pippa overcame these feelings and sensations and through the care and friendliness of the teachers and with the guidance and support of a mentor, she began to progress as a teacher. Once more, the diversity of the educational space is worth noting in Pippa's account:

'One of the things for me was how the group was so diverse. I'd never met a transgender woman. My second week there, this woman walked down to the bus station with me. We walked together and she said, "I'm going to tell you something now. You might not know this, but I used to be a man." Talk about having a big mouth! I said, That's why you've got such a beautiful figure!'

An important aspect of diversity is that we are continuing to discover the enormous and expanding variousness of what it means to be human. Further and adult educational spaces can be significant in expanding students and teachers' horizons in this regard. Pippa goes on to describe how more transgender women joined the group:

'We ended up with perhaps six or seven transgender women coming and joining the group which was very difficult as other women had been fleeing domestic violence and things like that. The transgender women for some at first did pose a threat. But everything turned out fine. I put that down to L___, the teacher, my mentor. She handled it so well. Because some of these women have gone years without having their own voice ... they'd attempted suicide, things like that. I'd been learning about creating a very easeful environment for these women. The learning there is about empowerment. L___ is brilliant at this and I'd like to think that I am as well now. I feel passionate about it.'

Pippa's account here reveals how adult educational space can provide healing and be 'easeful' at the same time not avoiding difficult and potentially confrontational relations in the classroom. This is the definition of 'differential space' as conceptualised by Lefebvre (see Chapter 7). The acceptance of difference here is balanced against the safety of all and this is only possible due to the skill and experience of the teacher. Pippa learnt from that and felt she had grown as a teacher herself. The course then enabled Pippa to travel from experiences of pain towards being able to support others and give them strength. Talking about one of the women on the course she states:

'There's a poem that one of them wrote for my birthday. It talks about an oak tree and the roots being very deep. And she had been physically abused by her partner. She left him. And she goes on to talk about how the branches can be broken but how the roots are still strong under the ground and how she's learnt to be strong because of me. And then underneath it just says: To Pippa, the strongest woman I know.'

The social benefits accruing from Pippa's transformative experiences are powerfully conveyed in her account. In her role as an educator, Pippa is able to bring her authentic self and her narratives into the classroom. Her passion and commitment, her love and care mean that she acts a catalyst for students' hope and inspiration.

Story-telling and sharing our stories is a transformative way to reimagine futures that may otherwise have been thought of as 'out of reach' and not for 'people like me'. Of course, the sharing of stories about our own learning journeys can be transforming for the storyteller as well as our students. The process of sharing a story which has been hidden is often very difficult. It may be that incidents have been hidden in shame for a long time. Going into these corners of life takes courage and sharing these stories can liberate people who are trying to overcome trauma to find peace and to move forward in hope. The act of telling our story out loud can give power to others who may have experienced similar circumstances.

The mutual sharing of stories enables people to reclaim their sense of identity by giving voice to that which is often unspeakable. This includes experiences of violence in its many forms which can leave a person broken. Creating a safe space in the classroom to share stories is therefore emotionally powerful and can be cathartic, validating, healing and empowering. Our individual stories allow a personal connection between different people that can lead to building deeper democratic truths and an expanding awareness of the diversity of the society and world we live.

Concluding thoughts

The COVID-19 pandemic has huge social justice implications for individual and collective health and the role of further education in supporting many communities' emergence from it will be key. As identified by Chowdhury (2020) the pandemic exposed a huge disparity in how the virus has impacted on different groups and has laid bare and exacerbated social inequalities across countries. Ethnic and religious minorities, indigenous people, migrants, old people, people with disabilities, prisoners and other marginalised groups have all been adversely affected due to their lower socio-economic status, lack of access to sanitation, healthcare and housing facilities and higher levels of unemployment. As such the impact of COVID-19 calls for a strengthened role for further and adult education in working for social justice in both redistributive (the need for additional resource) terms and relational (through transformative pedagogical approaches) ways.

Support for colleges to be able to offer educational space that is conducive to transformative teaching and learning has never been more urgently needed. Such educational spaces nurture hope, solidarity, care and love, and connect the lives of students and their educational journeys closely to the teaching and learning. Such spaces support student dialogue – allowing students to express their feelings, reflect on the barriers to their learning and enabling teachers to develop educational resources and experiences that will allow students to flourish.

Further and adult education provides a multitude of social benefits that have often been diminished because of the lack of focus on the importance of human emotional engagement. The quotation from Biesta at the beginning of this chapter emphasises the importance of keeping the purpose of educational endeavour in mind if we are to realise the full potential of a 'good' education. Our position is that further and adult education is deeply wedded to social justice and this purpose is an integral part of the educational experiences it can offer. As we have argued, an instrumentalist purposing of education has pushed aside a greater transformative prize that in its holistic nature has remained largely unmeasured – precisely because it cannot be quantified in a form that the current FAP apparatus recognises. This chapter has highlighted how transformative teaching and learning can be a powerful tool to address the issues of social injustice that plague our society and that this is a worthy goal. The next chapter will explore the role of leadership in extending and embedding transformative educational practice in further and adult education settings.

6

Transformative teaching and learning and education leadership

> Leaders who do not act dialogically, but insist on imposing their decisions, do not organize the people – they manipulate them. They do not liberate, nor are they liberated: they oppress.
>
> Paulo Freire, *Pedagogy of the Oppressed*

Introduction

This chapter starts with a quotation from the hugely influential book *Pedagogy of the Oppressed* by Paulo Freire (Freire, 1995, 178). Freire's writing connects strongly with the central concerns of this book, in particular the connection between further and adult education, social justice and hope. In the quotation above, Freire is reflecting on the nature of leadership when it is orientated towards tackling and ending oppression to bring about social justice. The passage clearly illustrates the egalitarian principles that define Freirean pedagogy while also signalling how concentrating power in the hands of individuals rather than sharing it, and imposing rather than negotiating meanings, will lead to oppressive rather than emancipatory outcomes. This chapter will look at the ways in which leadership is typically conceptualised in further (and to a lesser degree adult) education settings and in so doing, will seek to answer questions relating to how it needs to work to create the conditions in which transformative teaching and learning can take place. It will also briefly outline the way colleges are governed and the impact of this since incorporation.

The incorporation of colleges under the 1992 Further and Higher Education Act placed leadership and governance on a new footing. A business ethos and practices from business management were very much to the fore in the new dispensation. Colleges were encouraged to take an entrepreneurial view of their provision: to grow new 'business', to expand provision in additional 'outlets' and to behave generally in a competitive and self-interested manner. While this may have had little impact where a town had only one college, in bigger conurbations, some colleges found themselves in direct competition with each other. In the last two decades, closures, mergers and takeovers have become familiar events and the restructuring of staff (often involving redundancies) common occurrences.

The Act also changed the composition of college governance decisively in terms of a new employment-related focus. Governing bodies were reconfigured to represent the interests of local employers and oversight by local authorities ended. In this way, the locus of decision-making and power was shifted from a local, democratically elected body (the local authority) and transferred to local employers and business interests. Each governing body had a chair and members, one of which was the college principal. In some colleges, the relationship between the principal and the chair of governors took on huge significance as, if it was too 'cosy', then proper levels of challenge and accountability failed to materialise (Gleeson et al, 2011). Some principals became adept at 'managing' the college governors.

More recently, changes brought about by the Education Act 2011 (HMSO, 2011) enabled the replacement of 'teaching' staff governors through a reference to a more generic 'staff' governors, meaning that the position of actual teachers on college governing boards is no longer guaranteed (see Sodiq and Abbott, 2018). In a context in which funding was prioritised above all in the running of institutions, and with a governing body making decisions about pay and conditions as well as growth and 'restructuring', it's clear to see how quickly educational considerations and the kind of values that we have foregrounded in this book could become marginalised and ignored.

Under the regime brought about by incorporation, colleges were paid to deliver 'units' of educational experience. In the early years of incorporation, providers were also incentivised to grow hugely. A broad pattern was established in which colleges were effectively contracted to deliver a set amount of courses for a set amount of money. The exact totals were reviewed and adjusted annually. Meeting targets and neither under nor over-recruiting became vital to maintain a stable financial position. Colleges were forced to recruit armies of administrators to oversee the gathering of complex data related to students, and the courses they were taking. In a role later taken by Ofsted, to start with the market regulator was the Further Education Funding Council. This body carried out periodic inspections to check on 'quality' and published their findings. The role of colleges' governing bodies in this environment revolved primarily around overseeing the smooth running of all these arrangements and being 'accountable' (although in most cases what this meant was extremely difficult to pin down).

In a competitive market context, senior leadership of a kind that foregrounded institutional responsiveness became necessary. As such, we would argue the dominant model of leadership that emerged in the competitive market environment established by the Act was more focused on institutional self-interest than the wider concerns of social justice and meeting community needs traditionally associated with further and adult education – and closely linked to transformative educational experiences. This dominant leadership model was a symptom of the emergence of the

FAP orthodoxy. It was orientated to bringing about efficiencies, organising performance data collection and the management of complex data-centric systems. It had to be. This was essential due to the instability of the further education funding regime and the short-term policy churn that has impacted in a variety of (often negative) ways on further and adult education over the past quarter century.

What's interesting about the reconceptualisation of the provider-as-business sparked by incorporation is that over the course of 30 years, it has been singularly unsuccessful. Colleges have closed and been merged and taken over. Big college groups have been established. Arguably, today, some of these are effectively too big to fail. The failure of the model was signalled by the launch in 2014 of a series of national Area Reviews, a programme of 'deep-dive' audit-based reviews triggered by concerns that too many colleges were failing to manage their finances successfully. The letter explaining the purpose of the reviews sent by David Collins, the newly appointed Further Education Commissioner signalled that 20 years after incorporation, the vision of a self-sufficient business-minded 'sector' had proved to be illusory:

> In most of the colleges I have visited to date, it would be true to say there hasn't been the level of challenge and scrutiny by the governing body that might be expected in an organisation that is dealing with financial concerns. This is often because some governing bodies do not have sufficient financial expertise within their membership to oversee complex multi-million-pound organisations. (BIS, 2015, 1–2)

The Area Reviews led to more mergers, closures and the consolidation of bigger college 'groups'. There was a widespread sense however that the inefficiencies uncovered in these reviews were really only a symptom of budget cuts and the byzantine and unstable funding regime that providers had been operating under for so long (see Smith, 2017).

In the marketised education environments of the early 21st century, the hegemonic model of leadership that is promoted and viewed as common sense is hierarchical. The stereotypical Chief Executive Officer (CEO) from this period is an entrepreneurial, ambitious, workaholic, decisive, self-promoting, self-aggrandising, single-minded individual who 'takes no prisoners'. This model is a product of the neoliberal mind-set we touched on in Chapter 1 and there are aspects of this model that clash directly with a project of transformative education. For a start, such a leader might be so orientated in her/his conduct that they have little or no understanding of the human and altruistic impulses that underpin transformative approaches. Also, on a more practical level, such a leader (and we may see examples of this is our current political leadership) is more likely to be interested in maintaining at least a surface appearance of pursuing the agenda set by the current skills discourse. In other words, we might expect such a leader to view further and adult education students as the raw material through which human capital is produced. S/he might also be the last person to actually consider sending their own children to learn in a further or adult education setting. They might see no distinction between performance data and the social reality of the teaching and learning going on in their college. The challenging financial circumstances that confront anyone leading a further or adult education provider, the need to balance the books, the regular re-structuring exercises and redundancies might also determine the character of such a leader. Unfortunately, incorporation required leadership of this kind and, arguably, it is still prevalent in colleges.

But leadership doesn't have to be viewed in this way. Rather than seeing it as the psychological characteristic or property of a single exalted individual who has clawed their way up a pyramid of power to the most senior position, leadership in further and adult education settings can be viewed as a characteristic of the actions of staff at all levels of an organisation (see O'Leary et al, 2019; Smith and Duckworth, 2020). Leadership can be synonymous with agency and professional autonomy. In an educational setting such as a college, thinking of leadership in this way fits better with an ethos in which all staff are there to facilitate the education of students in a nurturing and co-produced transformative educational space. This isn't to say that complex organisations like colleges do not require senior leaders – of course they do – but the manner in which those individuals lead and the guiding principles of their work, are only one element of leadership when social practices and cultures (the *processes* of education) are more important than 'productivity' (the outcome data that reductively signify students' educational experiences).

Starting with the role of the senior leadership team (SLT), this chapter will look at the different strata of leadership and theorise the current and possible relationship of each level to transformative education. Following on from Chapter 5, we will explore the constraints SLTs operate under and the demands they face as they strive to sustain a values-driven approach shaped by a commitment to social justice and we will comment on some of the strategies they can utilise. We will then go on to theorise how teachers can exercise leadership in their practice by foregrounding the necessity of focusing on students' needs through the lens of transformative teaching and learning. In many cases, this might put their practice in tension with college regimes orientated around conformity to funding, accountability and performance cultures.

Historical perspectives

The Further and Higher Education Act of 1992 scaffolded not just particular purposes for education and for learning and teaching but particular meanings around how institutions should contribute to these meanings and how those institutions should be led. The Act brought together the complexity and diversity of further education, which included everything from offender learning to second-chance adult education and work-based learning, under a single umbrella 'sector'. The designation of 'non-Schedule 2' qualifications (so-called 'leisure' courses that would no longer be centrally funded) was an attempt to streamline provision that had hitherto developed in an organic way. Instead, the drive was to fund only qualifications that could be more easily mapped against an instrumentalist purpose. The Act also contributed to the exclusion of the notion that social justice was in any way an integral element of the social value produced by/through further and adult education.

There are several ways in which national policies and funding constrain transformative education and senior leaders are the chief mediators of these constraints. The first is curricular. It has now become universally accepted that only some courses (notably those with accreditation) are funded in further and adult education. Funding arbitrates what's possible. It is important to remember that, prior to incorporation, lots of other 'leisure' courses were also funded. These did not necessarily include a qualification. Courses like pottery, yoga and a range of other 'leisure' courses over night fell outside the 'Schedule 2' category and were no longer funded. This was a crucial moment in the tightening of what was deemed to be useful and, consequently, of the instrumentalisation of further and adult education.

The assumptions underpinning this move were twofold: first that courses without accreditation and that had no 'official' assessment could not be measured in terms of 'quality' of delivery. Secondly, there was an assumption that courses – often catering for community groups, the elderly and others who might in neoliberal terms be regarded as not economically viable individuals – were of little or no value to wider society because they offered no qualifications that related directly to the employment market. This strengthened an architecture that was (and still is) largely blind to the social benefits of education, how it delivers on many levels relating to health and well-being and can operate as an equaliser – putting right some of the social inequality that a rigidly structured schooling system causes.[1]

While New Labour policies (1997–2010) attempted to reconnect further and adult education to ideas of social justice through, inter alia, the Skills for Life initiative, an instrumentalist emphasis was maintained. The austerity measures then introduced in the wake of the financial crisis, from 2010, when the Conservative-Liberal Democrat coalition came to power, have shaped policy decisively in this respect. Colleges bore much of the brunt within the education system, suffering successive rounds of cuts to funding which resulted in a further narrowing of provision and substantially reduced numbers of adult students. Despite that, the social justice work being undertaken by colleges was thrown into relief and given new meaning and impetus as the home circumstances of many students were made grimmer. Despite their more limited resources and the financial instability introduced by austerity, colleges responded as best they could, as they strove to meet the needs of their communities as well as the demands of the state.

By 2015, cuts to further and adult education budgets had resulted in a big increase in the number of colleges facing financial deficit (NAO, 2015). This situation was the catalyst for the post-16 so-called Area Review Programme that ran from September 2015 to middle of 2017. Interestingly, rather than acknowledging that the financial squeeze put on colleges by austerity measures might have impacted negatively on their 'performance' as educational institutions, the area reviews instead shifted the focus on to colleges as part of a regional infrastructure tasked with delivering skills – and found them wanting in this regard. The aim of these reviews was to 'move towards fewer, larger, more resilient and efficient providers, and more effective collaboration across institution types' (BIS and DfE, 2016, 3). They had a familiar instrumentalist theme as these bigger college groups would then be expected to: 'deliver high quality education and training which supports economic growth'. (BIS, 2015, 2). As well as further curtailing the autonomy of colleges, supposedly assured by incorporation, the area reviews signalled that the distinctive local identity of individual colleges was to be further eroded by government policy. This had implications for college leadership and for the ability of colleges to focus on meeting the needs of their local communities.

This potted history provides some important insights into the role of college SLTs in this period. Once incorporation put colleges on a competitive footing as stand-alone institutions, the function of SLTs has been to mediate policy change and manage resource. But since 2010, their role has refined to presiding over a steady contraction of funding and resources. This is a long way from the glamour of the incorporated principal's role circa 1993. That was, it seems, just an enticing dream.

Leadership orthodoxy and the architecture of further and adult education

As a starting point, it's useful to return to the two versions of further and adult education that we introduced this book with. As we explained, the two versions aren't totally distinct in the experience of teachers and students. They merge into one another and in local contexts, one or other may be more dominant. But that is not to underestimate the monocular fixity of policy. Policy in this area is almost exclusively focused on the skills and productivity discourse and has been, to the exclusion of all alternatives, for at least a decade (since 2010) and arguably longer.

One way of thinking about leadership is to frame the discussion within this context and conceptualise it along a continuum between two poles. At one end is the idea, largely promoted by government policy at this point as 'commonsense' and indeed, absolutely necessary. That is the view that further and adult education is first and foremost a sector of different institutions that are competing with each other and against 'benchmarks' to turn out students with qualifications that meet the skills needs of local industry and the nation. As we have seen, at its worst, this position treats students' own interests as if they are irrelevant and issues of social justice as, at best, secondary. It also views teaching and learning primarily in transmission terms, and if students are 'disengaged', it locates the fault in them, rather than in the curriculum and what they are being expected to benefit from. This version sees students as human capital to be shaped for some 'greater cause' and in so doing it objectifies them.

At the other end, we have presented a version of further and adult education that currently nests, in the interstices, in pockets within this first version. In what remains of adult education in England, this version is still writ large. This version can be viewed through the lens of transformative education and is all about students' interests and development. In this second version, the curriculum is problematised and questioned, as is assessment. This version also rejects an absolutist view of teaching and learning: in order to meet students' needs, it strives to experiment in an ongoing interaction with students' progress. This version acknowledges that people learn differently, and that some students' learning can be disrupted by didactic approaches or approaches that fail to connect with existing knowledge and experience. Taking account of these things is seen as necessary and as contributing positively to learning.

Behind each of these views, we can perceive a set of assumptions about society and the world more broadly. At one end of the continuum, the view is that there is no alternative to the current state of the world and how it is governed. This position views inequality as a product of the unequal distribution of 'talent' and 'intelligence'. The existing social order therefore mustn't be challenged as it expresses in some way a 'natural' or even a 'God-given' moral order. In many ways, this position is increasingly difficult to sustain. As the histories of empires across the world are re-visited and challenged and as climate change confronts humankind with catastrophe irrespective of national boundaries and wealth, it has become untenable. Like a castle made of sand, the waves are lapping at its edges, and it is beginning to melt into the sea. The focus on climate and ecology in the G7 summit in June 2021 shows how dramatically commonsense and established economic models are going to have to change – despite reluctance on the part of the world's most powerful governments (Schomberg, 2021).

But unfortunately, there are still loud voices that oppose these changes. The climate change deniers are an example. As economies of the world have largely founded their growth on the use of fossil fuels, it's clear why some individuals, corporations and governments might not want to acknowledge that it's time to stop using them. Indeed, they might want to invest heavily in producing knowledge and in funding organisations specifically to counter such arguments. Further, they might want to resist any attempt to be held accountable for the ecological damage the oil industries are responsible for. Above all, those who see the way the world is as 'natural', 'inevitable' and/ or 'justifiable', are desperate to resist facing up to the need to change the way the global economy works.

The other end of the continuum acknowledges all of this. It starts from an outward-looking premise that the current social order is unequal, not because the talented have worked their way to the top, but because, those with access to the best resources ensure that they keep a hold on them and protect their position. It's important to state here that we are not focusing only on a national picture: this argument is drawing on what we know of inequality in the world more broadly. At the level of nation, ultimately it connects with how, historically, Britain cast an imperial net across much of the globe, sucked the natural resources out of the countries it colonised and when it withdrew, established a set of relations that helped it to maintain the dependency of those nations and the inequality established by the Empire (Hickel et al, 2022; Hirsch, 2019; Akala, 2018). The world view underpinning transformative teaching and learning does not blame the poor for being poor or the vulnerable for being vulnerable. It seeks instead to meet student needs and catalyse students' inherent learning abilities while also addressing the social conditions that give rise to inequality. With these contrasting and conflicting world-views in mind, we can return to exploring educational leadership.

The way further and adult education is currently set up, central government is disproportionately empowered to affect how colleges and other providers organise their educational offer. As we have already outlined, the FAP apparatus functions to perpetuate this centralised power relation. An annualised re-assertion of (national) instrumentalist policy aims, vividly articulated in the Skills White Paper of January 2021 in which 'good governance and leadership' appears to be subject to the central role of employers and the establishment of employer-led standards (DfE, 2021, 8) dominates further and adult education at the expense of other purposes. Clearly, this limits colleges' independent ability to address the local circumstances including those related to social justice.

In structural terms then, transformative teaching and learning can be said to be disabled or, at least, marginalised by the current FAP regime. That doesn't mean transformative education has been extinguished: depending as it does on micro interactions between teachers and students it could never be shut out entirely but, it can be confined to individual interactions. Within colleges, this has structural consequences. Arguably, it limits the impact of transformative teaching and learning to the successful assimilation of previously marginalised individuals into an existing social order, rather than enabling an organisational effort that moves beyond this to question existing social structures.

Rethinking leadership as a quality of action rather than a role

The current world-wide crisis in models of leadership and legitimacy of leadership (even in societies founded on democratic principles) points to problems arising from the understanding of leadership as a quality of individual character. The seriousness of this crisis is clear when we understand that the performativity that so disfigures the educational landscape, all of the effort that goes into 'proving' that targets have been met and budgets balanced, the fabrication, concealment, the duplicity and the steady drift away from integrity can all be seen as characteristic of the way governments now operate in what some commentators have branded our 'post-truth' age (see Foroughi et al, 2019; Hopkin and Rosamond, 2018; Spector, 2020). In the experience of one of us (Rob), the duplicity of leaders – the misrepresentation of achievement data during the first 5 years of incorporation – led directly to more than one hundred redundancies and almost closed the college down; all while the college leaders maintained that finances were 'buoyant' (see Smith, 2015). Worryingly, a feature of institutional crises under market cultures is that they only become apparent after the event, as there is an institutional compulsion to disguise poor performance for as long as possible.

In England, the discourse of character-building that originates in public schools and was perpetuated through Empire, is a major contributor to the previous model. The literature that focuses on the psychology of leadership centres on individualised models even when theorising leadership orientated to meeting the needs of others (for example 'connective' and 'altruistic' leadership in Lipman-Blumen (1998) and Salas-Vallina and Alegre (2018). There is also a literature on 'transformative leadership' (for example, Shields, 2010) but this still locates it as originating in the traits of individuals with a senior organisational role.

Rather than emphasising the importance of individual leadership as character-based and hierarchical, we want to think about leadership as a quality of action that does not depend on a position within an institutional hierarchy. This is not to downplay the importance of senior leaders and their decisions within colleges. As we have already outlined, their outward-facing role, shielding their institutions from the worst excesses of blunt and clumsy policy is vital. Rather, it is a way of recognising how leadership on the part of teachers and the facilitation of that is crucial if further and adult education settings are to be conducive to transformative educational experiences. Teachers' leadership means being able to work against the grain of instrumentalist education policy by insisting on viewing their students as people with histories, biographies communities, hopes and dreams.

College leadership orientated by principles of social justice can suffuse college cultures, encouraging staff at all levels to act in ways that are informed by explicit values (see three specific examples of this kind of leadership in Smith and Duckworth, 2020). The impact of this on students emerges strongly in the Transforming Lives research. Whether this then connects and brings about change in local communities and wider society depends on the collective energies and organisation that individual students connect with once they venture beyond college walls. Ultimately, despite the prevailing policy context, leadership that is committed to social justice will foster the kind of critical consciousness we have provided evidence of and will continue to promote socially just practices and tackle social issues relevant to their communities informed by an optimism of the heart.

It's important to flag up here how this view of college leadership orientated to achieving social justice and transformative education is viewed with great suspicion by central government. Many adult education providers draw heavily on their historical heritage and the cultural capital embedded within that is an important resource in the assertion of their relevance and meaning. In recent years, some of these institutions have received special attention from (seemingly) hostile funding bodies (see Smith and Duckworth, 2020). As mentioned in Chapter 1, the adult education budget has suffered cuts of around 40% since 2010 and 16–19 funding of 24%. As a result, all colleges have been forced to strategise and calculate for the future while being hemmed in by an unreliable and unstable funding environment.

As we explained in Chapter 5, the Transforming Lives research provides powerful evidence that the demands of the FAP apparatus make an organisational focus on social justice: one that operates at every level of the college and informs interactions between staff and staff (all staff, not just teachers and managers) and staff and students – extremely difficult. The competitive market environment also means that discourses of 'putting the student first' might signal a deep commitment to social justice but can also operate as a discursive veneer in which 'equality, diversity and inclusion' have become hollow commodified tropes and empty words. If leadership as a quality of action within colleges is to facilitate transformative education then this requires the penetration of these values throughout organisational strata. The role for senior leaders is to ensure that the organisational culture of the colleges they work in privileges this. This suggests, not only that they act as a buffer between teachers and the pressures and demands of the FAP apparatus, but that they play an active outward-facing role in fighting for a broader conceptualisation of what further and adult education is here to achieve.

Teachers often are able to engineer their own transformative pedagogical leadership in their classrooms, whatever the institutional culture is like. Obviously though, their jobs can be a lot easier if they are not continually battling against a senior leadership that views funding, so-called accountability and performance as sovereign. Jez was a teacher of Level 1 and Level 2 Business students. He described his 'passion' as teaching these lower levels. Initially, a huge part of his role is confidence-building:

'They've had quite a negative experience of education so far. They come to college lacking in academic confidence. That's not to say that they don't have the skills and the qualities to succeed academically and professionally. I see it as my job initially to build that confidence in their own academic ability to build their confidence, using their experiences, using what they've been through … to empower the students.'

We can see some of the key ingredients in Jez's account. First, there is a given: Jez's belief in his students, his assumption that they have the potential to achieve. Then there is the acceptance of and engagement with their experiences and 'what they've been through' as the foundation from which the learning can progress. This bridging of the gap between the spoilt identity of the student who thinks they can't learn and the student who not only believes they can but is willing to try demands a particular kind of space. Jez describes it in the following way:

'It's about instilling the confidence in those you've got in front of you to give them the power to drive their own bus as it were … I was talking to my Level 1 students this morning … How are you going to know how to (be an independent learner) … if you've not done it and messed up? In my experience, you will learn from your mistakes and as long as you do … I create a safe space to fail … And when they mess up, I say Let's look at this. How are we going to do this differently? I don't see it as me and them. We are all one. If one of my students gets kicked, I limp … We work together.'

The centrality of removing students' vulnerability and thereby freeing them to 'make mistakes' in order to learn is a basic but vital aspect of an educational space that strives for transformative potential. The egalitarian ethos between student and teacher is also emphasised. Jez conceptualises his role through the metaphor of driving a bus:

'So initially I am driving the bus, I am showing them where the gear stick where the steering wheel is, but as their confidence builds and they get more familiar with their surroundings and my expectations (which are quite high by the way) they take over the reins and start driving the bus. So they dictate which way they want the course to go, what units they want to do and they present that argument to me in an adult way.'

There is a strong ethic of care in this: aspects of mentoring and of nurturing autonomy are clearly apparent. Interestingly, continuity, the ability to progress over several years one level at a time is another feature. The teacher/student relationship provides the cohesion over an extended period. In 'putting right' damage done in previous educational experiences, Jez is working for social justice, to challenge the inequality of a situation in which students feel they have been written off.

What we're suggesting here is that leadership (whether 'senior' or not) cannot be divorced from the tenor of the relationships within which it is embedded. Echoing Gewirtz (1998) for Raelin (2010), social justice is about distribution but also demands a critical (re)examination of relationships. It is expressed and produced by the relationship between *I* and *the other*. A concept that Raelin has drawn from Buber (1959, 1961). This brings us back to objectification. In transformative teaching and learning teachers and students strive to relate to others through I/thou rather than I/it relationships: 'The I-thou ... is based on an authentic recognition of the self in the other that can arise from genuine dialogue' (Raelin, 2010, 8). The flip-side of I-thou relationship, an I/it relationship would be where the I, the teacher for example, regards the student as not having the same needs, desires, ambitions and human qualities as themselves and allows this attitude to permeate the way they relate to the student, as somehow lesser than themselves. This could then be reasonably expected to impact on the student's progress and, ultimately, achievement.

Another way of seeing this is as the objectification of students: their enmeshment in a commercial and data-driven set of relationships in which, as enrolled students, they are monetised. Following that, we must also recognise that the exploitation and objectification of staff (all staff, including teachers) also logically undermines any college's claimed commitment to social justice and undercuts any claims being made about 'putting students first'. If staff feel exploited or objectified then their relationship with students can only ever be It/thou. And if students are also being objectified, this relationship reduces further to It/It: an embattled interaction between two alienated and consciously objectified beings.

Admittedly, this is a tension that further and adult education teachers have wrestled with ever since the funding methodology integrated achievement into its formula. Certainly, this tension sheds new light on the damage to educational relationships caused by FAP-orientated cultures. There is evidence to suggest that in order to escape such cultures many teachers retreat into the sanctuary of the classroom which becomes a cloistered space in which egalitarian relations can be materialised (see O'Leary et al, 2019).

The insistence that leadership is a quality of action rather than being the lionised personal characteristic of an individual allows us to re-evaluate the role and achievements of teachers in further education who, for more than a quarter of a century have striven to safeguard the needs and interests of students. If transformative teaching and learning exists as a continuum with (re)learning how to learn at the start flowering into a re-positioning of the self that is allied to the awakening of critical consciousness, then spoon-feeding and teaching to the test will only ever be experienced as alienating.

Lucinda is a teacher in offender learning and works with high-risk male offenders from 21 years upwards. She teaches them in prison and when released; she works in a multi-agency team with the probation service, social services and the police. Lucinda describes how she didn't have a straight trajectory into teaching. She left school and found employment and at 21 joined a night class and then went on to do a degree. During working for her degree she had a child, and she describes how she tells the learners her own journey and how her circumstances 'didn't stop her'.

Lucinda describes how many of the men she teaches have mental health issues and a history of drug and alcohol abuse. A pivotal part of her role is working effectively in partnership to meet the complex needs of her students in a holistic way. Some of the courses she delivers are tailored to their specific needs, for example, parenting and family relations courses. This is motivational as it links to the learners' lives and motivations. Vital to her role is supporting the men to be empowered to live independently when they are released. Lucinda works with the housing office to deliver a course on looking after the home which includes safety, cooking and basic budgeting. Lucinda shared many examples of learning being transformative:

> 'The biggest jump I've seen was an Entry 1 learner to Level 1 within twelve months. And then they were released from jail and wanted to continue their education with me outside jail. I secured two offenders places on a Foundation Degree, something that both thought was totally out of reach and they weren't aware of what paths to take to do that and it's given them confidence in their own ability So it's not beyond anybody to do that, to achieve anything.'

The offender learning setting offers clear examples of how re-connecting with education, or in some cases learning to read and write for the first time, can be life-changing. Often, in Lucinda's account there are examples where family circumstances also have an impact. The leadership Lucinda shows in her account stems from her refusal to judge the students. She uses her own story as an example to her students, saying: 'It's never too late for anybody. I was an adult learner at university'. She sees her role as opening her students' line of sight to a pathway that can lead them to a different life:

'One (student) was in jail for nearly ten years. He has four brothers and they are in prison as well and his dad. He said to me he didn't want that to be him. He'd already served a long sentence. He was only young. He was still under thirty and he didn't want that to be his life forever. And so he made the change. When they know they can make the change, that's when it happens. If they come out of prison saying I'm going to end up going back, often they do.'

The combined prison population in England and Wales is the biggest in Europe at just under 80 000 (MoJ, 2021A).[2] In 2019, the 'proven re-offending rate' was more than 25% (MoJ, 2021B), so clearly, transformative educational experiences have a vital role to play for individuals and their families in terms of wider social costs and also the pressure they put on the public purse.

The transformative educational experiences that Lucinda facilitates are hugely beneficial to the men involved but also to society as a whole: 'when you give them a positive experience, when you can show them that they can achieve in education, once they see it on a certificate, you can show them: that's when their confidence boosts. It's not out of reach then.' Lucinda cares and works in a non-judgemental way wherein empathy and hope is instilled in the students. They can then see a pathway forward and can reimagine a life away from crime where they have agency and can play a positive role in their families and communities.

As a teacher in offender learning, we would argue that Lucinda evidences the kind of leadership that is focused on the socially just aims of creating the conditions in which positive change can come about for her students. In this context, institutional leadership that is geared towards creating the conditions in which such transformations can take place revolves around sustaining a culture in which individuals at all levels are cognisant of the structural pressures that threaten to deform the bigger educational purpose. The role of senior leaders – in Lucinda's case, these might include the Prison Governor – in particular should be about enabling the agency of teaching and other staff to preserve these conditions by recognising the rehabilitative value of education and by acting as a buffer between teachers and a policy environment that in the criminal justice system gives primacy to punishment and seemingly cannot distinguish between skilfully wrought market strategies and the provision of high-quality teaching and learning.

Transformative teaching and learning, leadership and localism

Leadership can also connect strongly with the local and regional identity of colleges. The Transforming Lives project foregrounded this localism as a key aspect of the distinctiveness of the educational experiences offered by further and adult education providers.

As we have suggested, the incorporation of colleges marked a key moment in the evolution of further education structures and cultures in England. Among other things, incorporation encouraged principals to view themselves as Chief Executive Officers (CEOs). With much more decision-making power in relation to strategic direction but also in determining the contracts of staff, senior leadership and management have a powerful impact on the social conditions in which teachers work. In the 1990s, this was shaped by funding that incentivised increased 'productivity', but now, with college funding more stretched than it has ever been and the social benefits provided by colleges needed more than ever, it is time for college leaders to use their incorporated powers to offer institutional environments that are conducive to transformative educational experiences. Teachers themselves obviously still control the key environment: that of the classroom. But the extent to which the differential space (as explored in the previous chapter and developed later in this) that they co-produce with students reflects the wider values and ethos of the college is dependent on senior leaders and their determination to safeguard the college from the negative effects of FAP tithe.

The staff survey that formed a part of the project touched on this when it asked survey respondents to indicate the extent to which they perceived their college leadership allowed them to realise different aspects of their role. This question sought to look inside college cultures in order to establish the extent to which teachers felt supported in their teaching.[3] The question was phrased so as to leave open the respondent's interpretation of 'leadership' – whether that was SLT, middle managers – or just individuals with the authority to affect how teaching played out (including teachers themselves).

As Figure 6.1 shows, a significant proportion of survey respondents saw college leadership as enabling them to meet learners' needs. This is encouraging even given the limitations of the sample. At the classroom level, this shows the teachers who are best placed to know and understand students' needs have a sense of agency. Survey data also revealed that those who believed that leadership allowed them to support their students in these ways were more likely to foster positive student-teacher relationships and a sense of 'belonging' in the classroom. That said, 40% thought that leadership only sometimes, rarely or never allowed them to meet students' needs. This high percentage is striking and suggests that for nearly half of

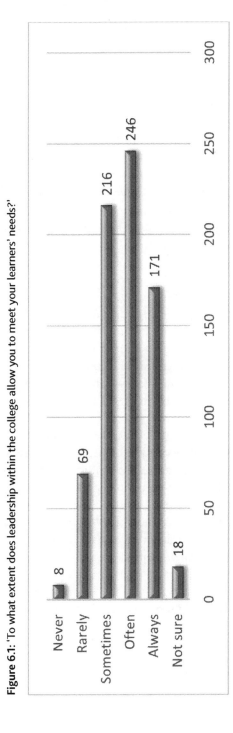

Figure 6.1: 'To what extent does leadership within the college allow you to meet your learners' needs?'

the respondents students' needs were at best a secondary consideration for college leadership. The data further indicates that there is a significant number of students whose needs are not being met and that these are the conditions created by the current regime of funding, accountability and performance.

A further survey question was forward-looking, focusing on the role of college teachers in facilitating the realisation of students' hopes for their future, see Figure 6.2. In many ways this question is probing at the heart of the purposes of further and adult education. It is asking teachers whether they feel they are supported to join with students in the pursuit of agreed aims. It is attempting to gain an overview of the extent to which students may be being subjected to a process that does not align with their hopes and interests. This might signal the extent to which colleges are seeing students through the distorting lens of FAP, seeing them in terms of 'progression' (how many consecutive years of funding income can be squeezed out of them) – in other words, to what extent they are objectified. Responses to this questions were varied. Over half of the sample of teachers believed that leadership did allow them to deliver these aspects of their role, 'often' or 'always'. Once more though, more than 35% believed that leadership allowed them to support students in achieving their aspirations only sometimes, rarely or never. The extent to which teachers held these beliefs once more affected the degree to which they attempted to foster positive student-teacher relationships and a sense of belonging in the classroom.

In our age of neo-liberalism and globalisation, the Freirean concept of transformation (see Freire, 1995), based on the premise that by overcoming oppression, oppressed people will move themselves *and their oppressors* towards true humanity, is attractive but is in tension with the competitive individualism that is deeply embedded in our education system. Arguably, it is this competitive aspect that fixates on assessment and ranks students, and that then labels a third of young people at 16 as 'unacademic' and in some way second-rate. In this context, if transformation and empowerment operate simply for some individuals and not others, they merely sustain the inequity of the bigger system. If individually focused rather than community-orientated, this kind of transformation may lead to a failure to engage in a broader commitment to social justice and positive change. The role of leadership in this context would seem to be best focused on supporting transformative education within the context of identified local needs.

According to the evidence from this project, further and adult education turns the deficit, negative self-worth and low self-esteem that students have had impressed upon them in their experience of schooling into a positive: enhancing their social integration, social mobility and agency with consequent knock-on effects for their families and communities. This requires us (and more importantly policy makers) to view further and adult education less as a 'sector' and more in terms of the basic units that provide

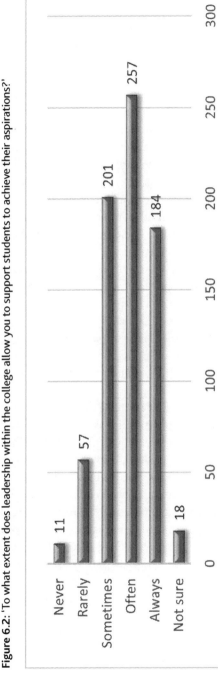

Figure 6.2: 'To what extent does leadership within the college allow you to support students to achieve their aspirations?'

the foundation for these transformative effects: a myriad of diverse local colleges and providers situated in local communities.

Further and adult education providers are first and foremost local institutions, and their leadership is most meaningful when this localism is foregrounded. They are well-positioned to connect with local employers in order to facilitate students' transitions into appropriate employment and/ or further study. This localism seems to us to be an important overlooked feature of what colleges do and where they are positioned educationally. The notion of the 'FE sector' dilutes this strength. The 'FE sector' is a rhetorical tool that supports the neoliberal instrumentalisation of further education.

The abstract space of the 'FE sector' is made 'real' through the FAP apparatus: the production (enforced via funding) and use of 'big (performance and accountability) data' and the feeding of this into the policy-making cycle. This bureaucratic work enables government and funders to view (potentially) transformative social processes in numerical forms (see O'Leary and Smith, 2012; Smith and O'Leary, 2013). This abstraction also impacts negatively on leadership in colleges. At its worst, it makes college SLTs minions of national instrumentalist policy which may work against local and regional interests and reduce teaching and learning to a technical 'delivery' process or an exercise in spoon-feeding and 'transmission'. Through abstraction, the complex socially interactive process that makes up teaching and learning in all its richness is reduced to numbers on a spreadsheet or worse still, a commodified set of qualification 'products'.

The evidence from our research counterposes this bleak and dehumanising abstraction with a different kind of space. Drawing once more from Lefebvre, we see transformative teaching and learning as reflecting what Lefebvre calls 'differential space'. He sees this as existing as potential within abstract space like a seed of the opposite: 'I shall call that new space "differential space", because, inasmuch as abstract space tends towards homogeneity, towards the elimination of existing differences or peculiarities, a new space cannot be born (produced) unless it accentuates differences' (1991, 52). If the abstract space of the 'FE sector' sees teaching and learning as corresponding to the transmission of knowledge, then differential space is a local space that is resistant to the external view of further and adult education as being about students acquiring skills for the national economy as though they were tiny cogs in a colossal mechanism. Differential space is the antithesis of abstract space and is a space in which critical pedagogy is espoused (see Chapter 7). This is an approach to teaching and learning that originates in Freirean pedagogy (Freire, 1995) and views students in a holistic way, as *coming from somewhere*, as reflexive and dialogical co-constructors of meaning and as people with biographies and an existing history as learners. It views teaching successfully as balancing a critical understanding of locality and the national policy context in which it takes place.

This perspective on leadership in colleges as first and foremost needing to meet local needs informed many of the teachers' accounts in our research. According to *AoC Key Facts* (2019, 22), 23% of 16–18-year-old students in colleges have learning difficulties and/or disabilities, compared to 20.9% of school students with special educational needs. Furthermore, as AoC research shows (AoC, 2019, 24), 16% of 16–18-year-old college students had previously been classified as qualifying for Pupil Premium and as eligible for free schools meals (FSM). By comparison, the number of students eligible for and claiming FSM in secondary schools is 12.4%. In other words, colleges cater for a much bigger proportion of young people from disadvantaged backgrounds or with learning difficulties and/ or disabilities than do schools.

Colleges' responsiveness to local circumstances goes largely unrecognised but leadership in this has an important socio-economic dimension in many instances. For some college teachers, dealing with the effects of austerity is a central element of this role. For example, in the North West, colleges have taken to providing free breakfasts for their students as many students were arriving on site unfed and not ready to learn because levels of household poverty were so high. A similar localised strategy involved providing uniforms for young people on one course that included a placement with external employers. This strategy came about in response to teachers noticing that a significant number of students had only one set of clothes.

In other cases, colleges' localised leadership came out of their rootedness in the history of their region. We saw earlier in Chapter 4 how Judith's practice as a teacher was grounded in a deep understanding of the North East. The narratives of participants in this area of the country all carried a historical subtext dating back to the Miners' Strike of the early 1980s. The mining villages surround Durham were severely affected by the pit closures that happened in the wake of the dispute. Many villages often depended on the mines as the main employers in the area. Consequently, pit closures resulted in mass unemployment and impacted massively on future job prospects. As identified by Hoffman et al (2019) an understudied but critical aspect of finding a career is the resource of social and cultural capital available to the job seeker. The college drew its demographic from surrounding (ex)pit villages and Judith was cognisant of that fact: 'We have to break the cycle of low aspirations in the North East because we've got whole generations now who don't work.'

Judith's understanding of her role is rooted in the location of the college and in the communities the college serves. In this case, her role involves addressing the legacy of the industrial strategies of 1980s Thatcherism when the largescale industries of motor manufacture, coal and steel production had public subsidies withdrawn. Some villages were entirely reliant on coal for employment so when the pits closed, this resulted in towns and villages losing huge numbers of jobs. The kind of educational leadership required in such local circumstances goes well beyond the individual, it has a strong collective dimension founded on care and altruism rather than self-interest.

The finding that colleges are going beyond funded provision in order to meet local student need with regards to meeting the needs of students from low-income backgrounds is also a strong theme in the account of Jacqui, a senior leader in a West Midlands college (whom we met in the last chapter). In her contribution, Jacqui outlined a number of initiatives that had strong elements of transformative teaching and learning. For example, the college had for a number of years provided community outreach specifically to target and recruit 'vulnerable' and 'disaffected' young people. Some of this provision was sports-focused and the idea driving it was that if these young people could be re-engaged through an attractive entry level course, which might then lead to them enrolling on other college courses. But there was a bigger motivation and that was connected to notions of the college as having a role in addressing issues of social deprivation and championing social justice and social cohesion.

> 'Our service ... it's half social work and half teaching. I mean who would pick up the pieces if we weren't here ...? Without us here? Mental health is massive, it's getting bigger. Social work. We find students places to live. We do all that wraparound service as well ... (Colleges) tend to be community hubs. Take Handsworth for instance ... people go there, we put on community events. It's a part of the community. I go back to mental health and loneliness – these are serious and growing things and further education is one of the only places that anybody can access, where people can interact and improve themselves. Without it, where do people without qualifications go?'

Jacqui's contribution was full of stories about young people who, through further education, found a positive way forward in life. She talked about her experiences of working with gang members in Birmingham. The previous excerpt presents the role of the college as much more than simply purveying courses to provide skills for employment. The 'wraparound' services offered by the college are plugging gaps left by the withdrawal of public funding for services like youth and community work. This 'sense of place' and the commitment to the communities the college has historically served is, like the pastoral work provided by teaching staff, 'under the radar' – not acknowledged by funders or government or, at best, viewed as an add-on. Jacqui on the other hand, sees these services as fundamental and positions the college as a hub that provides social cohesion and a range of other social benefits. She goes on to highlight how these wraparound services are under threat due to funding cuts:

'What they have done is cut our funding and our ability now to go out and run taster programmes for those we can get off the streets ... [W]ho there's a good chance they're not going to stay longer than a couple of weeks. But if you could get them and give them a try and if that doesn't work they could try something else ... Just give them that space of ten weeks. We used to get European funding for it and government funding ... I've put classes on in community centres in their areas ... we've done all of that extra work ... but the cuts mean it's less and less. Cutting the funding now, all you're doing: what it's going to cost in national health and health and social care!'

The first part of this passage depicts the college as undertaking outreach work in areas within the city and for young people who are at risk of becoming so-called NEET (not in education employment or training). Once more a sense of commitment, a residual civic duty motivates the senior leaders of the college to lay on taster courses as a way of re-engaging young people who have lost any sense that education can connect meaningfully with their lives. Leadership in this instance means recognising that the college has a preventative role in addressing social problems that, if left unaddressed would incur bigger (social but also financial) costs in the future. The funding and performance focus on the 'here and now' is found wanting from this perspective. Further and adult education is a vital resource for these transformative journeys. Indeed, as social and economic inequities increase between and within countries there is a need to take action. Policies designed to improve literacy and to enhance opportunities for transformative education need to be tightly bound to challenging poverty.

Jacqui's account positions education at the college as an avenue through which students can gain access to social and other forms of capital. This involves them building new relationships with their teachers and peers that allow them to develop their confidence and reposition themselves through routes into education and employment that may have previously been outside their world picture. Many of the students voiced how they had felt isolated in their communities. The friends they made at college became their support mechanism. Social capital is a resource which was accumulated through the relationships formed across the field of education. It offered many of the students a support mechanism throughout their trajectories and beyond. The students empowered themselves to navigate through difficult circumstances which included addictions, violence and trauma and austerity, through the bonds of friendship formed in the classroom. For some of the students in Jacqui's account, the social capital provided by the college filled a vacuum that would otherwise be filled by external affiliations and gang membership. Jacqui's account points up the importance of social capital in supporting marginalised groups of students into education and onto trajectories that offer hope.

Most importantly, the leadership shown by Jacqui's college derives from a determination to address need despite the funding, accountability and performance apparatus. There is an evident tension between the provision she talks about and the narrative of marketisation in which colleges now operate. In such an environment, the overriding concern of teachers and managers is how to navigate the (often debilitating) external pressures of incessant policy intervention and the restrictive FAP. As the previous discussion demonstrates, despite these pressures, colleges continue to pursue a fundamental purpose, in healing the damage caused by schooling and supporting students to positively reconstruct their identities as learners.

Incorporation and its attendant, ever-changing FAP technology, enshrined an orientation towards central policy prescription, which represents a barrier to the advancement of social justice in college leadership. In this context, leadership which supports transformative teaching and learning as an important dimension of educational practice (by principals, senior leaders, managers, teachers and other staff) emerges locally, through institutions and the actions of individuals, against the grain of national-level policy.

Concluding thoughts

Leadership will continue to be a vexed issue in further and adult education for as long as the competitive market structures, propped up by the funding and performance apparatus, persist. While the area reviews signalled an acknowledgement that competition between institutions alone had failed to produce the kind of entrepreneurial colleges unreliant on public funding that incorporation was premised on (see Smith, 2017), colleges are still in thrall to efficiency and the responsiveness demanded by the whims of centrally designated policy. If anything, the area reviews have only served to consolidate a late twentieth century organisational model: through merger and take over, the growth of bigger and bigger college 'groups' – one college group currently spans from the North East to the West Midlands. The dominance of this model signals decline: its raison d'être is a reduction of funding overall. Since 2015, the policy emphasis on Apprenticeships, with the employer 'in the driving seat' (Cui and Smith, 2020) also seems to signal a governmental disregard for further and adult education colleges and their historical links with vocational education.

Leadership in such circumstances presents a huge challenge for establishing learning environments in which transformative education can flourish. Mel, the principal of one of the small number of remaining adult education colleges in England was one of the senior leaders that we talked with.

Mel talks with great knowledge and passion about the importance of upholding the social justice values that have been rooted in the college since its inception:

> 'It was really about enabling working class people ... to have the opportunity of learning, living and working together in an educational community. Social justice values are what the college is all about ... and the object of leadership is to bring that to life in the college ... we see that as really important in modelling what that means. The essence of that is how we behave and how we behave with each other and what we expect not just in the day-to-day objectives but also in the kind of culture we create in the college and how that impacts on the students that come here.'

She speaks about education as a complex, interactive social process in which the college engages with the whole person of the student:

> 'It really is a holistic process ... not only about what they're learning but also empowering them through their knowledge and understanding of how the world works, particularly in the context of power and power inequalities from which many of our students have had challenges throughout their lives.'

Mel's account illustrates that despite enormous challenges – mainly it has to be said contrived by funders and policy makers, it is possible to lead in a way that distributes leadership as a quality of action underpinned by the kind of values that nurture transformative educational experiences (see Smith and Duckworth, 2020).

Responding to the FAP apparatus requires close attention, effort and hard work being as it is in unrelenting tension with the kind of personalised, holistic educational experiences that engender transformation. A model that adapts Gronn's (2002) notion of 'distributed leadership' is called for. A model in which college SLTs are outward-facing, fighting for funding, for proper recognition for further and adult education and building collective non-competitive alliances with other colleges, seems essential. Reflecting on 25 years of change, it seems remarkable that the key adversary of the employers' organisation (the AoC) has shifted since 1992 from being the trade unions to being the various funding bodies and departments of government that have been responsible for the attrition we have witnessed. Principals and others have an important role in the coming fight-back.

As important is their role in protecting the teaching and learning environments that students encounter and that requires them to respect their teaching staff, to mediate the worst excesses of the FAP apparatus and to facilitate teachers' pedagogical leadership. Cushioning teachers from the kind of pressures that lead to spoon-feeding, cynical recruitment practices and other strategies that effectively objectify students is vital. If the central role of colleges' SLTs is to safeguard students' educational interests, then transformative teaching and learning becomes possible as leadership is distributed to all staff and meeting students' needs is positioned centre stage.

When we look at transformative education and the role leadership has to play in facilitating it, the requirements are as simple as they are daunting. A consciousness on the part of all staff of the possible negative impact of the ways funding and performance measuring impacts on teaching and learning needs to be constantly refreshed. At present, this issue is barely acknowledged. Like an elephant in the atrium, everyone knows it, but it remains taboo. Leadership in this context is about addressing these issues openly and, to return to the Freirean quotation that opened this chapter, to act dialogically, to organise and liberate. To tear the corporate veil and make the negative impact of the FAP regime visible is one of the biggest challenges facing further and adult education colleges and it is an essential step for meaningful leadership if transformative teaching and learning is to be allowed to flourish.

So what is transformative teaching and learning? Extending our theoretical and embodied understandings

There are more things in heaven and earth, Horatio,
Than are dreamt of in your philosophy.
William Shakespeare, *Hamlet* (1.5.167–8),
Hamlet to Horatio

Introduction

Starting with this quotation from Shakespeare's *Hamlet* is a way of signalling that if you are reading this chapter in the way you would open a dictionary to find a definitive meaning for the term: transformative teaching and learning, then you are likely to be disappointed. In this conversation with Horatio, Hamlet is discussing the appearance of his father's ghost and explaining that some things are mysterious, they belong to an area of human experience that we have yet to understand and for which there is as yet no scientific explanation. That doesn't mean that these phenomena are not talked about though. Throughout this book, we've referred to transformative teaching and learning and transformative education and we believe the accounts we have shared will be recognisable to you the reader.

The drive to nail down in scientific terms or to define using language may be (as yet) a vain attempt. Meanings can be richly and fully conveyed without being solid, absolute or definitive. It may be that where there is an emotional, spiritual or an affective aspect to the phenomena or where 'belief' is playing a role, then that complicates things further. That may be another reason to feel for a poetic understanding or to argue that the incorporation of a poetic sensibility becomes necessary. A Shakespearean quotation then seems more than appropriate.

All that isn't to say that we won't be building on the examples given so far and trying to piece together a set of indications and suggestions. But in all cases, these efforts will be describing the conditions in which educational interactions occur that give rise to something that resonates beyond the classroom walls, and that is more mysterious than what can be observed. One can attempt to observe and to read the signs, but rather like the electron in the Heisenberg principle, looking for it will affect it and, potentially, change it.

A key question about transformative teaching and learning, like any other concept, is this: 'who is doing the defining and to what purpose? Whose agenda does it serve?' The reason for this is that, broadly speaking in England and the UK more widely, we have been conditioned into thinking about the education of adults and school leavers as being mainly or solely about employment and as being about 'skills'. As such we have lost sight of a broader sense of personal development which can and does connect to employment, but which sees beyond that.

Looking at the language relating to, for example race and ethnicity, we can see how meanings and use changes and how language is in a perpetual dialectic with human consciousness and human society. Like any other term, transformative teaching and learning can only ever be an attempt to identify an experience that others recognise and feel able to attach the label to. This means that the term may have resonance for some people (teachers and students) and carry very specific meanings associated with their experiences. For people who feel that their lives have been transformed through further educational experiences, there will be a specific and individual understanding. For others, for example, policy makers, government ministers who may or may not have any direct experience of further an adult education, the use of the *transformative* tag may simply serve a rhetorical purpose: using transformation in a sentence to argue for something makes the argument harder to challenge as transformation is (presumably) something that no one would argue against – particularly if positive and negative attributes are seen as inherent in the individual. That makes the failure of having no or few grades from school an identity to be escaped from.

This chapter will revisit current theorisations of transformative education and position our work within that field. At the same time, we will flesh out a distinctive theorisation drawing on a range of theoretical perspectives as we pull together the themes from the teachers and learners' chapters and probe the interconnected nature of transformative teaching and learning. The chapter will build on and sharpen the theorisation of the narratives in Chapters 4 and 5. Those chapters touched on Bourdieu's theory around symbolic violence and the social divisions fostered by a hierarchical education system that views further and adult education primarily through the lenses of social class and 'skills'. It also began to develop a Lefebvrian idea of differential space as part of what makes the teaching and learning transformative. This chapter will connect these ideas to other 'versions' of transformative learning and show the connection to critical pedagogy as well as developing additional theoretical strands.

We think that a key thing about teaching and learning in general is the *and*. We are not talking about one activity overseen and practised by a single person, but about the intersection of two interacting activities, often involving a group of people. Theoretical discussions about each half of the formula have seesawed backwards and forwards for decades, arguing that one end is more important than the other. So, recent government policy has stressed the teaching end of the seesaw: knowledge and didactic approaches in classrooms being positioned as most important (Gibb, 2017). As we have seen, one function of this model (the current model which privileges teaching and the transmission of knowledge) is that it allows for measurement of performance – so it is intimately connected to the FAP apparatus that underpins marketisation. But, countering this, there is also a tradition of lifelong learning that sees us all as 'hard-wired' to learn as a species: a capacity that naturally extends throughout our lives (Biesta, 2006) – that approach might seem to suggest that learning can still take place whatever the experience of teaching or even without teaching (by another person).

From our research in further education, we position transformative teaching and learning as social, as interactive and as being as much about the quality and dynamic of the relationship between teacher(s) and student(s) as about the qualities or characteristics of either. Our research showed how both sides of the relationship were important. The teacher crucially was important in establishing the conditions, the student then had the key role of responding and moving forward while becoming increasingly independent.

The problem with any formula that says: *transformative teaching and learning* = *XY* – is that it stands as an umbrella label that suggests that a million different experiences that involve the interaction of a million different micro-components can be 'named' and gathered together under a single label. In truth, as soon as you individualise and contextualise transformative teaching and learning it starts to feel less solid. Think about all the different variables: this teacher rather than that one; these students rather than those; this year group rather than that one; this lesson on that topic; this college rather than that one; or how about Tuesday morning rather than Friday afternoon?

The dynamic and interactive process of each part of the teaching and learning process is shaped by all those factors. Who is it say which one or which combination of different factors are the magic ingredients? It's important to note here also that we are not just talking about individual students. The paradox of researching individual cases of transformative teaching and learning is that in focusing on single cases, it quite frequently became clear to us as researchers that there was usually a wider social or collective element that played a significant part in the experience. If you consider for a moment, this is hardly surprising. All of the people we interviewed had families, parents, friends, siblings, children, classmates – all of whom had the potential to play a significant role in producing the conditions that led to and catalysed an educational experience, making it meaningful and creating a space in which that experience brought about a change of direction and a renewed perspective on the future as offering hope.

We see teaching and learning as two interacting and intertwined experiences that exist in a space and time in which the laws of physics, clock, calendar and timetable time are suspended and remade. The teaching element and the learning element don't even always coincide. So trying to understand the process through neuroscience is a worthy aim, but efforts to date have ended up reducing the mystery of consciousness – which as far as we know is only explicable at the quantum level – to the grinding of gears in a nineteenth century automaton.

For the previously presented reasons then, we are not going to attempt to present a single definitive formula for transformative teaching and learning. Instead, we want to try to develop a broad, shared understandings of it through interpreting our research data using different theories and ideas. We will frame the discussion by positioning it on the periphery of current debates that seek to understand learning by conceptualising cognitive processes and 'how the brain works'. We will then provide a range of interpretations to try to illuminate its different elements.

Transformative teaching and learning and 'the student's brain'

There is a body of work and a school of thought that sees transformative teaching and learning simply as very effective learning or even only as students passing the assessments on their courses successfully. This school of thought approaches teaching and learning as being mainly about every teacher understanding how every student's brain learns and then teaching in ways that uses that understanding to ensure progress. This neurological school of thought is attractive to some commentators as it appears to offer the promise that teaching and learning can be 'scientifically' and objectively defined, and thereby offer us all a clear and definitive approach to education (presumably regardless of context or all the variables previously mentioned). The implication is that the physiological and neurological structure common to all human brains should mean that we can discover a universal set of parameters/approaches that will be successful if applied to teaching and learning because 'that is how the brain works'. This seems to be the aim in the literature around, for example 'cognitive load' theory (see Sweller et al, 2011).

In a high stakes competitive environment like the one that schools, colleges and now universities are locked into, the allure of this 'silver bullet' view of teaching and learning is powerful. In terms of a teacher-centred and a knowledge-rich curriculum, it also appeals to educators and educationalists who see the control and regulation of young people (how they behave, what they should know, the parameters of their aspirations for their futures, their deference to authority) as a key purpose of education.

There are a number of real problems with this idea. The normative assumptions behind it are worrying. For a start, it seems to rely on a set of metaphors of the brain as operating like a computer, with circuit boards, start-up programs, RAM and storage space. There is a scene in the film *The Matrix* – which works a bit like this. Rather than going to a classroom with a teacher, the hero of the film, Neo, has a 'bio port' – a kind of USB slot in the back of his head. A terrifying needle-like connector like a jack-plug for an electric guitar is plugged into his skull and the person who might otherwise be a teacher simply selects the knowledge files from a data base and presses a button so that they are uploaded into Neo's brain.

This provides a clue as to what happens to the teacher's role once we have nailed 'how the brain works' in teaching and learning (if that were ever to happen, an idea that we find incredible): the complex, socially situated practices of teaching and learning vanish to be replaced by a technical exercise as simple as pushing a button on a keyboard. If there was such an approach that worked, teaching and learning as we know it would vanish. The process of learning would be an invisible seamless process – rather like uploading files onto a computer. Societies would be transformed. Schools, colleges and universities would be redundant. Or at least, their curricula would be entirely social rather than being about knowledge.

The 'how the brain works' fad is founded on the assumption that our in-species sharing of an organ (the brain) provides a short-cut to understanding the best way to learn. A very simple analogy can undermine that idea. Understanding how the body works doesn't result in all students excelling in sports. The 'how the brain works' approach will never remove the need to cater for students' diversity. This Holy Grail of teaching and learning does not then offer a universal solution. In other words, either how the brain works is an approach that offers universal application to everyone, or it acknowledges how each person's brain works is slightly different. In which case, we are back to 'differentiation' – catering for the learning needs of individuals.

It is important to understand that the 'how the brain works' silver bullet is positioned in a field of different educational ideas and that there is a political dimension to the debate. Many who support the idea (in these islands) think that the experience and understandings built up by decades of research into education is useless or too 'ideological'. In this, the so-called objectivity offered by 'how the brain works' is another way of dismissing social factors (like class, race, poverty, access to resources and the discriminatory educational systems, practices and cultures that feed into these) as insignificant or at any rate, not as important as the teacher and teaching, the school or schooling.

Just imagine that the neurological 'how the brain works' research produced a single, fool-proof and definitive recipe for teaching and learning. Imagine that this was disseminated to all schools and colleges. It is an approach then that is written into syllabi and Initial Teacher Education courses as the way to set up and run teaching and learning (incidentally systematic synthetic phonics has this status currently). The question then is: what happens when this foolproof hundred per cent 'scientific' approach doesn't work with all students? The answer is that it ends up, ultimately, back with a problematisation of the individual. Presumably, if some students don't thrive on it, then that will be because there is something wrong with their brains.

There are echoes here of what happened to children from the Windrush generation in the early 1970s in England who were judged to be 'educationally subnormal' and taken out of mainstream schools (see Coard, 1974 and McQueen, 2020). There are current versions of this mind-set of 'blaming (and penalising) the student' approach. For example, think about the current debate on the necessity of excluding and isolating some students who are viewed as 'disrupting' the smooth running of schools.

Another problem with the 'how the brain works' approach is how it ignores the nature of language and treats language as if it were maths. It is possible to express simple ideas with great clarity in language just as, in maths simple sums communicate precise facts. But this isn't the same for complex ideas. And that's because language works in a referential and signifying way: a speaker (or writer) makes a statement, and this is 'received' (variously and divergently) by the person or people who are listening or reading it. The transmission of meaning here is not perfect. It isn't telepathy. In everyday language interactions, people interpret meanings differently. So imagine what can happen when teachers start introducing new words and ideas.

What this means is that even if some clever educational neuro-guru discovers 'how the student's brain works', the complexity of language and its built-in slipperiness means that even then, with the teacher holding the Holy Grail firmly in one hand, it still doesn't guarantee the kind of frictionless transmission of knowledge that some people seem to imagine. While teaching and learning involves language it can never achieve 'perfect' transmission. That's not how language works.

The key thing to understand about the normative 'how the brain works' approach is that it is conjectural knowledge. Also, it becomes destructive if it is used to the exclusion of other approaches that attempt to address the myriad variables of any teaching and learning situation as it appears to be premised on the idea that human consciousness in all its diversity can be by-passed for a purpose and that teaching and learning can become a curriculum delivery system. That problem begs several questions: why would anyone want to change teaching and learning into something like the 'banking' model that Freire criticised? A further question also arises: what gets lost when teaching and learning is viewed in this way?

The UK adult education tradition and transformative learning

The tradition of transformative education in the UK is significant. As we touched on in Chapter 1, some of this is bound up in institutions and the values that informed their establishment: the small number of adult education colleges all have such historical roots. Fircroft College, for example, was founded in 1909 by George Cadbury, a son of the Quaker founder of the Cadbury's chocolate factory in Birmingham. From early on, the underpinning educational principles of the college were informed by the thinking of the Danish educational philosopher, Nicolaj Grundtvig, founder of the folk high school movement.

Grundtvig's educational philosophy foregrounded critical citizenship and rejected competition as a basis for social and educational interaction in favour of collectivism and cooperation. Grundtvig's philosophy also dismissed what Freire later called the 'banking model' of education: the transmission of inert knowledge from teacher to student via rote-learning. Instead, he saw learning as a social practice: interaction, discussion and debate between people of different backgrounds was viewed as essential.

Of course, the principles espoused by Grundtvig that inform the cultures of Fircroft and to a great extent the other adult education colleges and adult education provision more generally are rooted in political values. Specifically, they assert egalitarianism and see this as a fundamental feature of a democratic educational ethos. Consequently, students coming from a range of backgrounds (both urban and rural) were seen as whole people who could benefit from discussion and experiencing a common life within a community. In an echo of what we have elsewhere called the ripple effect, the aim was never to help students transcend their social background but through education to enable them to contribute to their communities' cultural capital and thereby safeguard democracy. Under this model, social mobility has a collective and local dimension that preserves cultural distinctiveness.

The social conditions co-produced by students and teachers in these educational settings are at a fundamental level conducive to transformative teaching and learning. Today, they naturally draw on both the historical traditions from which they sprung but also some of the international theorists that will be covered in the rest of the chapter. There are some important names and theorists that could be named here, drawn from a large group. In Raymond Williams' terms, adult education is a 'cultural field' and as such holds a historical position within the current politics of culture. It has to be said that in England at least, there is a sense that adult education does not occupy the position it once did, largely because of neoliberal policies. But its roots are still strong and the reason for that is that they derive from powerful political ideas.

The son of a Welsh railway worker, Raymond Williams is recognised as one of the foremost Left intellectuals of the latter part of the twentieth century. In the years after World War II, after graduating in English, he 'chose to opt not for university research but for adult education' (Williams, 2015, viii) and became a tutor for the Workers' Educational Association. As such he combined fierce political acumen with intellectual endeavour and grounded both in his experience as a practitioner in adult education which he viewed as representing 'a vital tradition which we are always in danger of losing and which we can never afford to lose' (1961, 2).

Connected to his important work on English literature, a key aspect of Williams' thinking came in his conceptualisation of culture not as something distinct from economy and politics but as overlapping and informing all aspects of personal and community life. So part of Williams' contribution is to conceptualise culture as reaching across all levels of human society. In this, he 'de-classed' earlier and more traditional and elitist thinking (as promoted by the poet T.S. Eliot for example) that saw culture through social hierarchy: as aesthetic production that only some people can appreciate, those same people being empowered to identify what was culturally valuable and what wasn't.

This contribution is hugely significant. Effectively, Williams' thinking sought to value 'the ordinary' and to challenge established ideas about what should be valued as culture. An example of this was his championing of film as an accessible and worthwhile cultural form. His position here can be seen as engaging in a struggle over what constitutes culture which is still relevant (see also McIlroy and Westwood, 1993). We can see this relevance in recent government interventions to consolidate a knowledge-rich curriculum (Gibb, 2017, 2021) and in GCSE English in England the prescription of 'classic literature' and Standard English (DfE, 2013, 3). It also clearly connects with the theoretical position that is so strong in the adult education tradition of teaching the 'whole' student: the importance of the placing and valuing of students' biography and experience in curriculum space. It is also fundamentally an egalitarian position which seeks to support student enquiry into why society is the way it is and to critically engage with how different groups are positioned, advantaged and disadvantaged within it.

Another thinker in the English tradition of adult education is Tom Lovett. Lovett's work around community education in Liverpool illustrates how the meanings of adult education are forged in the furnace of particular, socially situated educational encounters. Through his experience in Education Priority Areas in Liverpool in the 1970s, Lovett conceptualised adult educators as social activists who listened to the views, mediated the issues and helped with the challenges faced by the parents of community school children. His experiences illuminated how adult education in a community school should not only serve the function of helping parents to 'understand and encourage the educational development of their children', but also to become 'deeply involved in the whole variety of problems facing such communities' (Lovett, 1971a, 183). Necessarily, the curriculum for this kind of education project could not be dictated from some remote central body. Instead it should arise out of discussion with parents/students and respond to their priorities. This in turn is likely to mean that issues such as poor housing, local amenities and in some cases, problems arising from poverty become a feature.

Lovett's thinking is strongly premised on the principle of 'learning through doing' Lovett, 1971b, 60). Consequently, he sees an overlap between community development and adult education. In common with many of the models of transformative education, Lovett's conceptualisation sees the 'Community Adult Educationalist' ultimately as a facilitator of action, someone who nurtures the awareness of adults in order that they can act and tackle the issues they face.

The final name we will mention here is Stephen Brookfield. Brookfield's work on critical reflection and the practice of adult education sits comfortably in a tradition in which the need for us to interrogate things we may regard as 'commonsense' has never been more urgent. In the field of critical pedagogy, adult learning and the initial teacher education of adult educators, Brookfield's work has been highly influential. Drawing on the tradition of critical theory and other European Marxist thought, Brookfield conceptualises learning as social and political. Building on the key engine for learning in initial teacher education: reflective practice – that has been increasingly colonised (and depoliticised), Brookfield carefully crafts the notion of critical reflective practice.

Critical reflective practice builds on reflective practice by adding an additional focus. Not only does the practitioner focus on their own practice in a given situation, but they also look beyond their immediate environment to scrutinise, for example, the impact of policy or to critique assumptions that mask ideological precepts. A key focus for Brookfield is the concept of hegemony – a term used by Italian philosopher/activist Antonio Gramsci to explain how ideology works insidiously to normalise sometimes extreme views and actions. For Brookfield a hegemonic culture is one in which people learn 'quite willingly' to assimilate dominant ideology. He explains that hegemony is 'the process by which we learn to embrace enthusiastically a system of beliefs and practices that end up harming us and working to support the interest of others who have power over us.' (2005, 94–5). Brookfield's emphasis on this self-interrogatory perspective particularly in relation to one's own assumptions and values is a way of counteracting hegemony.

Critical reflective practice can be seen as building on reflective practice, its less politicised sibling, through an insistence on the political nature of the workplace and society in general. In the field of adult education, the orientation to action of reflective practice moves beyond mere personal development and instead becomes a political commitment. There are strong links here to the emancipatory thinking of Freire and others. The practitioner (experienced or novice) is invited to reflect on their practice as contextualised within broader social structures of inequality and oppression. In this way, Brookfield asserts the aim of critical reflective practice as being not just to improve individual practice – after all, that might mean simply becoming more efficient at a practice of questionable social value – rather, the practitioner is encouraged to view their practice as a means of challenging social structures and values that are seen as contributing to the unfreedom of individuals.

The transformative aspect of Brookfield's thought positions learning in a broader social and political context. Countering the individualism and self-interest of the neoliberal *weltbild*, Brookfield asserts that learning and personal growth through critical reflective practice are an 'irreducibly social' and collegial process (Brookfield, 1997, 19). Brookfield's work also focuses on informal adult learning as learning is seen as a natural human activity that has been politically structured and purposed in particular, constraining ways. Working in a range of different academic settings in the United States for many years, Brookfield's most recent work focuses on tackling race and whiteness in educational settings (see Brookfield, 2018) – and feeds into the urgent issue of racism highlighted by the murder of George Floyd and the Black Lives Matter movement.

The following sections will build on these important insights from the UK tradition of adult education by looking at transformative teaching and learning through a variety of different theoretical lenses.

The project's theoretical lenses

Our research was founded on a simple premise: that for some people further and adult education provides a lifeline and a (re)introduction to learning that has the power to transform their lives. Our research has illuminated how this happens (frequently and unacknowledged) in further and adult education colleges. We knew this from our personal and professional experience of working in it as teachers and we wanted to explore how common these stories were but also to look for and identify patterns in them. In addition, we wanted to find out how transformative learning connected to transformative pedagogical approaches (if it does).

Transformative teaching and learning and critical pedagogy

In this section, we will give an overview of some of the different thinking that has been done about critical pedagogy before connecting it to our ideas on transformative teaching and learning.

The first theoretical lens we want to use to describe transformative teaching and learning is that of critical pedagogy. Critical pedagogy originates in the hugely influential work of Paulo Freire (1995). Freire's work sprung from his educational experiences with indigenous and marginalised people in the highly stratified society of Brazil. A Portuguese colony, Brazil was a country built on the labour of people enslaved in Africa and transported across the Atlantic. In addition, like all of the 'New World', it was also founded on the denial of the human rights of the existing indigenous people. In this context, Freire's successful model of literacy education with indigenous and disenfranchised people was political. Indigenous poor people were dehumanised in Brazilian society. For Freire their education involved reversing the negative self-image imposed by the dominant cultures of the western colonising people. Ultimately, this led to Freire being exiled to Chile and as neoliberal dictatorships took hold in Latin America (aided and abetted by the United States government), he was expelled from Chile as well.

The principles of a Freirean critical pedagogy centre on 'conscientisation' – consciousness raising (or 'a "coming to awareness" of self and other in the world' (Kress, 2011, 262) through dialogical, problem-posing educational experiences. This involves students learning to look again at their own experiences and values and to disentangle these from the messages they are given about themselves by a wider society that doesn't value them. In other words, at the heart of Freire's practice as a teacher, was a view of knowledge as material that the student acted upon and brought meaning to. Freire rejects education as transmission of knowledge – what he brands the 'banking concept of education'; instead he sees inquiry, the quest to know, as a profound feature of what it is to be human: '[k]nowledge emerges only through invention and reinvention, through the restless, impatient continuing and hopeful enquiry that humans pursue in the world and with each other' (Freire, 1995, 26). It's significant that Freire aligns learning with hope. Learning is not mechanistic. It is connected to the world, a view of our place in it and in our ability to act. The purpose is freedom: emancipatory development. That idea: that education should contain within it, for individuals and groups of people, the means of achieving freedom is a central principle that appears again and again in different versions of critical pedagogy that have emerged since Freire.

Freire's influence has been international. Bell hooks is one advocate, coming at it from a black, feminist perspective which also brings with it a quality that we might call spirituality:

To educate as the practice of freedom is a way of teaching that anyone can learn. That learning process comes easiest to those of us who teach, who also believe that there is an aspect of our vocation that is sacred;

who believe that our work is not merely to share information but to share in the intellectual and spiritual growth of students. To teach in the manner that respects and cares for the souls of our students is essential if we are to provide the necessary conditions where learning can most deeply and intimately begin. (hooks, 1994, 13)

What's interesting here is how the student's growth takes precedence over an insistence on what knowledge they should be learning. This student-centredness (as opposed to a knowledge-centredness or even a teacher-centredness) is a key value in critical pedagogy. And it connects strongly to transformative teaching and learning. But that isn't to dismiss the importance of knowledge.

Henry Giroux is another North American educational theorist who focuses on critical pedagogy. His perspective is useful because he too links critical pedagogy to successful democracy:

My view of critical pedagogy developed out of a recognition that education was important not only for gainful employment but also for creating the formative culture of beliefs, practices and social relations that enable individuals to wield power, learn how to govern and nurture a democratic society that takes equality, justice, shared values and freedom seriously. (Giroux, 2011, 3)

If we try to connect this to what we have learnt about transformative teaching and learning, we can see how Giroux regards moral and social critique as an integral aspect of teaching and learning. Furthermore, for Giroux, any transformation is not just personal and individual; instead it ripples outwards: the transformation of the individual has the potential to change the social, to change the world. As with Freire and hooks, Giroux's starting point is that the world order needs to change, that it is inherently unjust and perpetuates inequality. He is concerned that democracy is under threat and that the meaning and purpose of public education have been hijacked by restrictive economic and political interests. Their influence is operating to stifle the potential for freedom in education and instead to position education as a system that serves and helps to preserve current systems and the power and privilege of certain groups in our society.

Giroux's advocacy of critical pedagogy is rooted in a strong critique of the way knowledge is thought about and used in modern western democracies. He is critical of the dominance of positivism – the perspective that sees objective and scientific 'facts' as the only evidence on which to base decisions. Underpinning this is the 'assumption that knowledge is objective and value-free' (Giroux, 2011, 26). To that extent, this version of rationality blots out values, it sees values as contaminating knowledge and understanding.

It's easy for us, post–COVID (if indeed the pandemic is over), to see how problematic such a view of knowledge is. In England, Government spokespeople used graphs, statistics and scientific experts from March 2020 through to April 2021 when the vaccination program appeared to lower the infection and death rates in the UK. But the messages were contradictory and unstable. The facts, it seemed, were not the only things guiding government decisions. There were economic reasons too. At one point, it appeared as though schools and colleges' primary purpose wasn't educational but was to warehouse young people and children so that their parents could go out to work to benefit the economy! Even the scientists failed to speak with one voice. Announcements about the relative safety of mask-wearing or the return to schools made by the Government Sage Advisory Committee were countermanded on a weekly basis by a Shadow Sage Advisory Committee of equally eminent (and somehow more credible) scientists.

For Giroux, the dominant positivist version of knowledge also fails to take proper account of history, for example by insisting on a single absolute interpretation of events. Any view that challenges this is vilified as political and partisan. Once more, this struggle over knowledge can be seen in recent history in the ongoing row about decolonising the curriculum. At the heart of these debates is the question of authority. It's clear enough that for those who view knowledge in terms of objective facts, learning English is the same as learning Maths. But the problem with authoritative knowledge in an educational context is twofold: i) it can never admit error; ii) learning it can only ever be rote-learning – the point is not to question but to accept. For that reason Giroux insists that critical pedagogy incorporates the interrogation of authority.

Giroux argues that it is vital to understand how culture shapes the everyday lives of people: how culture is a site for ongoing struggles over meaning, identity and social practices. He insists on the need to recognise the 'educational force of our whole social and cultural experience [as one] that actively and profoundly teaches' (2011, 52).

What's important in this idea is that it connects classroom interactions to a mode of social being. In other words, pedagogy is a medium through which power, knowledge and being/becoming are articulated. How does this look in the classroom? For example it might foreground discussion between small groups of students about issues where they share their existing knowledge and try to connect that to new ideas presented by the teacher. It might also involve teachers inviting students to challenge different ideas.

A didactic approach, a classroom with a teacher standing at the front and talking for half an hour while the students sit in silence listening and following the teacher with their eyes, seems inimical to such a pedagogy. Rather, it elevates teaching to an event like a spectacle or even (in the reverence and authority granted the teacher) worship: where else do people gather as a collective in silence to listen to the views of one individual?

For some people, discussion of issues and ideas is a behaviour learnt at home from the dinner table. The main aim of the discussion may not be to 'win' the debate, or 'destroy' someone else's arguments, it is, rather to explore an issue: to take it in turns testing out thinking and ideas and different ways of expressing them. Children may not really understand that their family culture may be different from that of others – but clearly, family habits that include discussion can be advantageous in school. Mainly because they are about sharing, expressing, critiquing and constructing ideas.

Giroux takes a position similar to Freire on knowledge:

> Rather than viewing teaching as technical practice, radical pedagogy in the broadest terms is a moral and political practice premised on the assumption that learning is not about processing received knowledge but about actually transforming it as part of a more expansive struggle for individual rights and social justice. (2011, 72)

What we can say about this in relation to existing teaching and learning practices in further and adult education in England is that teachers, by and large, are not always or even often supported to enquire into the external forces and factors that shape what they do. The goals that further and adult education teachers are supposed to harness their energies to are often either remote and abstract (skills shortages, 'productivity', the 'sunlit uplands' of the post Brexit era) or brutally utilitarian: making young people 'employable'. The model of teaching and learning underpinning this is transmission, Freire's famous 'banking' model. As such, it takes no account of the hopes, desires and (even) interests of the students as human beings. They are instead viewed as an abstract faceless mass, who are to be processed by further and adult education.

It's not only the students who are dehumanised though. Teachers also suffer in this arrangement. Once learning has been reduced to the morbid recycling of dead information that is not to be interpreted, critically re-articulated or re-invented, the teacher becomes a mortician responsible for preserving the corpse of knowledge. Teaching and learning in this context is alienating and dehumanising.

Critical pedagogy is the opposite of this. Rather than reducing teachers to technicians, it sees them redefine their roles as engaged public intellectuals capable of teaching students the language of critique. This classroom practice is imagined as a first step to students' social agency, an opening of the door that connects education to new possibilities of social change. In short, critical pedagogy embraces the prospect that human societies have to change and adapt and that moving away from the current model of 'progress' is a necessity.

Transformative teaching and learning and powerful knowledge

Both Freire and Giroux emphasise the importance of focusing on knowledge. Clearly, any focus that takes students' interests as a priority is likely also to have a critical eye on the knowledge that students are going to encounter. This is one reason why the idea of a 'knowledge-rich' curriculum is so suspect. If politicians are going to pronounce what knowledge is worth knowing and what isn't (there are many examples, see Gove on Dryden and Pope in English or recent debates about Mozart versus Stormzy in music), then clearly, knowledge and knowing are now being viewed as political territory to be fought over.

Kincheloe (2008) is another important writer who focuses on this. Like other theorists, Kincheloe's position draws on his personal extensive experience of involvement with other cultures, other peoples and other languages (2008, 16–19). He doesn't see this as just an appreciation of different ways that human societies interact with and shape the world, but instead uses it to frame a critique of capital and the dominant forms of economic and political government in the Western world. He sees these systems as underpinned by a particular set of philosophical and political ideas about knowledge. He sees this way of understanding and of acting in the world as a pathway leading to a cliff edge.

For Kincheloe, critical pedagogy centres on the knowledge systems that need to be critiqued and the new ways of knowing and the new knowledge that is needed if we are to i) address the historical injustices meted out against people and peoples whose interests have not fitted the requirements of this dominant order and ii) safeguard a future for the planet that is sustainable and that is founded on ending human suffering.

It's interesting how important these bigger perspectives are. They give us a point of reference, a beacon on the horizon to steer towards. But we also need theories and ideas that relate more closely to the actual experience of teaching and learning in classrooms and mediating the given curriculum.

Lingard's work on 'productive pedagogies' in Australia is an important contribution in that regard. Lingard's work (2005) critiques the relationship and interaction between curriculum, pedagogy and assessment. Lingard acknowledges the idea that some knowledge is 'powerful knowledge' (an idea from Young, 1958, 2007). This knowledge emphasis is important for us for two main reasons: first it recognises that our society is divided by social class, wealth and race (among other characteristics) and that as a part of this, some knowledge is given more value and this (arbitrary) value is affirmed by curricula. Also, it recognises that this knowledge belongs to no one, just like any knowledge it can be acquired and used and interpreted and re-fashioned and that can be done in the interests of a fairer society that meets the needs of all its people.

We might take an example from the classics – works of literature from the Greek and Roman Empires, writers and thinkers like Homer, Martial,

Ovid and Cicero. Or we might point to particular examples from English literature: Shakespeare, Dryden, Dickens, D.H. Lawrence that seem to be cited often by politicians who have enjoyed exclusive education at expensive public schools like Eton. We sense that this knowledge somehow belongs to a socially superior culture. To know it well would be to have access to a set of stories, a language, possibly even a way of thinking that opens doors into the culture of a more privileged section of society.

Although we might hate D.H. Lawrence, find Cicero boring and detest the high status that these writers are given (I mean, what's wrong with *The Simpsons* or *Watchmen*?), to deny our students access to these cultural reference points is to stop them from being able to make their own judgements but also to perpetuate the 'ownership' of this knowledge and thereby to fail to engage in a struggle to change the current disequilibrium.

Lingard's concept of 'productive pedagogies' connects with Young's 'powerful knowledges' by saying that making explicit cultural knowledge as part of assessment can lead to more equitable outcomes. For Lingard, 'authentic pedagogy' and 'authentic assessment' include high order thinking and boosts the achievements of all students including those from disadvantaged backgrounds.

This is an important reminder that any discussion of transformative education needs to focus not just on how teaching and learning happens but on what knowledge is the focus. Care (see later in the chapter) alone isn't enough. It's an important, even a vital component. But ensuring that the curriculum is sufficiently challenging is equally important otherwise there are social justice implications and a risk that existing structures of inequality will be reinforced. One thing that can be said at this point is that whatever the knowledge content, a key task of the teacher is to mediate it.

In the following sections we are going to move from discussing knowledges to looking at the negative impact of existing patterns of teaching and learning that result from narrow ways of looking at knowledge and education – like those associated with the 'how the brain works' school of thought. Any attempt to identify what transformative education is, necessarily has also to mark out what it isn't. Our claim has never been that all further and adult education is transformative. Indeed, our research has sought to highlight the stories of people whose experiences have been positive in a context which often appears to be shaped by some overwhelmingly negative structural features. We will explore these in the next section.

Transformative teaching and learning and symbolic violence

While the work of Mezirow (1990) and Illeris (2014) among others seeks to present a set of universal principles that underpin transformative learning, our work sees context as a fundamental component in any understanding of what transformative teaching and learning means. Our usage of the term in relation to further and adult education comes from the contextual frame we outlined at the beginning of this book. It is a policy context in which further and adult education has been stripped of its broad educational and social value and instead been re-cast as instrumental, as being about the skills of the nation rather than the hopes of individuals and communities. It is also a context in which, to be in any way transformative, college teachers have to undo the damage done by the age-staged tyranny of achievement that structures schooling in the UK (Mansell, 2007).

In that sense further and adult education can be either restorative or can exacerbate the scholagenic experiences of young people who come away from schooling with low levels of achievement feeling stigmatised and alienated. Our research data provides evidence of the importance in transformative educational experiences of a strong emphasis on building confidence to renew learning identities as a consequence of the 'symbolic violence' many students have experienced in their schooling. If teaching in further and adult education begins by trying to address the damage done by students' experiences of education to date, our responsibility as teachers and researchers is to explore how that damage has been done, what did the damage and how that damage can be put right.

The concept of symbolic violence that we are drawing on originates in Bourdieu and Passeron (2013). They write about the symbolic system that education draws on to impose meanings on learners. They see education as imposing a standard culture whose values reflect the social structure and the power relations that underpin it. In other words, in a socially unequal society, education can perpetuate a stratification of individuals in a way that serves to replicate existing social inequalities.

It's also important here though to be clear that violence comes in different forms or modalities and can have different rhythms (Collins, 2008). Many of us who were at school in the 1970s in the UK habitually witnessed teachers hitting other children and may even have been beaten, smacked, given the 'pump' or caned ourselves. Today, few people would support the maxim '*spare the rod and spoil the child*' and it is important that we acknowledge that as a society we have moved on from the knowledge encapsulated in this proverb. For some of us, looking back, how physical violence can be reconciled with pedagogy can be extremely difficult to understand.

I (Rob) have friends who still carry the emotional scars of being beaten by teachers when, actually, what they needed was emotional support and understanding. Some of them still hold anger and resentment in their hearts towards the teachers who beat them.

I (Vicky) remember a board duster hitting my head in primary school because I didn't get the maths question right, forgetting my PE kit in seniors and being hit before going into the second-hand box for shorts and a tee-shirt, and the history teacher who bruised the back of my legs with his whack in front of the class because I was talking; this happened to my mates too and with the humiliation we smiled it out not to lose face; but inside I shrank. It is through further education that I (Vicky) reclaimed my body back in the care and goodness of the teachers who spoke to me and did not seek to hurt me with their words or hit me.

Once we have accepted that today, this kind of use of physical violence is not only damaging, but is unlawful and has no place in educational contexts (and surprisingly, some people still find that difficult), then we need to start looking at other forms and modalities of violence. While corporal punishment has been largely recognised as damaging (Gershoff, 2017), Bourdieu and Passeron's concept of symbolic violence sees the coercion and damage we associate with physical violence also operating at the level of culture. This form of violence connects back to the discussion about knowledge – about what is valued and what is de-valued in educational contexts. Bourdieu's notion of cultural capital may have been taken up (although misinterpreted) by Ofsted, but symbolic violence to date, has been entirely ignored by government. Our argument is that although physical violence has disappeared from our classrooms, this other form of violence is widespread. It impacts on 16-year-old students entering further education and in many cases the impact continues throughout their time in colleges.

A good example of symbolic violence can be seen in the teaching of English and in debates around the 'decline' in the standard of written and spoken English which are long-standing. But more recently, evidence has surfaced of a policing of language use, the 'banning' of certain words and phrases in classrooms, the exclusion of students' dialect. The basis for this is that Standard English is 'naturally' (and by implication morally) superior and that regional varieties are an inferior subspecies of the Queen's English. It is notable that no one with a knowledge of linguistics believes this. David Crystal, one of England's most celebrated language expert refutes it (Crystal, 2019). What we regard as Standard English and the grammar we regard as 'standard' have historical origins sustained by economic and political force. Bennett et al, (2022) and Cushing (2020, 2021) among others have written extensively about how the enforcement of this particular view of subject English in the classroom has oppressive and alienating overtones. It can systematically disenfranchise some students by ruling the language that connects them to their social class or ethnicity (and therefore to their identity) as substandard. This then is symbolic violence – particularly if accompanied by a justification that presents the Standard English as 'natural' and even morally superior.

It would be wrong to claim that experiences of symbolic violence in education are confined to schooling. Indeed, arguably, the current further education system in England is as or more susceptible to the commonsense ideas that impose meanings and curricula on students in ways that do not best serve their interests. One way of viewing the way symbolic violence plays out in further education (and to a different extent in adult education provision) is through student objectification – a concept we will develop here. By objectification, what we mean here is that students are not given the proper level of dignity that people are entitled to. Instead they are viewed as objects, to be moulded and coerced: cogs in a bigger machine that may or may not serve their better interests. There are at least three forces of objectification – a triple-lock of symbolic violence – that students in further education can be said to be (potentially) subject to.

The first layer of objectification is located in the 'skills' discourse outlined earlier. While not singling out or categorising individuals, this neoliberal ideological perspective provides a commonsense framework for understanding further education as being centred on producing 'skills' in other words as human capital production. Such an understanding objectifies and dehumanises students.

The second layer of the triple-lock is more substantial and structural in the sense that it is strengthened and perpetuated by the current qualifications framework and the expectations, ways of thinking and student learning trajectories that these give rise to. We can see this second layer of objectification in the qualification framework that enforces a binary perception of young people as being either 'academic' or 'vocational' (Payne, 2010). This is also a feature that has been reinforced by the stratification of colleges on a lower rung of the status ladder in the education 'market'. For further education students, this layer of objectification, that puts a focus on vocational learning, categorises them as 'low achievers'. The clumsy academic/vocational split is not neutral and further education students are effectively 'classed' by it (Thompson, 2009).

A third layer of the triple-lock in further education is also a consequence of the competitive marketisation that providers operate in. A key aspect of the incorporation of colleges was that it introduced a transactional aspect to the relations between students and providers. This supposedly privileged students through their choice as 'consumers', but a more significant effect was to incentivise teachers and managers in further education to view the recruitment of students in funding terms, as a 'bums on seats' exercise that prioritises the generation of college income.[1]

In our research with teachers, an alarming number believed that course funding 'always' or 'often' impacted on their freedom to meet their learners' needs and support students to achieve their aspirations. This was something they had to actively resist in order to foster positive student-teacher relationships or a sense of belonging in the classroom. This effect of funding arrangements has not been acknowledged by any government minister in the last two decades, which is worrying as it positions students as a means of obtaining and increasing college income: a priority that can and does over-ride the educational interests of the students themselves.

Transformative teaching and learning emerges from this research as, above all, an overturning of the symbolic violence embodied in this triple lock of objectification. Indeed, the triple-lock makes it seem miraculous that this kind of teaching and learning is taking place at all in further education settings. Our research, however, provides evidence that it is. Teachers in colleges break the triple-lock when they seek to overturn the scholagenic damage caused to students' learner identities, when they incorporate students' biographical experiences into the curriculum and when they strive to establish egalitarian relations within their classrooms. This makes radicals of all further education teachers that do; it flags up how their everyday practice can challenge and overturn the damaging and socially divisive effects of our current educational system.

Transformative teaching and learning and affect

Affect is a word with a broad meaning which we want to touch on as being important in transformative educational experiences. Focusing on the affect in the learning environment is to take account of the importance of the 'feel' or emotional atmosphere of the learning space. It includes emotion as a central embodied aspect of teaching and learning: the idea that learning is felt and experienced – in other words, that it is embedded in a social frame. We would argue that what is often marginalised or absent in further and adult education policy is an understanding and real appreciation of the emotional realm of learning and with that a deeper insight into a humanistic perspective of students learning which validates their experiences as truly agentic and transformative.

But affect is not the same thing as emotion. Massumi states that emotion and affect 'follow different logics' (Massumi, 1995, 88). Instead he makes the case for affect as being connected to the intensity of an experience, an intensity that is felt as bodily sensation and that is not always recognised as such.

There are other definitions. Gregg and Seigworth also see affect as unconnected to 'conscious knowledge' and suggest instead that: 'affect … is not objectifiable and quantifiable as a thing that we then perceive or of which we are conscious'. Instead, they see it as '[a] visceral force … that can serve to drive us toward movement, toward thought and extension' (Gregg and Seigworth, 2010, 1).

For Sara Ahmed, affect is 'what sticks, or sustains or preserves the connection between ideas, values and objects' (Ahmed, 2010, 29). In this description, it's possible to imagine how students pick up that the educational experience they are involved might not actually be about *them*, but is, instead, about the school or college or other educational institution and its interests. That feeling, that intangible sense might be hammered home as one knowledge-based lesson after another rumbles on despite them not understanding, giving the overall impression that not only is the spectacle not *about* them, it is not *for* them either. In that sense, affect is a feature of the ordinary and the everyday (Stewart, 2007). It shapes who we are, without us necessarily being aware of that.

If we use the idea of affect and focus on the importance of the emotional environment when learning, that helps us to perceive how transformative teaching and learning works against the grain of a 'bums on seats' approach: as an antidote to the performance data that colleges are forced to produce in the current marketised set-up. It helps us see that the Further and Higher Education Act of 1992, created the conditions that shape teaching and learning in negative ways: demanding a focus on targets, paperwork and the production of performance data. That focus might make colleges look good but that has often been at the expense of students' interests.

We also connect it with the need to counteract the damage that is done to some young people and adults' learner identities by the rigid and assessment-heavy system of schooling that has been constructed over the last thirty years. Taking affect into account in teaching and learning often involves addressing students' all too common scholagenic feelings of being 'stupid' – feelings that students may not themselves be conscious of. Youdell (2011) uses a storytelling approach to bring together a range of evidence from different research sources, in a vignette called *Falling* in which she presents:

> [T]he contemporary education landscape dominated by national testing regimes; the ways that attainment in these tests demarcates educational possibilities and impossibilities; the complexities and opacities of schooling's systematized practices; how responsibility for educational successes and failures is individualized; the ways that particular identities are made and given bounded meanings within and beyond schools; the dynamic between how schools recognize or cannot recognize students and students' own identifications and the practices that flow from this dynamic; the way that the minutiae of everyday life in school is implicated in framing and constraining 'who' a student can be, even when this is nothing more than a simple look; and the way that feeling is an integral part of the experience of these processes. (Youdell, 2011, xi)

This picture has a strong resonance with further and adult education as well. The 30-year market experiment heralded by incorporation has shifted colleges' focus to meeting their own needs first and foremost and away from meeting the needs of students and their communities. What we need to consider is how an overemphasis on measurement through assessment as demanded by our current marketised system of education has a side effect on the feel (or 'affect') of educational space.

A pedagogical approach that is sensitive to affect, the emotional temperature and feel of the learning space, is one that is attuned to the alienation that many students are subjected to and that remains the bedrock of their educational experiences. Pippa's account reminds us of the bodily courage it takes to walk through the doors of the college in order to enroll on a course. Confidence is *felt*. It is a bodily experience. In precisely the same way, anyone who is repeatedly subjected to an experience that hammers home to them that they don't understand and (even) are not capable of understanding, will *feel* that. To that extent, confidence-building, a key feature of adult learning (see Norman and Hyland, 2003) can be viewed as an element of an affective pedagogical approach and part of the process of becoming that transformative teaching and learning catalyses.

The judgemental pedagogical gaze

There are two further concepts we would like to develop here that connect with affect. The first is the idea of the gaze. The second which is linked (through the communication of judgement) is that of the micro-aggression.

The gaze is a concept developed by Foucault among others to explain how people internalise a sense that they are under surveillance and therefore conform to expected norms and regulatory systems of behaviour. For Foucault, this is one way of explaining how power works. In his famous analysis of a prison with a central watch-tower that can see into every cell, he talks about the impact of this panopticon as it instils in the prisoner: 'a state of conscious and permanent visibility that assures the automatic functioning of power' (Foucault, 1995, 201). In educational settings, the gaze works in a similar way. Foucault sees the school as a space in which students are subjected to a 'perpetual comparison' and in which regular assessment and measurement of learning creates an affective environment akin to an 'uninterrupted examination' (Foucault, 1995, 186).

Foucault writes about examinations as working as part of a 'normalising gaze', a surveillance practice that makes it possible to qualify, to classify and to punish. The normalising gaze makes individuals feel their visibility and through that makes them feel how they are differentiated and judged. Because of stories that repeatedly surfaced in our research about being labelled at school, feeling stigmatised and internalising teachers' judgements of being 'thick', we theorise that teachers' attunement to teaching and learning as embodied experience is vital. This is not only about trying to set the temperature and work to establish a particular atmosphere in educational spaces, but it extends to how teachers relate to individual students on a one-to-one basis.

The importance of the judgemental pedagogical gaze (the JPEG) is explained by the way schooling conditions students. Imagine the dynamic between the teacher and a student that is repeatedly shaped by assessment. In a self-reinforcing loop, a student's work is judged to be a particular grade. It's not difficult to see how that could congeal into a cycle of expectation and limitation. Soon this becomes the expectation of both student and teacher. In this light, the judgemental pedagogical gaze can be seen as the evaluation and assessment that teachers make that is visible and consciously or unconsciously registered by the student. The judgemental pedagogical gaze establishes the basis on which the educational encounter develops (or doesn't).

In that sense, the gaze can be seen as operating in the same way as micro-aggressions. Micro-aggression is a term often used in literature and research into racism (Kohli and Solorzano, 2012; Huber and Solorzano, 2015; Pierce, 1974). These are small interactions with a big significance: a casual snub, a 'dirty' look, or 'behaviours or statements that do not necessarily reflect malicious intent but which nevertheless can inflict insult or injury' (Runyowa, 2015) or that can communicate disapproval, dislike, discomfort and prejudice.

Adam's story, Anita's story and Rithenella's story all provide examples of this kind of mini-assault: educational moments in which a teacher's judgement has operated not explicitly through a pronouncement of ability (although that may have previously occurred) but through the withdrawal of affirmation and/or an implicit labelling that is then felt to inform all future interactions.

This reading suggests that in transformative teaching and learning, teachers have to be highly sensitive to the messages of assessment and judgement that they might be (unwittingly) communicating. Put another way, rather than making judgement of ability a feature of their practice, they might instead cultivate micro-affirmation in all their personal interactions with their students. This connects with a cluster of connected themes that resonated powerfully in our research: belief, hope and care.

Belief, hope and care

Our research revealed that underneath the policy discourse of 'skills' and 'employability' there were powerful, often hidden, social practices and lived human experience where those important attributes might have been acquired but only as part of a process of becoming more human. Typically, those experiences were not only 'student-centred', but they went beyond and even worked against the tick-box approaches to assessment and learning that the current marketised system encourages.

How could something as unscientific as 'belief' affect the educational experiences and achievements of a student? After all, alongside love and other human qualities and emotions, belief isn't something that is measurable. In our research, student participants identified individual teachers who catalysed the change in their attitude to learning and their confidence in themselves as learners. In explaining what it was about the class or the learning experience that helped to spark the change, they also frequently commented that the teacher 'believed' in them. An example from the research would be Herbert.

Herbert's story provides another example of how further and adult education can offer people the chance to shape their own lives and pursue a fulfilling career. Herbert told us about his experience of dyslexia and how further education played a role in helping him realise his talents first as a bricklayer and then, as a photographer. As a member of the generation about whom Bernard Coard's seminal text *How the West Indian Child is Made Educationally Subnormal in the British School System* (Coard, 1971) was written, Herbert's experience at school followed a worryingly typical pattern.

'I didn't really learn much at school. I had two CSEs. They treated me okay. Some didn't treat me that well because I was a difficult child. Not difficult due to playing up or being violent but difficult through learning and that was because of my dyslexia – which I didn't know about then … I think if you are an artist, school doesn't give you the options to explore yourself. When I left school I couldn't really read that well. It makes you think like you're nothing really.'

Leaving school at 16 with a couple of CSEs (as opposed to O Levels – which were the qualifications that led to A level), Herbert went on to do a bricklaying course and to become a builder. Building work was a good option for him at that time as it virtually guaranteed employment. But while this made him a living, he cherished the idea of becoming a photographer and took up photography in his spare time. This dream became a reality when he returned to college to study – this time for a career that he knew he could find fulfilment in.

'When you're at school it feels like it's for the government. Whereas, when you're at college you feel: this is for me, it's my livelihood. It's going to be my future … (My college tutor), she was a brilliant woman; she had time for life, for people. *It was her. It was really her.* She saw dyslexic people as having a gift. So when I went to university I was grateful for being dyslexic, because dyslexic people have a creative mind and that comes through in my photographs.'

What is striking in Herbert's interview is the weight he attaches to his tutor's view of him. A clear marker in the learning experience within this account is the moment at which the teacher helps Herbert transform the dyslexic label into a positive attribute rather than a deficit. In her interactions with Herbert, this teacher communicated belief. The strength that Herbert draws from this he still carries with him today, years later. Herbert's story also tells us something about the interaction between individual people and the 'education-is-for-employment' discourse. At 16, young people can be sucked into this and may feel they have no option. The skills discourse is, after all, founded on fear: fear of unemployment, fear of being (or remaining poor), fear about the future.

Another way of looking at it is that Herbert's bricklaying skills freed him to choose another option. Knowing he could always fall back on bricklaying for income, he navigated a route to pursue a meaningful vocation while maintaining a safety net. Either way, his story illustrates the higgledy-piggledy relation between employment, earning and the drive and ambitions of the individual as they ricochet off each other in the passage of time. Above all, this, the reality of education and employment across time, reveals how startlingly inadequate a linear system of education is that aims to rank and categorise young people according to their qualifications as though fixing them at that age is in any way sensible. Let us also remember that Herbert's schooling was in the 1970s. The trajectories from education into employment in those days was much smoother and more stable than they are today.

Just because a teacher's 'belief' in students cannot be measured, of course that does not mean it can't have a powerful and positive impact. Interestingly, the power of belief can be evidenced from scientific literature and the field of medicine. A paper by Chen et al (2019) published in *Nature Human Behaviour* investigates the placebo effect. The paper centres on a trial in which doctors were given either placebo pills to prescribe or pills with an active ingredient. What their research showed was that during a consultation, the belief of the doctor that the medicine given to the patient would be effective had an impact irrespective of whether the patient was given a placebo or genuine medicine. They pinpoint 'subtle changes in (doctors') facial expression behaviours' and conclude that 'healthcare providers' behaviour and cognitive mind-sets can affect clinical interactions' (Chen et al, 2019, 1,295).

Here we appear to see confirmation of the potential impact of 'affect' and of the power of language, body language and facial expression that all combine to have a positive effect. Furthermore, we might interpret this evidence of the impact of 'belief' as the flipside of the notion of micro-aggressions: rather than the deliberate or unconscious communication of disapproval, dislike and prejudice, transformative teaching and learning rests upon the conscious and unconsciously communicated 'unconditional positive regard' (see Rogers, 2007, 241) that is registered by students in discrete moments of what we might call *micro-affirmation*.

What might that mean in terms of the ground we have already covered? The ingredients clearly include what Crownover and Jones (2018) refer to as 'relational pedagogy' (see also Ljungblad, 2019), a particular kind of nurturing relationship that is carefully calibrated by a teacher who is willing to get to know their students, who is interested in them and their lives. This kind of pedagogy is founded on I/Thou rather than I/it relationships (see Buber, 1959). In our research, a great number of the teachers we talked to from further and adult education providers viewed their students holistically. They undertook a range of pastoral activities: contacting absent students, counselling them when domestic circumstances were difficult, helping and advising them in their relations with other agencies (the police, the local council, social workers and so on); in some cases, they helped with accommodation issues and even bought groceries and paid for food.

All of this activity was deemed by many teachers to be part of the teaching role and addressing those needs a prerequisite for learning to take place. It's important to note here that in some colleges, pastoral concerns were taken on by a separate 'non-academic' team, but in most colleges, teachers found themselves taking on these responsibilities and meeting these needs. This connects powerfully to the pedagogy of 'care' which is championed by Nel Noddings (2005) among others.

That college teachers' work is frequently 'under the radar', and can centre on the biographical background of individuals is key in any analysis of these aspects of relational pedagogy. Holistic approaches were identified in much of the research produced in the Transforming Learning Cultures (TLC) in the further education strand of the Teaching and Learning Research Programme (TLRP) that ran between 2001–08 (for example, Hodkinson, Biesta and James, 2007; Gleeson and James, 2007). This is a model of professional practice that is focused on the needs of students as a necessary precursor to learning. It pays close attention to student biographies (Biesta and Tedder, 2007) and addresses issues arising with a view to scaffolding the classroom experience. In many cases, without this scaffolding, further education students would find it difficult to engage in learning.

We would position care as a key aspect of adult learning (Duckworth and Smith, 2019). To return to the quotation from Hamlet at the start of this chapter, there is something ineffable in this, something difficult to pinpoint, something once again which is a human quality rather than a 'skill', a competence or a practice underpinned by professional standards. The insights into critical pedagogy that we gathered at the beginning of the chapter need to be kept in mind though. As Lingard (2005) points out, care alone is not enough, it needs to be the framing for students' encounters with challenging (and powerful) knowledges. 'We believe that teachers should be praised for ... their commitment to social support for the students but that the absence of intellectual demand, connectedness and working with and valuing difference carries with it significant social justice concerns' (Lingard, 2005, 179). The challenge then, is to meet those needs, to build that confidence and to foster student autonomy. If transformative teaching and learning is to yield concrete social benefits, then all that work must connect with specific goals. That means that challenge is essential. The educational gains made can only reach full fruition if they re-connect with the lifeworld outside the classroom and if the student returns to the world in order to contribute to it and bring their new knowledge and understanding to bear on it.

Hope is the final ingredient. Here we are drawing on the thinking of Ernst Bloch, a critical theorist from the last century, who writes powerfully about the connection between hope and agency. For Bloch, hope:

> [I]s indestructibly grounded in the human drive for happiness and ... has always been too clearly the motor of history ... when the will had learnt both through mistakes and in fact through hope as well, and when reality did not stand in too harsh a contradiction to it, (it) reformed a bit of the world; that is: an initial fiction was made real. (Bloch, 1986, 443)

Bloch sees hope as a powerful quality of the human spirit, a positive orientation towards the future that can bring about change in the world. For Bloch, hope is an attitude and emotion that drives agency and the ability and need to act. He sees it as an inherent 'drive' in people which is, however, disrupted and undermined by the economic and political discourses and conditions of the historical period we are living through. Commenting on the way Bloch conceptualises hope, Thompson makes explicit how hope can be catalysed: '[h]ope has to be learned ... It does not just come about automatically but is the produce of experience, failure and resistance to an everyday acceptance of reality ... Hope therefore learns but it also teaches as well as constitutes its own conditions' (Thompson, 2013, 7).

Transformative teaching and learning is a pedagogy that embeds belief, hope and care – all of which work to challenge the objectification and stratification that students may have been conditioned to feel are inherent aspects of educational experiences. For these students, by locking them out of learning, this feeling effectively turns educational space into dead or purgatorial space, space in which they are ware-housed prior to being slotted into employment. The next section will explore aspects of transformative teaching and learning and spatiality in more detail.

Transformative teaching and learning and spatiality

For further education in particular, the sense that a college is an integral part of the local social landscape, part of a publicly owned infrastructure that is there to serve the communities in which it is situated has been seriously eroded by marketisation. This point was borne out for us when filming an introductory video for the Transforming Lives project. On a Sunday morning, standing outside a college in Birmingham, speaking about the important role colleges play in transformative education, we were distracted by the sounds of knocking. A member of the college's estates staff remonstrated through the ¾ inch plate glass of the foyer: *You can't film here.* Rob walked over to explain the project but was told: 'you can't film here. This is private property. Move away or I'll call the police'.

The encounter was symbolic of a broad and deep shift in the way colleges view themselves. As a semi-privatised version of organising the public good of further education, incorporation legally altered the feel of this educational space (see Smith, 2015). A new corporate space was produced, one that featured self-promotion and a consciousness of a college's commercial image, a space filled with the language of funding, of targets, of contact hours and contracts, success and progression rates. The glossiness of incorporated further education space is best exemplified in the newly built colleges that sprang up across the country under the Building Colleges of the Future initiative (2008–09). A detailed critique of some aspects of these buildings can be found elsewhere (Smith, 2017B), but in this context, it needs to be noted that behind the glazed facades and mall-like atria that were such noticeable features of these buildings, there were some serious design short-comings in relation to teaching and learning spaces. Despite this feel of institutional and corporate spatiality, teachers and students in classroom spaces were still able to experience transformative teaching and learning. In this section we will explore how.

Henri Lefebvre's work on time/space and affect (Lefebvre, 1991, 2004, 2014) can also provide some important insights into transformative teaching and learning. Lefebvrian thinking combines a critique of the 'monster' of capital (Lefebvre, 2004, 55) with an insistence that every moment carries within it the potential for change. And while he sees the influence of capital as deforming what it is to be human, he also never loses sight of the potential for humans to transform the world and themselves in positive ways.

The place of colleges in their local contexts seems to us to be an important overlooked feature of what colleges do. The idea of the 'FE sector' plays a (negative) part in this. The 'FE sector' is really a rhetorical tool that evokes a generalised, decontextualised meaning on a hugely diverse set of institutions and educational settings. The 'FE sector' is what Lefebvre (1991) calls an 'abstract space'. This space is conjured up as 'an impersonal pseudo-subject' which conceals 'state (political) power' and in it 'lived experience is crushed' and 'vanquished' (Lefebvre (1991, 49–51). The abstract space of the 'FE sector' is a policy-makers' tool. It is the space in which colleges compete against each other as required and shaped by the FAP apparatus. This bureaucratic work enables government and funders to view transformative social processes in numerical forms (see O'Leary and Smith, 2012; Smith and O'Leary, 2013). This is the abstract space in which transformative teaching and learning is displaced by a technical 'delivery' process or a spoon-feeding/transmission approach to education. Through abstraction, the complex and nuanced social process of transformative teaching and learning that we have detailed in this chapter, in all its richness, is reduced to numbers on a spreadsheet.

Our research counterposes this bleak and dehumanising picture with a different kind of space. Drawing once more from Lefebvre, we see within transformative teaching and learning echoes of Lefebvrian 'differential space'. This suggests that the transformative classroom is a particular kind of social and learning environment. But this is a familiar educational environment to teachers who have worked in schools and colleges in super-diverse cities like Birmingham, Manchester and London. These environments, mixing male, female and LGBTQ+ students and students with backgrounds that reach out to different countries across the world, are common and where they work well, have a lot to teach other less diverse settings.

As a first step, to establish a differential educational space necessitates the reasoning out, establishment and agreed implementation of ground rules on behaviour. A way of behaving is essential if transformative teaching and learning is to take root. For equity to flower in the classroom, the diverse attitudes, expectations and opinions of students and teachers (and possibly the culture of the college) must be interrogated. This classroom is a space in which students are supported to use their lived experience as the raw material from which to understand who they are, what the world is and from there, what the world could be. Because transformative teaching and learning spaces attempt to realise a way of interacting with each other that allows everyone to benefit and the different skills and dispositions to be celebrated, they model the desirable qualities of democratic interaction: they look to the way social relations in wider society could and should be. In that sense, transformative teaching and learning is not some kind of teaching technique rather it is focused on producing new and critical relations between the student and knowledge and the student and the world.

As differential space is collective, the transformative power it offers is not just transformative of the individual. Differential space is also a space in which the 'otherwising' touched on by Kincheloe (2008) is a feature. The diverse classroom, peopled by students from a wide range of backgrounds, offers a unique social/educational space in which social cohesion can be enhanced and students can become familiar with the richness of others' backgrounds. Sadly, here we start to see the huge negative impact of the kind of monocultural classrooms that selection (through grammar schools) and wealth (through fee-paying and private 'public' schools) bring about. Those educational environments appear instead to be finely tuned to re-producing society as it is. At their worst, they promote a narrow view of the world that is not interested in changing existing inequalities or ending human suffering but instead seeks to support and sustain the current social order and the knowledges that underpin it.

Differential educational space is qualitatively different. It does not position knowledge as inert matter to be transmitted by the teacher to the student who must then be assessed on the accuracy of how it has been 'learned'. Rather, it leans towards a position in which every student's encounter with knowledge has the potential to critique it, to change it, to build on it, to reach beyond it. As such, it is space that opens out from the classroom and provides the possibility of transformation of the social forces and structures that created the inequality to start with. In our research, transformative teaching and learning connects strongly to differential space.

Concluding thoughts

Every student in further and adult education is entitled to ask the question: 'what do you want me educated *for*?' If the answer to this question centres on 'the economy' as opposed to individual and broader social benefits, then we shouldn't be surprised if that fails to motivate and inspire the student, after all, it is part of an objectifying discourse. What's more, it certainly 'classes' the student because young people from middle-class and wealthy backgrounds are simply not going to be subjected to any such direction. Instead, they will be encouraged to aim high and steered towards the high-salaried careers deemed to be appropriate to their social stratum.

Furthermore, this question confronts our collective failure to take into account how our knowledge and understanding of global economy has moved from the 1990s view that global competition has to guide all our actions. It is hazardous indeed to maintain the view that our national energies need to focus on drawing in as much investment and being as competitive (in terms of so-called 'productivity') as we can, rather than addressing a much more challenging set of realisations: that global resources are finite, that global inequality has increased and that this in itself is not only unjust but poses significant hazards.

Transformative teaching and learning may start by tackling scholagenic damage through restorative approaches (relearning the ability to learn). For some students it involves a kind of deconditioning: a breaking of bodily hexis and educational habitus that has effectively disabled any progress or self-belief in the relevance and joy of learning. Transformative teaching and learning depends on restimulating hope. It necessitates rebuilding students' confidence and the reconstruction of positive learning identities, but it isn't limited to those aspects. In providing students with the learning tools and confidence to approach knowledge in a critical way, it aspires to build the potential for growth and change in the knowledges and practices that shape our society. Transformative teaching and learning is a starting point from which students can make changes in their lives, re-orientate their thinking and begin to see themselves as capable of acting to secure a different future for themselves. But for some students, this can connect to them becoming agents of hope within their communities and for society at large.

For further and adult education teachers of all subjects, there is a question similar to that for students: 'what do you want me to educate *for*?' In a world gripped by economic and ecological uncertainty and disfigured by social inequality, poverty, injustice and human suffering, simply teaching to get students through an assessment to achieve a qualification is no longer enough. How could it be, when we are no longer able to make an accurate judgement about what jobs there are likely to be in the next 50 years? All teaching now needs to frame subject knowledge with broader powerful knowledges that equip students with an understanding of how the dynamic of cultural capital works and the kind of criticality they will need in a world where patterns of life and work are changing so rapidly.

Transformative teaching and learning takes account of these questions and positions the interests of the student centrally, within a frame that is local, national and international. Combining different elements of the ideas and theories of the thinkers whose work we have touched on, we see transformative teaching and learning as a social and pedagogical practice that exists along a cline: having at one end students who are helped towards an appreciation of themselves as being successful learners (rather than failures) and at the other, students who may have refashioned their learning identities and gone on to develop a critical view of themselves and of society and the world. Indeed, some students find their perspectives on the world are changed and politicised. There are strong links at this end of the continuum with Freirean precepts. This basically plots a pathway in which the learner identity runs parallel to knowledge content, a pathway that starts off as learning (again) how to be a learner and continues developing a consciousness of the factors local, national and international that have impacted on students' lives and the lives of others.

We have also explored the importance of the teachers' pedagogical role, in particular the way in which teachers need to deploy nuanced and individualised strategies in order to create the social conditions in which transformative educational moments can occur. This pedagogy operates through the embodied knowing of these practitioners and against the grain of existing policy knowledge systems. Transformative educational experiences are largely hidden from view because their impact falls outside the metrics that drive further education policy and underpin funding in the UK. Their wider significance remains unmeasured by blunt assessment. For us, this is a failure of the regulatory FAP apparatus that shackles providers. Viewing further education programmes through the lens of transformative teaching and learning enables a reclaiming of educational space and purposes that offers renewed hope and dignity which open opportunities for students in higher education, employment and beyond (Duckworth and Smith, 2018b).

The open-ended nature of transformative teaching and learning also needs to be clarified. Transformative teaching and learning is not a single event of revelation and transformation: transformation is a process and just like learning it doesn't occur instantly for all students. Indeed arguably, if we are all still learning, then we are all still changing. Our engagement with our communities in collective struggle isn't something that all of us are always fully engaged in. The idea of struggle might seem irrelevant to us: after all, we are encouraged through the property market to re-locate ourselves away from 'problem' areas and we may find comfort in living alongside people from our own class background and heritage. Even then though, we remain aware that there is a balance that tips back and forth between keeping one's own body and mind together and in looking beyond that balancing act to the needs and interests of others within and without our immediate circle and community.

What this points to is that transformative teaching and learning is a collective experience that pierces a hole through our acceptance of the 'way things are' and, that reaches towards ways of thinking and being that may be at the moment 'beyond our philosophy' as Hamlet put it. Transformative teaching and learning, the potential that it signals for change within us and the problems it flags up with marketised educational systems and practices that objectify students and teachers, all signal the possibility and indeed the necessity of societal change.

8

What needs to be done

Making the classroom a democratic setting where everyone feels a responsibility to contribute is a central goal of transformative pedagogy.

bell hooks, *Teaching to Transgress*

Teaching to Transgress is an important book by the black thinker, prolific writer and activist bell hooks who died in 2021. In the book, hooks, like Dewey, Freire and others, see transformative teaching and learning as intimately connected with democracy. She shares her experiences as a young black woman growing up in the racially segregated southern states of the United States. She grew up wanting to teach and wanting to write and as she points out: '[f]or black folks teaching – educating – was fundamentally political because it was rooted in antiracist struggle' (hooks, 1994, 2). hooks' experience of learning in segregated classrooms and being taught by black teachers was liberatory and for her, the classroom was a 'place of ecstasy – pleasure and danger' (hooks, 1994, 3). Teaching to transgress sees hooks sharing her experiences as a teacher and theorising a praxis in which the classroom becomes a 'differential space', in Lefebvrian terms: a space which foregrounds and takes full account of gender, sexuality, race, social class – all of the characteristics that mark us as individual members of the human family. At the heart of this is a determination to co-produce classroom spaces as microcosms of democratic human interaction. This classroom space is one in which students are active and feel a responsibility to participate, this responsibility is something hooks sees as radiating out from the classroom and as a product of transformative teaching and learning. For hooks, transformative education is necessary if we want our democracy to be fully representative, for it to thrive.

This connection between the purposes of teaching and learning in the classroom and the impact of this for and in wider society has been a strong theme throughout this book. We have presented a picture of how further and adult education has been reframed and debased by a market fundamentalism that has swept across 'Western' societies. None of us should make the mistake of thinking this has only happened in education. Ask a nurse, ask a social worker, ask a police officer, ask a midwife, ask almost anyone working in what used to be called the public sector. Funding-centredness has become central to so many of our institutions and the tentacular grip of managerialist practices has deformed and distorted cultures and practices in those fields in just the same way. Our problem is that this is presented to us as an inevitable extension of the modern world.

In further and adult education in England, there have been particular consequences that we see as of particular relevance to understanding transformative teaching and learning and its importance. Students have been increasingly positioned as a 'classed' political category whose individual interests can be disregarded in the pursuit of an instrumentalist agenda. In its rawest form, this instrumentalist perspective is focused simply on fashioning a slipway from education into employment for the young people within this category. To that extent, the history, identity and meaning of colleges and those of the people who work and study in them are irrelevant. In hooks' terms, this instrumentalism turns classrooms from spaces of liberation and the nurturing of democratic practice into spaces of domination.

As the FAP apparatus finds so many colleges wanting with regards to efficiency and solvency, this is not a consequence of 'the invisible hand of the market' or of shifts in the demand for particular courses. Rather it reflects (grotesquely) the impact of a remote distributive mechanism that engineers annual instability and uncertainty with calculated indifference. Reductions in funding since 2010 and the charade of the area reviews suggest that if colleges were to disappear tomorrow, government ministers wouldn't blink. Indeed, that might explain the determination to put employers 'in the driving seat' and the channelling of funding towards work-based learning and apprenticeships. Our theorisation of transformative teaching and learning involves recognising and addressing all of these factors. Transformative teaching and learning is not a politicisation of further and adult education, it is founded on a recognition that it is already politicised.

It is extraordinary that, according to our research, we have reached a situation in which one of the first tasks of further and adult education teachers is to undo the damage done by schooling. The impact of scholageny (marketised teaching) is still barely acknowledged – but its effects are real and lasting and until it is properly recognised, it will continue to damage the lives and life chances of large numbers of people. But dealing with that damage is only the first significant step. As we have outlined, for some of the research participants, the moment of claiming a position in the-world-as-it-is is the extent of their journey. For others, transformative teaching and learning encompasses not just a change in their place in the world but a changed view of the world as well and a sense that the world itself needs changing.

Starting in the classroom, this book has provided an overview of the fundamentals of a pedagogical approach that can be implemented by teachers to create the conditions in which transformative teaching and learning can take place and take effect. We have outlined how teachers are hindered in producing these conditions at the local level in colleges and other providers.

We have also detailed the constraints on leadership in further and adult education providers. Throughout, we have stressed the need for a shift in values so that teachers are supported to focus on pedagogy.

But these aspects are dwarfed by the pressing need for a change of focus in funding systems. That change should be motivated by a recognition that the current FAP apparatus is destructive of the respect and dignity that should be afforded further and adult education students: it objectifies them. The current FAP apparatus also dehumanises staff, undermining their professionalism and integrity and trampling underfoot the purposes of education that brought many of them into teaching in the first place. Through its burdensome bureaucracy, its one-dimensional metrics and its hideous systemisation of the living, breathing human process of education, the current FAP apparatus corrupts the very thing it claims to measure. As such, it is destructive of transformative teaching and learning and the conditions transformative education needs to flourish. Furthermore, it perpetuates policy thinking that appears to be incapable of recognising the broader social benefits that education brings about.

We recognise that a shift in policy like this would require an unprecedented realignment of government thinking. It would require policy makers and government ministers to have Dweck's 'open mind-set' and to be prepared to challenge some fundamental assumptions. The current context is one in which much of the effort of teachers is expended in nurturing hope and self-belief in students who have been convinced through repeated experiences of assessment and systematic labelling that they are not good at learning. The schooling career of a child is now measured and audited from Year 1 to Year 11 and beyond. But one serious consequence of a linear framework with its normative schedule of what-should-be-learnt-by-when is that approximately a third of students who have not been able to 'keep up' and match this norm enter colleges at the age of 16 feeling like failures. This normative framework means that further and adult education teachers typically spend time and energy helping students walk away from the spoilt identities that they bring with them from schooling.

For us, this gives a precise, situated meaning to transformative teaching and learning – one that cannot be detached from the further and adult education context as it operates today in England. If schooling was not as rigid in its imposition of what should have been learnt by what age, then this aspect of further education work would not be in evidence. The need for transformative teaching and learning at this end of the continuum originates in patterns and cultures of assessment. To that extent transformative teaching and learning is essential to address the scholagenic effects of schooling for some students.

Our argument in this book has been that further and adult education is for everyone and has never been just about 'skills'. It can provide a model for a renewed understanding of lifelong learning in which transformative teaching and learning could and should be the norm – enabling it to increase exponentially colleges' contributions to the social and economic benefits they already make.

Transforming further and adult education into a truly egalitarian experience fostered by colleges and other providers requires a funding regime that nurtures and supports a holistic and integrated approach. This includes ensuring equality in educational and related resources (for example; between schools, further education and higher education), equality of respect, knowledge and recognition of learners and the communities they hail from; a rebalancing of power away from central government to bolster locally orientated autonomy in further education and equality in care, hope and love.

Transformative teaching and learning can be seen as a barometer of the extent to which our society is open to change and is forward-looking. It reflects the idea not just that individuals are capable of changing who they are, their 'subjectness' and position within their family, community and society more broadly, but the extent to which the community and society of which they are a part are responsive to those changes. Viewed in this way, transformative teaching and learning is the dynamic space of change, the pivot on which students' emergent identities and perspectives and who they are and how they face how the world is catalysed to change it. The challenge is to raise awareness of the damage that is being done and of the huge social benefits of further and adult education that are currently ignored. This book is an attempt to make a small contribution to meeting that challenge.

To return to the bell hooks quotation at the start of this chapter, being the teacher in further and adult education is about creating the conditions in which learning can take place for all students. If respecting and safeguarding the souls of students is the opposite of objectifying them and seeing them as income or as receptacles for 'skills', then it is about safeguarding their souls as well.

What needs to be done

Clearly, there are huge structural changes that underpin many of the ideas for change that arise from the Transforming Lives research. For a start, the governing human capital discourse that objectifies teachers and students in further and adult education needs to be subordinated to a much richer and more holistic way of talking about further and adult education that upholds a perspective that it benefits the lives of real people and communities in more complex and profound ways. In addition, – and this is an equally big ask – the current marketised structure with its accompanying funding, accountability and performance apparatus should be overhauled and, preferably dismantled or at the very least neutered.

We are not so naïve as to believe that such a huge recalibration is going to take place any time (very) soon, as the fundamentalism that sees these structures as beneficial and necessary is deeply embedded in our political and economic life. But that cannot stop us from reimagining and insisting on the necessity of change.

While we wait for such fundamental change, a levelling up is required by which the work that further and adult education undertakes is properly recognised and funded. Further and adult education has a history of catering for the needs of students from low-income households. Many colleges address these needs through their pastoral teams and by providing meals, and other basic support. The wraparound role of colleges in addressing students' needs must be acknowledged as an important aspect of pedagogy – by government, by funders, by Ofsted. We need a funding model that takes proper account of these socio-economic factors. If students are coming from low-income backgrounds and have additional needs associated with poverty, poor mental health and difficult home circumstances, then colleges need to be properly funded to address these. In this way the contribution made by further and adult education colleges to social justice can be properly supported.

Colleges and other further and adult education providers have to re-build damaged learner identities as a precursor to providing courses and qualifications. This often operates at the level of re-engagement but is an essential first step. Nowhere is this recognised in the current funding model. The vital restorative pedagogical work that further and adult education teachers have to undertake means that additional time is necessary if students are to be given equal opportunities to achieve the qualifications they take. Therefore, providers need to be freed up from the prescriptive time-limits that are imposed on the courses they offer – that are imposed irrespective of the (educational and socio-economic) backgrounds of the students they provide for. The annual cycle of funding is a part of the way colleges are straight-jacketed in what they are able to achieve. These cruel and unjust restraints fail to take account of student needs and reduce further and adult education's potential to bring about social mobility.

Leadership in further and adult education providers needs rethinking. Colleges have a key role that makes them much more than a component in the supply of 'skills' for employers. The wider social and health benefits of further and adult education require the involvement and coordination of local authorities. The ability of colleges to address social inequality needs to be enhanced. For those reasons, college governance needs to be locally and democratically reconfigured. There is a danger that the current move towards delegating some further education provision (through combined local authorities for example) will result in a locally managed replication of national government's traditional supply-side policy model. Twenty-five years of weighting governing bodies with the voices of employers has produced scant benefits – particularly in terms of curriculum.

The teachers in further and adult education who understand how flawed the current apparatus is should be valued and supported more, by and through research by employers' organisations, by local authorities and by central government. In our view it is imperative that these same teachers are supported to take on senior roles to ensure continuity in their understanding of transformative teaching and learning feeds and to ensure it feeds upwards and, ultimately, puts them in positions in which they can leaven the worst excesses of institutional leadership which, in the pursuit of 'balancing the books' poisons the conditions in which transformative teaching and learning takes place.

We propose a localised further and adult education system in which colleges and other providers are viewed as important epicentres of social inclusion and cohesion that connect to schools pre-entry and employers and HE on exit and that are accessible to people of any age to access in order to achieve the personal and/or professional development they need to thrive. Funding needs to address and reflect this.

Further and adult education providers should be re-positioned locally as *the* non-linear model of education that is required for the twenty first century. Policy and funding need to acknowledge the important role colleges are playing by providing flexible and part time routes not just as an additional part of a linear system. We support campaigns that assert everyone should have the Right to Learn (Right to Learn, 2021) which drawing from the 2019 Lifelong Learning Commission calls for everyone to have a statutory right to learn whatever their age or background.

The Transforming Lives research is one example of a growing body of research coming from grassroots further and adult education staff. We see it as a model of participatory knowledge production and meaning making, that, as the bell hooks quotation at the start of the chapter underlines, feeds into a vision of a democratic society in which all voices are heard. To further this aim, we urge and support all further and adult education staff to get involved in practitioner research through one of the many groups that are springing up online and on social media.

To make change possible, we need to build the knowledge base. If you are a teacher in further and adult education, use your experience, connect with others, learn about knowledge production, undertake further study and formalise your understandings by carrying out research. Further and adult education needs you.

Notes

Chapter 6

1   It is interesting that the social welfare aspect of schooling has emerged as an important aspect of school work during the COVID-19 pandemic. The government attempt to balance the economic and instrumentalist value of schooling (children's supposed long term interests in getting qualifications) with the wider social benefits for them of being in school for their mental health and in order to be fed – provided an interesting spectacle.

2   In comparison, Germany, with a population of 83 m, has only 45,000 people in prison.

3   Findings are shown below each item (with the number of teachers shown after bars).

Chapter 7

1   For a lengthier discussion of symbolic violence and transformative teaching and learning, see Duckworth and Smith, 2018b.

References

Ahmed, S. (2007) 'A phenomenology of whiteness', *Feminist Theory*, 8(2): 149–68.

Ahmed, S. (2010) 'Happy objects', in Gregg, M. and Seigworth, G.J. *The Affect Theory Reader*, Durham NC: Duke University Press.

Ainley, P. and Bailey, B. (1997) *The Business of Learning*, London: Cassell.

Akala (2018) *Natives: Race and Class in the Ruins of Empire*, London: Two Roads.

All-Party Parliamentary Group on Social Mobility (APGSM) (2012) *Seven Key Truths about Social Mobility*, [online] available from: https://www.raeng.org.uk/publications/other/7-key-truths-about-social-mobility [accessed 22 June, 2021].

Association of Colleges (AOC) (2019) *Key Facts 2018/19*, [online] available from: https://www.aoc.co.uk/sites/default/files/College%20Key%20Facts%202018-19.pdf [accessed 2 June, 2021].

Ball, S. (2003) 'The teacher's soul and the terrors of performativity', *Journal of Education Policy*, 18(2): 215–28.

Ball, S. J. (2005) *Education Policy and Social Class*, London: Routledge.

Barad, K. (2007) *Meeting the Universe Halfway*, London: Duke University Press.

Barry, B. (1989) *Theories of Justice*, London: Harvester Wheatsheaf.

Barton, D., Hamilton, M. and Ivanic, R. (2000) *Situated Literacies: Reading and Writing in Context*, Abingdon: Routledge.

Barton, D., Ivanic, R., Appleby, Y., Hodge, R. and Tusting, K. (2007) *Literacy, Lives and Learning*, London: Routledge.

Bauman, Z. (2001) *Liquid Modernity*, Cambridge: Polity Press.

Beauchamp, M., Barling, J., Li, Z., Morton, K., Keith, S. and Zumbo, B. (2010) 'Development and psychometric properties of the transformational teaching questionnaire', *Journal of Health Psychology*, 15(8): 1123–34.

Becker, Gary, S. (1993) *Human Capital, a Theoretical and Empirical Analysis with Special Reference to Education*, London: University of Chicago Press.

Beckert, J. (2020) 'The exhausted futures of neoliberalism: From promissory legitimacy to social anomy', *Journal of Cultural Economy*, 13(3): 318–30.

Beetham H. and Oliver M. (2010) 'The changing practices of knowledge and learning', in R. Sharpe and H. Beetham (eds) *Rethinking Learning for a Digital Age*, London: RoutledgeFalmer, 155–69.

Belfield, C., Farquharson, C. and Sibieta, L. (2018) *2018 Annual Report on Education Spending in England*, Institute for Fiscal Studies, funded by the Nuffield Foundation, [online] available from: https://www.ifs.org.uk/uploads/publications/comms/R150.pdf, [accessed 12 October 2021].

Bennett, P., Lambert, L. and Smith, R. (2022) *Rethinking and Reviving Subject English: The Murder and the Murmur*, London: Routledge.

Bernstein, B. (1971) 'On the classification and framing of educational knowledge', in M.F.D. Young (ed.) *Knowledge and Control: New Directions for the Sociology of Education*, London: Collier MacMillan, 47–69.

Bernstein, B. (2000) *Pedagogy, Symbolic Control and Identity: Theory, Research, Critique* (revised edn), London: Rowman & Littlefield.

Biesta, G. (2006) 'What's the point of lifelong learning if lifelong learning has no point? On the democratic deficit of policies for lifelong learning', *European Educational Research Journal*, 5(3/4): 169–80.

Biesta, G. (2010) *Good Education in an Age of Measurement*, Boulder: Paradigm Publishers.

Biesta, G. (2015) 'What is education for? On good education, teacher judgement, and educational professionalism', *European Journal of Education*, 50(1): 75–87.

Biesta, G. and Tedder, M. (2007) 'Agency and learning in the lifecourse: towards an ecological perspective', *Studies in the Education of Adults*, 39(2): 132–49.

BIS and DfE (Department for Education) (2016) *Reviewing post 16 education and training institutions: Area reviews*, [online] available from: https://www.gov.uk/government/publications/reviewing-post-16-education-and-training-institutions-list-of-area-reviews/reviewing-post-16-education-and-training-institutions-areareviews-waves-1-to-5, [accessed 8 June, 2021].

Blair, Tony (1996) Speech given at Ruskin College, Oxford, 16 December, 1996, [online] available from: http://www.leeds.ac.uk/educol/documents/000000084.htm [accessed 26 May, 2021].

Bloch, E. (1986) *The Principle of Hope, Volume 1*, Cambridge, MA: MIT Press.

Bourdieu, P. (1994) 'Structures, habitus, power: Basis for a theory of symbolic power', in Bourdieu, P. and Passeron, J-C. (2013) *Reproduction in Education, Society and Culture*, London: Sage.

Bourdieu, P. and Passeron, J-C. (2013) *Reproduction in Education, Society and Culture*, London: Sage.

Bowles, S. and Gintis, H. (1976) *Schooling in Capitalist America: Education Reform and the Contradictions of Economic Life*, New York: Basic Books.

Bratich, J. (2018) 'Observation in a surveilled world', in N. Denzin and Y. Lincoln (eds) 2018, *The SAGE Handbook of Qualitative Research*, London: SAGE, pp 911–45.

Breunig, M. (2005) 'Turning experiential education and critical pedagogy theory into praxis', *Journal of Experiential Education*, 28(2): 106–22.

British Educational Research Association (2018) *Ethical Guidelines for Educational Research*, [online] available from: https://www.bera.ac.uk/researchers-resources/publications/ethical-guidelines-for-educational-research-2018 [accessed 26 March, 2022].

Brockmann, M. and Smith R. (forthcoming) '"Invested" partnerships as key to high-quality "expansive"apprenticeship programmes', *Learning and Work* (under review).

Brookfield, S. (1995) *Becoming a Critically Reflective Practitioner*, Mahwah, NJ: Jossey Bass.

Brookfield, S. (1997) 'Assessing critical thinking', *New Directions for Adult and Continuing Education*, 75: 17–29.

Brookfield, S. (2005) *The Power of Critical Theory for Adult Learning and Teaching*, Maidenhead: Open University Press.

Brookfield, S. (2018) *Teaching Race: How to Help Students Unmask and Challenge Racism*, Mahwah, NJ: Jossey Bass

Brown, L. (ed.) (1993) *The New Shorter English Dictionary*, Oxford: Clarendon Press.

Buber, M. (1959) *I and Thou*, Edinburgh: T&T Clark.

Buber, M. (1961) *Between Man and Man*, London: Fontana.

Buchmann. C. and Diprete, T. (2006) 'The growing female advantage in college completion: The role of family background and academic achievement', *American Sociological Review*, 71(4): 515–41.

Campbell, D.T. (2011) 'Assessing the impact of planned social change', *Journal of Multidisciplinary Evaluation*, 7(15): 3–43.

Campbell, S., Greenwood, M., Prior, S., Shearer, T., Walkem, K., Young, S., Bywaters, D. and Walker, K. (2020) 'Purposive sampling: Complex or simple? Research case examples', *Journal of Research in Nursing*, 25(8): 652–61.

Carr, W. and Kemmis, S. (1986) *Becoming Critical: Knowing Through Action Research*, London: Falmer Press.

de Carvalho, E. and Skipper, Y. (2019) '"We're not just sat at home in our pyjamas!": A thematic analysis of the social lives of home educated adolescents in the UK', *European Journal of Psychology of Education*, 34: 501–16, available from: https://doi.org/10.1007/s10212-018-0398-5.

Cassidy, D. (2009) *Beyond Uncertainty: Heisenberg, Quantum Physics, and The Bomb*, New York: Bellevue Literary Press.

Centre for Social Justice (CSJ) (2016) *Selective Education and Social Mobility*, [online] available from: https://www.centreforsocialjustice.org.uk/wp-content/uploads/2018/03/161201-Grammar-School-Report.pdf [accessed 26 June, 2021].

Chen, P.A., Cheong, J.H., Jolly, E. Elhence, H., Wager, T. and Chang, L.J. (2019) 'Socially transmitted placebo effects', *Nature Human Behaviour*, 3: 1295–305.

Chowdhury, K. (2020) *Has COVID-19 Highlighted Social Injustice Built into our Cities?*, [online] available from: https://www.cebm.net/2020/10/has-covid-19-highlighted-social-injustice-built-into-our-cities/ [accessed 29 June, 2021].

Coard, B. (1971) *How the West Indian Child is Made Educationally Subnormal in The British School System: The Scandal of the Black Child in Schools in Britain*, London: New Beacon for the Caribbean Education and Community Workers' Association.

Coffield, F. (2008) *Just Suppose Teaching and Learning Became the First Priority*, available from: http://weaeducation.typepad.co.uk/wea_education_blog/files/frank_coffield_on_teach_and_learning.pdf, [accessed 11 May, 2021].

Collins, R. (2008) *Violence*, Princeton: Princeton University Press.

Crawford, C., Dearden. L., Micklewright J. and Vignoles A. (2016) *Family Background and University Success*, Oxford: Oxford University Press

Creswell, J. (2003) *Research Design: Qualitative, Quantitative and Mixed Methods Approaches*, London: Sage.

Crownover, A. and Jones, J.R. (2018) 'A relational pedagogy', *Journal of Thought*, 52(1–2): 17–28.

Crystal, D. (2019) *The Cambridge Encyclopedia of English Language*, Cambridge: Cambridge University Press.

Cui, V. and Smith, R. (2020) *The Factors Affecting the Quality of the 'Off-The-Job' Element of Apprenticeships in the West Midlands Region*. London: Gatsby Foundation.

Cushing, I. (2020) 'The policy and policing of language in schools', *Language in Society*, 49(3): 425–50.

Cushing, I. (2021) 'Policy mechanisms of the standard language ideology in England's education system', *Journal of Language, Identity and Education*, available from: https://doi.org/10.1080/15348458.2021.1877542.

Daley, P. (1998) 'Black Africans in Great Britain: Spatial concentration and segregation', *Urban Studies*, 35(10): 1703–24.

Davies, W. (2014) *The Limits of Neoliberalism*, London: Sage.

Davis, A. (2001) *Women, Race and Class*, London: Women's Press.

((deMarrais, K.G. and LeCompte, M. (1995) *The Way Schools Work: A Sociological Analysis of Education*, 2nd edition, White Plains, NY: Longman.

Department for Business Innovation and Skills (BIS). (2015) *Area Reviews and the Reshaping of the College Sector. Letter to Principals 30 October 2015*, [online] available from: https://www.gov.uk/government/publications/area-reviews-and-reshaping-the-college-sector-fe-commissioner-letter-march, [accessed 9 December, 2021].

Department for Children, Schools and Families (DfCSF) (2009) *Improving the Attainment of Looked After Young People in Secondary Schools*, [online] available from: https://assets.publishing.service.gov.uk/government/uploads/system/uploads/attachment_data/file/190241/01048-2009.pdf, [accessed 11 June, 2021].

Department for Education (2015) *Post-16 Work Experience as a Part of 16 to 19 Study Programmes and Traineeships: Departmental Advice for Post-16 Education and Training Providers*, London: Department for Education, [online] available from: https://dera.ioe.ac.uk/22421/1/130332015_DfE_dept_advice_post-16_WEx_-_final.pdf [accessed 18 June, 2021].

Department for Education and employment (DfEE) (1998) *The Learning Age*, [online] available from: https://dera.ioe.ac.uk/15191/6/9780101379021_Redacted.pdf [accessed 26 June, 2021].

Department for Education (2013) *English Literature GCSE Subject Content and Assessment Objectives*, [online] available from: https://assets.publishing.service.gov.uk/government/uploads/system/uploads/attachment_data/file/254498/GCSE_English_literature.pdf, [accessed 15 December, 2021].

Department for Education (2016) *Revised GCSE and Equivalent Results in England, 2014 to 2015*, [online] available from: https://www.gov.uk/government/uploads/system/uploads/attachment_data/file/494073/SFR01_2016.pdf, [accessed 11 May, 2021].

Department for Education (2021) *Skills for Jobs: Lifelong Learning for Opportunity and Growth*, [online] available from: https://assets.publishing.service.gov.uk/government/uploads/system/uploads/attachment_data/file/957810/Skills_for_jobs_lifelong_learning_for_opportunity_and_growth__print_version_.pdf [accessed 1 June, 2021].

Department for Education and Science (DES) (1999) *The Moser Report*, [online] available from: http://www.educationengland.org.uk/documents/moser1999/moser-report.html [accessed 26 June, 2021].

Department for Education and Science (DES) (2002) *Success for All*, [online] available from: https://dera.ioe.ac.uk/4736/1/SOR_189_1.pdf [accessed 12 June, 2021].

Department for Education and Science (DES) (2005) *14–19 Education and Skills*, [online] available from: http://www.educationengland.org.uk/documents/pdfs/2005-white-paper-14-19-education-and-skills.pdf, [accessed 20 April, 2021].

Dewey, J. (1916) *Democracy and Education*, Norwood, Mass: Macmillan.

Diprose, K. (2015) 'Resilience is futile', *Soundings*, 58(58): 44–56.

Dorling, D. (2011) *Injustice: Why Social Inequality Persists*, Bristol: Policy Press.

Duckworth, V. (2013) *Learning Trajectories, Violence and Empowerment Amongst Adult Basic Skills Learners*, Research in Education. London: Routledge.

Duckworth V. and Smith R. (2017a) 'Adult literacy: Further education as a space for resistance', *RaPAL*, 93: 9–17.

Duckworth, V. and Smith, R. (2017b) *Further Education in England – Transforming Lives and Communities: Interim Report*. Project Report. UCU.

Duckworth, V and Smith, R. (2018a) 'Transformative learning in English further education', in C. Borg, P. Mayo and R. Sultana (eds) 2018, *International Handbook on Vocational Education and Training for the Changing World of Work*, London: Springer, pp 151–77.

Duckworth V. and Smith R. (2018b) 'Women, adult literacy education and transformative bonds of care', *Australian Journal of Adult Learning*, 58(2): 157–83.

Duckworth, V. and Smith, R. (2018c) 'Breaking the triple lock: Further education and transformative teaching and learning', *Education & Training*, 60(6): 529–43, available from: https://doi.org/10.1108/ET-05-2018-0111.

Duckworth, V. and Smith, R. (2018d) 'Further educations: Transformative teaching and learning for adults in times of austerity', in E. Boeren and N. James (2018) *Being an Adult Learner in Austere Times*, London: Palgrave-Macmillan.

Duckworth, V and Smith, R. (2018e) 'Creative dissemination, learners' lives and further education', in B. Grummell and F. Finnegan (eds) *Doing Critical and Creative Research in Adult Education*, London: Sense.

Duckworth, V. and Smith R. (2019) 'Research, criticality & adult and further education: Catalysing hope and dialogic caring', in M. Hamilton and L. Tett *Resisting the Neo-Liberal Discourse in Education: Local, National And Transnational Perspectives*, London: Policy Press, pp 27–40.

Dweck. C. (2006) *Mindset*. New York: Random House.

Foroughi, H., Gabriel, Y. and Fotaki, M. (2019) 'Leadership in a post-truth era: A new narrative disorder?', *Leadership*, 15(2): 135–51.

Foucault, M. (1982) 'The subject and power', *Critical Inquiry*, 8(4): 777–95, [online] available from: www.jstor.org/stable/1343197 [accessed 31 May, 2021].

Foucault, M. (1995) *Discipline and Punish*, London: Vintage.

Freire, P. (1995) *The Pedagogy of the Oppressed*, New York: Continuum.

Fuller, A. and Unwin, L. (2003) 'Learning as apprentices in the contemporary UK workplace: Creating and managing expansive and restrictive participation', *Journal of Education and Work*, 16(4): 407–26.

Gershoff, E.T. (2017) School corporal punishment in global perspective: prevalence, outcomes, and efforts at intervention, *Psychology, Health & Medicine*, 22(sup1): 224–39.

Gewirtz, S. (1998) Conceptualizing social justice in education: Mapping the territory, *Journal of Education Policy*, 13 (4): 469–84.

Gibb, N. (2017) 'The importance of knowledge-based education', available from: https://www.gov.uk/government/speeches/nick-gibb-the-importance-of-knowledge-based-education, [accessed 11 May, 2021].

Gibb, N. (2021) *The Importance of a Knowledge-Rich Curriculum*, [online] available from: https://www.gov.uk/government/speeches/the-importance-of-a-knowledge-rich-curriculum, [accessed 15 December, 2021].

Gillborn, D. (2008) *Racism and Education: Coincidence or Conspiracy?* London: Routledge.

Giroux, H. (2011) *On Critical Pedagogy*, London: Continuum.

Gleeson, D., Abbott, I. and Hill, R. (2011) 'Governing the governors: A case study of college governance in English further education', *British Educational Research Journal*, 37(5): 781–96.

Gleeson, D. and James, D. (2007) 'The paradox of professionalism in English further education: a TLC project perspective', *Educational Review*, 59(4): 451–67.

Glynn, S. (2005) 'East End immigrants and the battle for housing: A comparative study of political mobilisation in the Jewish and Bangladeshi communities', *Journal of Historical Geography*, 31(3): 528–45.

Goodley, D., Lawthom, R., Clough, P. and Moore, M. (2004) *Researching Life Stories: Method, Theory and Analyses in a Biographical Age*, Abingdon: Routledge.

Goodson, I. and Sikes, P. (2001) *Life History Research in Educational Settings*, Milton Keynes: Open University Press.

Gregg, M. and Seigworth, G.J. (2010) *The Affect Theory Reader*, Durham NC: Duke University Press.

Gronn, P. (2002) 'Distributed leadership as a unit of analysis', *The Leadership Quarterly*, 13(4): 423–51.

Guardian 2001. 'Towards a national debate', available from: https://www.theguardian.com/education/thegreatdebate/story/0,9860,574645,00.html, [accessed 27 December, 2021].

Habermas, J. (2006) 'Euroskepticism, Market Europe, Or a Europe of (World) Citizens?', in G. Schott and J. Habermas (eds) *Time of Transitions*, Cambridge: Polity Press, pp 73–88.

Hanley, L. (2007) *Estates: An Intimate History*, London: Granta.

Hansard (2018) 'Improving Education Standards', Volume 650: debated on Thursday 29 November, 2018 [online] available from: https://hansard.parliament.uk/commons/2018-11-29/debates/03D364AB-E6D1-45BD-80E2-90082F93D5FF/ImprovingEducationStandards [accessed 31 May, 2021].

Harvey, D. (2005) *A Brief History of Neoliberalism*, Oxford: Oxford University Press.

Henehan, K. (2020) *Class of 2020 Education Leavers in the Current Crisis*, London: Resolution Foundation, [online] available from: https://dera.ioe.ac.uk//35542/1/Class-of-2020.pdf [accessed 27.11.21].

Herndl, C. and Nahrwold, C. (2000) 'Research as social practice', *Written Communication*, 17(2): 258–96.

Hickel, J., Dorninger, C., Wieland, H. and Suwandi, I. (2022) 'Imperialist appropriation in the world economy: Drain from the global South through unequal exchange, 1990–2015', *Global Environmental Change*, 73: 1–13, available from: https://doi.org/10.1016/j.gloenvcha.2022.102467.

Hirsch, A. (Host) (2019) 'We need to talk about the British Empire', [audio podcast] Audibles, available from: https://www.audible.co.uk/pd/We-Need-to-Talk-About-the-British-Empire-Audiobook/B081581253 [accessed 16 June 2021].

His Majesty's Stationery Office (HMSO) (1946) *Youth's Opportunity. Further Education in County Colleges*, Ministry of Education Pamphlet No 3, London: HMSO.

Her Majesty's Stationery Office (HMSO) (2011) *Education Act 2011* (c.21; s.49). London: HMSO.

Hodkinson, P., Biesta, G. and James, D. (2007) 'Understanding learning cultures', *Educational Review*, 59(4): 415–27.

Hoffmann, N., Wright, T.B. and Gatta, M. (2019) 'Ethnographies of work and possible futures in new ways meaningful first career', in A. Mann, P. Huddleston and E. Kashefpakdel (eds) *Essays on Employer Engagement in Education*, London: Routledge, available from: https://doi.org/10.4324/9781315144115.

Holloway, J. (2002) *Change the World without Taking Power: The Meaning of Revolution Today*, London: Pluto Press.

Holmes, A.D.G. (2020) 'Researcher positionality – a consideration of its influence and place in qualitative research – a new researcher guide', *International Journal of Education*, 8(4): 1–10.

hooks, b. (1994) *Teaching to Transgress. Education as the Practice of Freedom*, London: Routledge.

Hopkin, J. and Rosamond, B. (2018) Post-truth politics, bullshit and bad ideas: 'Deficit fetishism' in the UK, *New Political Economy*, 23(6): 641–55

Huber, L. and Solorzano, D. (2015) 'Racial microaggressions as a tool for critical race research', *Race Ethnicity and Education*, 18(3): 297–320.

Huddlestone, P. and Laczik, A. (2019) 'Employers at the heart of the system? The role of employers in qualification development,' in A. Mann, P. Huddleston and E. Kashefpakdel (eds) *Essays on Employer Engagement in Education*, London: Routledge, available from: https://doi.org/10.4324/9781315144115 [accessed 30 November, 2021].

Hyland, T. and Merrill, B (2003) *The Changing Face of Further Education*, London: Routledge.

Illeris, K. (2014) *Transformative Learning and Identity*, Oxon, England: Routledge.

Institute for Fiscal Studies (2016) *Family Background and University Success: Differences in Higher Education Access and Outcomes in England*, [online] available from: https://www.ifs.org.uk/publications/8791 [accessed 2 April, 2021].

Jarvis, P. (2004) *Adult Education and Lifelong Learning: Theory and Practice*, London: RoutledgeFalmer.

Johnstone, L. and Boyle, M. (2018) 'The power threat meaning framework: An alternative nondiagnostic conceptual system', *Journal of Humanistic Psychology*. Doi: 10.1177/0022167818793289.

Kaur, B. (2021) *Educational encounters, hybrid identities and spectral traces: Contesting the myths of Aston through the accounts of South Asian Muslim women*, PhD thesis, Birmingham: Birmingham City University.

Keddie, A. (2012) 'Schooling and social justice through the lenses of Nancy Fraser', *Critical Studies in Education*, 53(3): 263–79.

Keep, E. (2006) 'State control of the English education and training system—playing with the biggest train set in the world', *Journal of Vocational Education & Training*, 58(1): 47–64.

Kennedy, H. (1997) *Learning Works: Widening Participation in Further Education*, London: Further Education Funding Council (FEFC).

Kincheloe, J.L. (2008) *Knowledge and Critical Pedagogy*, London: Springer.

Kincheloe, J.L., McLaren, P., Steinberg, S.R. and Monzó, L. (2017) Critical pedagogy and qualitative research: Advancing the bricolage, in N.K. Denzin and Y.S. Lincoln (eds) *The SAGE Handbook of Qualitative Research*, (5th edn), Thousand Oaks, CA: Sage, pp 235–60.

Kohli, R. and Solórzano, D. (2012) 'Teachers, please learn our names! Racial microaggressions and the K-12 classroom', *Race Ethnicity and Education*, 15(4): 441–62.

Kress, T.M. (2011) 'Inside the "thick wrapper" of critical pedagogy and research', *International Journal of Qualitative Studies in Education*, 24(3): 261–6.

Leach, L. (2013) 'Participation and equity in higher education: Are we going back to the future?' *Oxford Review of Education*, 39(2): 267–86.

Learning and Work Institute (2018) *Learning, Work, and Health: The Next 70 Years*, [online] available from: www.learningandwork.org.uk/wp-content/uploads/2018/10/Learning-Health-and-Work-the-next-70-years.pdf [accessed: 3 June, 2021].

Lefebvre, H. (1991) *The Production of Space*, Oxford: Blackwell.

Lefebvre, H. (2004) *Rhythmanalysis*, London: Continuum.

Lefebvre, H. (2014) *Critique of Everyday Life*, London: Verso.

Leitch, S. (2006) *Prosperity for All in the Global Economy: World Class Skills*, London: HM Treasury.

Lingard, B. (2005) 'Socially just pedagogies in changing times', *International Studies in Sociology of Education*, 15(2): 165–86.

Lingfield, R. (2012) 'Professionalism in the further education', in The Lingfield Report, London: DBIS.

Lipman-Blumen, J. (1998) 'Connective Leadership: What Business Needs to Learn from Academe', *Change The Magazine of Higher Learning*, 30(1): 49–53, available from: Doi: 10.1080/00091389809602592.

Ljungblad, A. (2019) 'Pedagogical Relational Teachership (PeRT) – a multi-relational perspective', *International Journal of Inclusive Education*. Doi: 10.1080/13603116.2019.1581280.

Lovett, T. (1971a) *Adult Education and the Community School*, [online] available from: https://academic.oup.com/cdj/article-abstract/6/3/183/321257, [accessed 14 December, 2021].

Lovett, T. (1971b) 'Community adult education', in S. Westwood and J. Thomas (eds) *The Politics of Adult Education*, London: NIACE, pp 59–69.

Lucas, N. and Crowther, N. (2016) 'The logic of the incorporation of further education colleges in England 1993–2015: Towards an understanding of marketisation, change and instability', *Journal of Education Policy*, 31(5): 583–97.

Luke, C. and Gore, J. (eds) (1992) *Feminisms and Critical Pedagogy*, London: Routledge.

Lupton, R., N. Heath and E. Salter (2009) 'Education: New Labour's top priority', in *Towards a More Equal Society? Poverty, Inequality and Policy since 1997*, J. Hills, T. Sefton and K. Stewart (eds) Bristol: Policy Press, pp 71–90.

McIlroy, J. and Westwood, S. (1993) *Border Country: Raymond Williams in Adult Education*, Leicester: National institute of Adult Continuing Education.

McQueen, S. (2020) *Small Axe: Education*, (television series episode). BBC.

Macedo, D. (1994) *Literacies of Power: What Americans are Not Allowed to Know*. Boulder, CO: Westview.

Mansell, W. (2007) *Education by Numbers: The Tyranny of Testing*, London: Politico.

Massumi, B. (1995) 'The autonomy of affect', *Cultural Critique*, (31): 83–109.

Merriam, S., Johnson-Bailey, J., Lee, M., Kee, Y., Ntseane G. and Muhamad M. (2001) 'Power and positionality: Negotiating insider/outsider status within and across cultures', *International Journal of Lifelong Education*, 20(5): 405–16, available at: Doi: 10.1080/02601370120490.

Mezirow, J. (1990) *Fostering Critical Reflection in Adulthood*, San Francisco: Jossey-Bass.

Mezirow, J. and associates (2000) *Fostering Critical Reflection: A Guide to Transformative and Emancipatory Learning*, Mahwah: Jossey-Bass.

Mezirow, J. (2009) Transformative learning theory', in J. Mezirow, and E.W. Taylor (eds) *Transformative Learning in Practise: Insights from Community, workplace and Higher Education*, Mahwah: Jossey-Bass, pp 18–32.

Ministry of Justice (MoJ) (2021A) *Prison Population Figures: 2021*, [online] available from: https://www.gov.uk/government/statistics/prison-population-figures-2021 [accessed December 19, 2021].

Ministry of Justice (MoJ) (2021B) *Proven Reoffending Statistics: October to December 2019*, [online] available from: https://www.gov.uk/government/statistics/proven-reoffending-statistics-october-to-december-2019/proven-reoffending-statistics-october-to-december-2019 [accessed 19 December, 2021].

National Audit Office (NAO) (2015) *Overseeing Financial Sustainability in the FE Sector*, [online] available from: https://www.nao.org.uk/wp-content/uploads/2015/07/Overseeing-financialsustainability-in-the-further-education-sector.pdf, [accessed 8 July, 2021].

Niemiec. C.P. and Ryan, R.M. (2009) 'Autonomy, competence and relatedness in the classroom: Applying self-determination theory to educational practice', *Theory and Research in Education*, 7: 133–44.

Niemiec, C.P., Ryan, R. and Deci, E. (2010) Self-Determination theory and the relation of autonomy to self-regulatory processes and personality development', in R.H. Hoyle (ed.) *Handbook of Personality and Self-Regulation*, Wiley online Library, available from: https://onlinelibrary.wiley.com/doi/pdf/10.1002/9781444318111.ch8 [accessed 21 May, 2021].

Noddings, N. (2005) *The Challenge to Care in Schools*, New York: Teachers College Press.

Norman, M. and Hyland, T. (2003) 'The role of confidence in lifelong learning', *Educational Studies*, 29: 261–72

Noys, B. (2013) *Malign Velocities, Acceleration and Capitalism*, London: Zero

O'Brien, M. (2007) 'Mothers' emotional care work in education and its moral imperative', *Gender and Education*, 19(2): 159–78.

O'Leary, M. (2013) *Classroom Observation: A Guide to the Effective Observation of Teaching and Learning*, London: Routledge.

O'Leary, M. and Smith, R. (2012) 'Earthquakes, cancer and cultures of fear: qualifying as a skills for life teacher in an uncertain economic climate', *Oxford Review of Education*, 38(4): 437–54.

O'Leary, M., Smith, R., Cui, V. and Dakka, F. (2019) *The Role of Leadership in Prioritising and Improving the Quality of Teaching and Learning in the Further Education Sector*, London: Further Education Trust for Leadership (FETL), available from: https://fetl.org.uk/publications/the-role-of-leadership-in-prioritising-and-improving-the-quality-of-teaching-and-learning-in-further-education/ [accessed 4 March, 2022].

OECD (2017) *Benchmarking Higher Education System Performance: Conceptual Framework and Data, Enhancing Higher Education System Performance*, OECD: Paris.

Ofsted (2008) The Annual Report of Her Majesty's Chief Inspector of Education, Children's Services and Skills 2007/08, [online] available from: https://assets.publishing.service.gov.uk/government/uploads/system/uploads/attachment_data/file/248394/1114.pdf [accessed 26 June, 2021].

Ofsted (2018) *The Annual Report of Her Majesty's Chief Inspector of Education, Children's Services and Skills 2017/18*, [online] available from: https://assets.publishing.service.gov.uk/government/uploads/system/uploads/attachment_data/file/761606/29523_Ofsted_Annual_Report_2017-18_041218.pdf [accessed 26 May, 2021].

Ofsted (2020) *The Annual Report of Her Majesty's Chief Inspector of Education, Children's Services and Skills 2019/20*, [online] available from: https://assets. publishing.service.gov.uk/government/uploads/system/uploads/attachme nt_data/file/939834/Ofsted_Annual_Report_2019-2020.pdf [accessed 31 May, 2021].

Parker, C., Scott, S. and Geddes, A. (2019) 'Snowball sampling', in P. Atkinson, S. Delamont, A. Cernat, J.W. Sakshaug, and R.A. Williams (eds) *SAGE Research Methods Foundations*, available from: https://dx.doi. org/10.4135/9781526421036831710 [accessed 4 March, 2022].

Paton, G. (2010) *Spending Review: Schools Budget Protected* [online] available from: https://www.telegraph.co.uk/education/educationnews/8076 309/Spending-Review-schools-budget-protected.html [accessed 19 December, 2021].

Payne, J. (2010) 'The unbearable lightness of skill: the changing meaning of skill in UK policy discourses and some implications for education and training', *Journal of Education Policy*, 15(3): 353–69.

Peters, M., Besley, T. and Paraskeva, J. (2015) 'Global financial crisis and educational restructuring', *Citizenship, Social and Economics Education*, 14(1): 15–18.

Pierce, C. (1974) 'Psychiatric problems of the black minority', in S. Arieti (ed.) *American Handbook of Psychiatry*, New York: Basic Books, pp 512–23.

Pink, S. (2007) *Doing Visual Ethnography: Images, Media, and Representation in Research*, (2nd edn), London: Sage Publications.

Plummer, K. (2001) *Documents of Life 2: An Invitation to a Critical Humanism*, London: Sage.

Prensky M. (2001) 'Digital natives, digital immigrants', *On the Horizon*. MCB University Press. 9(5), available from: www.marcprensky.com [accessed June, 2017].

Raelin, J. (2010) 'Imagine there are no leaders: Reframing leadership as collaborative agency', *Leadership*, 12(2): 131–58.

Randle, K. and Brady, N. (1997) 'Managerialism and professionalism in the "Cinderella service"', *Journal of Vocational Education and Training*, 49(1): 121–39.

Reay, D. (1998) '"Always knowing" and "never being sure": Institutional and familial habituses and higher education choice', *Journal of Education Policy*, 13(4): 519–29.

Reay, D. (2000) '"Dim dross": Marginalised women both inside and outside the academy,' *Women's Studies International Forum*, 23(1): 13–21.

Richmond, T. (2018) *The great training robbery: Assessing the first year of the apprenticeship levy*, London: Reform, [online] available from: https://ref orm.uk/research/great-training-robbery-assessing-first-year-apprentices hip-levy [accessed 15 May, 2021].

Right to Learn (2021) *Our Launch Statement*, [online] available from: https://right2learn.co.uk/what-we-do/, [accessed 14 July, 2021].

Rogers, C. (2007) 'The necessary and sufficient conditions of therapeutic personality change', *Psychotherapy: Theory, Research, Practice*, 44(3): 240–48.

Rorty, R. (1999) *Philosophy and Social Hope*, London: Penguin.

Runyowa, S. (2015) 'Microaggressions matter', *The Atlantic* [online] 15 September, available from: https://www.theatlantic.com/politics/archive/2015/09/microaggressions-matter/406090/, [accessed 14 May 2020].

Ryan, R and Deci, E. (2000) 'Self-determination theory and the facilitation of intrinsic motivation, social development, and well-being', *American Psychologist*, 55(1): 68–78, available from: Doi: 10.1037110003-066X.55.1.68.

Salas-Vallina, A. and Alegre, J. (2018) 'Unselfish leaders? Understanding the role of altruistic leadership and organizational learning on happiness at work', *Leadership & Organization Development Journal*, 39(5): 633–49, available from: https://www.emerald.com/insight/content/doi/10.1108/LODJ-11-2017-0345/full/html [accessed 4 March, 2022].

Sandel, M. (2021) *The Tyranny of Merit: What's Become of the Common Good?*, London: Penguin.

Schomberg, W. (2021) 'More needed: G7 nations agree to boost climate finance', *Reuters*, [online] available from: https://www.reuters.com/business/sustainable-business/g7-leaders-commit-increasing-climate-finance-contributions-2021-06-12/ [accessed 26 June, 2021].

Sellen, P. (2016) *Teacher Workload and Professional Development In England's Secondary Schools: Insights from TALIS*, Education Policy Institute, available from: https://epi.org.uk/wp-content/uploads/2018/01/TeacherWorkload_EPI.pdf, [accessed 28 May, 2021].

Shepherd, J. (2012) 'Pupil behaviour worse since abolition of caning, warn teachers', *The Guardian*, [online] available from: https://www.theguardian.com/education/2012/apr/04/corporal-punishment-student-behaviour-worse, [accessed 31 May, 2021].

Shields, C.M. (2010) 'Transformative leadership: Working for equity in diverse contexts', *Educational Administration Quarterly*, 46(4): 558–89.

Smith, R. (2007A) 'Of "duckers and divers", mice and men: The impact of market fundamentalism in FE colleges post-incorporation', *Research in Post-Compulsory Education*, 12(1): 53–70.

Smith, R. (2007B) 'Work, identity and the quasi-market: The FE Experience', *Journal of Educational Administration and History*, Special Practitioners' Research Edition, 39(1): 33–47.

Smith, R. (2015) 'College re-culturing, marketisation and knowledge: The meaning of incorporation', *Journal of Educational Administration and History*, 47(1): 18–39.

Smith, R. (2017) 'Area reviews and the end of incorporation: A Machiavellian moment', in M. Daley, K. Orr and J. Petrie (eds) *The Principal*, London: UCL IoE Press.

Smith, R. (2017B) 'Building colleges for the future: Pedagogical and ideological spaces', *Journal of Education Policy*, 32(6): 855–70.

Smith, R. and Duckworth, V. (2020) 'Digital research as a resource for reimagining further education', in A. Bulajić, T. Nikolić and C. Vieira (eds) *Navigating through Contemporary World with Adult Education Research and Practice,* Belgrade: Institute for Pedagogy and Andragogy.

Smith, R. and Duckworth, V. (2019) 'Transformative Teaching and Learning in Further Education Summative report for the University and College Union Transforming Lives and Communities project'. London: UCU, available from: https://www.ucu.org.uk/media/10385/Transformative_teaching_and_learning_in_further_education_july_2019/pdf/transformativeteachingandlearninginfurthereducationjuly2019 [accessed 4 March, 2022].

Smith, R. and Duckworth, V. (2020) *Leadership, Further Education and Social Justice*, London: Further Education Trust for Leadership.

Smith, R. and O'Leary, M. (2013) 'NPM in an age of austerity: Knowledge and experience in further education', *Journal of Educational Administration and History*, 45(3): 244–66.

Social Mobility Commission (2019) *The Adult Skills Gap: Is Falling Investment in UK Adults Stalling Social Mobility?* London: Social Mobility Commission.

Sodiq, A. and Abbott, I. (2018) 'Reimagining academic staff governors' role in further education college governance', *Research in Post-Compulsory Education*, 23(1): 138–57.

Soja, E. (1996) *Thirdspace: Journeys to Los Angeles and Other Real-and-Imagined Spaces*, Oxford: Blackwell.

Soja, E. (1989) *Postmodern Geographies*, London: Verso.

Spector, B. (2020) 'Post-truth claims and the wishing away of brute facts', *Leadership*, 16(1): 9–24.

Standing, G. (2011) *The Precariat, the New Dangerous Class*, London: Bloomsbury.

Staufenberg, J. (2021) 'The slow death of adult residential education?', *FE Week*, [online] 18 May, available from: https://feweek.co.uk/2021/05/18/the-slow-death-of-adult-residential-education/, [accessed 26 June, 2021].

Stewart, K. (2007) *Ordinary Affects*, Durham NC: Duke University Press.

Street, B. (1990) 'Putting literacies on the political agenda', *RaPaL Bulletin*, No. 13, in M. Herrington and A. Kendall (2005) (eds) *Insights from Research and Practice: A Handbook for Adult Literacy, Numeracy and ESOL Practitioners*, Leicester, NIACE, pp 25–36.

Sweller, J., Ayres, P. and Kalyuga, S. (2011) *Cognitive Load Theory*, London: Springer.

Thomas, L. (2012) 'Building student engagement and belonging in Higher Education at a time of change', [online] available from: https://s3.eu-west-2.amazonaws.com/assets.creode.advancehe-document-manager/docume nts/hea/private/what_works_final_report_1568036657.pdf, [accessed 28 October, 2021].

Thompson, R. (2009) 'Social class and participation in further education: evidence from the Youth Cohort Study of England and Wales', *British Journal of Sociology of Education*, 30(1): 29–42.

Thompson, P. (2013) 'Introduction: the privatization of Hope and the crisis of negation', in P. Thompson S. and Zizek (eds) *The Privatisation of Hope*, Durham, NC: Duke University Press.

Tuckett, A. (1991) 'Counting the cost: Managerialism, the market and the education of adults in the 1980s and beyond', in Westwood, S. and Thomas, J.E., *The Politics of Adult Education*, London: NIACE.

Vincent, C. and Ball, S.J. (2007) ' "Making up" the middle-class child: Families, activities and class dispositions', *Sociology*. 41(6): 1061–77.

Virilio, P. (2006) *Speed and Politics*, Los Angeles: Semiotext(e).

Watt, N. (2013) 'Boris Johnson invokes Thatcher spirit with greed is good speech', *The Guardian*, [online] 27 November, available from: https:// www.theguardian.com/politics/2013/nov/27/boris-johnson-thatcher-greed-good, [accessed 21 May, 2021].

Whieldon, F. (2020) '64 colleges running out of cash which is "more than we thought" admits official', *FE Week*, [online] 26 November, available from: https://feweek.co.uk/2020/11/26/64-colleges-running-out-of-cash-which-is-more-than-we-thought-admits-official/, [accessed 29 November, 2020].

Wilkinson, R. and Pickett, K. (2010) *The Spirit Level: Why Equality is Better for Everyone*, London: Penguin Books.

Williams, R. (1961) An Open Letter to WEA Tutors, [online] available from https://weaeducation.typepad.co.uk/files/raymond-williams-an-open-let ter-to-wea-tutors-1.pdf, [accessed 15 December, 2021].

Williams, R. (2015) *Keywords: A Vocabulary of Culture and Society*, Oxford: Oxford University Press.

Williamson, G. (2021) Education Secretary at HEPI conference: Learning from the crisis (speech), [online] available from: https://www.gov.uk/gov ernment/speeches/education-secretary-at-hepi-conference-learning-from-the-crisis [accessed 25 June, 2021].

Willis, P. (1977) *Learning to Labour: How Working-Class Kids Get Working Class Jobs*, Westmead, Farnborough: Saxon House.

Wolf, A. (2011) *Review of Vocational Education – The Wolf Report*, London: DfE.

World Health Organisation (WHO) (2000) *Women's Mental Health, an Evidence-Based Review*, [online] available from: https://www.who.int/ mental_health/media/en/67.pdf [accessed: 26 June, 2021].

Yarrow, K. and Esland, G. (1998) 'The Changing Role of the Professional in the new FE', Unpublished Conference Paper, BERA Conference, Queen's University, Belfast.

Youdell, D. (2011) *School Trouble: Identity, Power and Politics in Education*, London: Routledge.

Young, M. (1958) *The Rise of the Meritocracy*, London: Pelican.

Young, M. (2007) *Bringing Knowledge Back In*, London: Routledge.

Index

diversity 105, 107, 117
Duckworth, V. 114
Duckworth, V. and Smith, R. 1, 25, 36, 38, 58, 67, 80, 89–90, 111, 113, 170, 176
dyslexia 72, 168–9

E

economic inequality 29
education
  banking model of 151, 155, 158
  competitive individualism 136
  'good' 95
  hope and 27
  ideological fog 9
  negative impact on students 11, 50–1
  purposes of 9, 95
  reproduction of social order 101
  schooling and 75, 76, 101
  social benefits of 124
  symbolic violence in *see* symbolic violence
  value of 109–10
  see also adult education; further and adult education; further education
Education Act (1944) 16
Education Act (2011) 121
education-is-for-employment discourse 168–9
education policies 99
Education Priority Areas 152
educational research *see* research project
egalitarianism 80, 90–1, 151
Eliot, T.S. 152
emotional capital 82
emotional environment 164, 165
employers
  colleges and 84–5
  further and adult education 1, 2, 15, 102
  further education providers and 17
empowerment 80
engagement 50
English for Speakers of Other Languages (ESOL) courses 13
ethnicity 103–7
  social class and 105
experiential capital 74
exploitative relationships 99

F

Family background and university success (IFS, 2016) 112
FAP apparatus 18–19, 143–4, 147
  constraints on teachers 88
  digitisation of knowledge production 55
  FE sector 138
  flaws 22
  government agenda 18, 19
  grade fabrication 30
  impact of 19–26
    portfolio passes 19–20

marginalisation caused by 127–8
  method of 29
  negative consequences of 19, 20, 94
  perpetuating centralised power relations 127
  teaching to test 30
  see also funding
FE sector 172
  abstract space of 138, 172–3
  notion of 24, 63, 138
  in policy discourse 63
film 152
Fircroft College 151
fossil fuels 127
Foucault, Michel 73
  the gaze concept 166–7
  school examinations 166
14–19 Education and Skills (DES, 2005) 101
free school meals (FSM) 139
freedom 155, 156
Freire, Paulo 79, 120, 136, 154
  critical pedagogy 155
Freirean pedagogy 138
Fuller, A. and Unwin, L. 84
funding
  of colleges 10, 22–23
  complexity of 19
  constrains 47, 124–5
  cuts in 3–4, 10, 22–3, 109, 122, 124–5, 129, 140–1
  of further and adult education 2, 10
  impact
    of austerity measures, impact of 124–5
    on students 47, 48
    on teachers 47
  instrumentalist skills agenda 47–8
  principles of 18–19
  process 10
  of research 27
  for student recruitment 163
  see also FAP apparatus
funding, accountability and performance *see* FAP apparatus
further and adult education 3–5
  active involvement in decision-making 78
  affirmative culture of 72
  architecture of 125–8
  bigger picture 2
  'bums on seats' knowledge-delivery system 2, 55, 163, 165
  counter-metrics 81
  data production 20
  funding 2, 10
    cuts in 22–3, 109
  further and adult, distinction between 3
  as homogeneously whole 63
  importance of 8